PASSAGES

Copyright © 2022 by Maurita Estes Stueck, with help from Katie McNeil, Lawrence Stueck, Linda Mahan, Sara Stueck, and the Girl Scouts of America

Design copyright © 2022 by Burns Studio Art
Cover copyright © 2022 by Lawrence Stueck

All rights reserved. No part of this book may be used or reproduced by any means, graphic, electronic, or mechanical including photocopying, recording, tape or by any information storage retrieval system without the written permission of the publisher except in the case of brief quotations embodied in critical articles and reviews.

Bilbo Books Publishing
www.BilboBooks.com
bilbobookspublishing@gmail.com
(706)549-1597

ISBN: 978-1-7364598-2-9

Printed in the United States of America

All rights reserved. Published in the United States of America by Bilbo Books Publishing - Athens, Georgia

Dedication

This book of writings is dedicated especially to
Wesley Carroll Mahan
May 17, 1984–October 31, 2020, Fort Collins, Colorado

Grandmother's Bio Written for Wesley Mahan

Baby Estes was born August 18, 1922, in St. Louis, Missouri, in the Children's Hospital. She was christened Maurita Fay, the first born to her parents. Her father, Wellborn Estes, and her mother, Clara Fay Ostner. Their home was at Hillandale, Potosi, Missouri.

Maurita was born in St. Louis as the little family has stayed in St. Louis about six weeks prior to the birth so that the arduous trip from Potosi could be made before the "due date".

Her paternal grandparents were Mr. and Mrs. John Wesley Estes (mother: Talullah Martha Carroll) of St. Louis. Her maternal grandmother was Louisa Cavanah Ostner of Charleston, Missouri. Grandfather Max Lee Ostner passed away a day or two after Maurita was born.

John and Linda Mahan wih Maurita and Wesley

Introduction

In August 2012, family gathered at Pine Winds in Estes Park to celebrate Mother's 90th birthday. We ate her favorite BLT sandwiches and ice cream.

Her gift to her four children that day were 3-ring binders titled *PASSAGES* with copies of ten of her writings and a picture from October 18, 1946, of Mother in her wedding dress. We knew that she had been writing memoirs in lifelong learning classes at her *alma mater*, Washington University. After her move to Ohio from Webster Groves in 2016, she began a writing group (PENS or FRIENDS group) with other members of the Middletown Branch of the American Association of University Women. As an AAUW member since 1943, friendships among these members had always been special and were the focus of much of her interest in women's rights and in supporting scholarships for higher education.

Although I typed a few of her last memoirs, I had no idea she had so many! A few of the stories were new to me, but many of them we heard growing up and having time with her during her 97-year life. In compiling this book, I have not edited these writings. A few contain some of the same memories and were written at different times for different groups but always for her family future readers. The same story can be woven with another memory to take a memoir in a different direction. These stories were brought into her writings from the extensive travel journals, scrapbooks, and photo albums saved through the years.

The final chapters titled *Philosophies* and *Other Writings* came about because she was always so interested in so many issues and had the years of wisdom to put things in historical context and perspective! Her Christmas letters to friends reflect her Christian ethic and the value she placed on maintaining relationships. The speech she gave in 1984 I never knew about, as I was busy with another move and baby. I realized that the writings she saved in organized files and the mementos in a large wooden box were of importance to her and should be shared with those who loved her.

Another memoir project of Mother's was a CD which grandson Wesley Mahan helped record with clips from 16mm films that her father began taking in 1930 and her narration of growing up in St. Louis and raising a family through 1971.

The pictures are added to share the importance of family, friends and places mentioned in the memoirs. They are just a few of the thousands that the family is fortunate to have in our archives (my basement). Genealogy was another interest of Mother's and the family trees and stories of ancestors are in other treasure chests.

We thought that sharing this collection would help preserve our family history and bring memories to family and friends who knew Mother and may consider ways to give their own gift of memoirs to their family and friends.

Enjoy!

Katie Stueck McNeil
September, 2021, Oxford, Ohio

Table of Contents

Growing Up..7

Raising a Family..83

Places I Have Lived................................141

Travels...203

Philosophies...251

Additional Writings...............................293

Addenda..309

Prologue to the Gift

Memoirs-writing for our children and our children's children. This was one of the classes of Lifelong Learning Institute several terms past. I signed up. Though I have kept diaries from time to time, made scrapbooks of most of our family vacations, written logs of sailing *Ceilidh* and *Christa Galli* and done some journaling periodically, I never had an ambition to be a writer. I have not had a writing class since Senior Composition in high school.

90th birthday gift of *Passages* to children

    I try hard not to talk about the past although everything I have to share is past. I do not want the past always to be present. This being said, I have come to the understanding that a "gift" to my children and their offspring might be not just wealth but an edition of the "memoirs" I have written in my Lifelong Learning terms. It is my hope that, dear Readers, you will have an understanding of the times I have embroidered my tapestry, my life's journey.

    I have lived nine decades. I stand on the threshold of the tenth as I give to you my "gift", the gift someone has call the "Perfect Gift". May you enjoy the PASSAGES!

August 18, 2012

CHAPTER ONE
Growing Up

Maurita Estes, 1926

In 2013 much is being learned about the need for our human species to be in touch with the natural world. I treasure my experiences at the Farm for giving me the opportunity to be a part of the natural world somewhat intimately. Being an urban child, I might otherwise have been deprived.

Early Years

Maurita lived with her parents for two plus years 12 miles out of Potosi at Hillandale in the home her father had built for his bride, intending to be a farmer applying his knowledge gained from taking an Extension Course from Missouri University. Family story has been told for years about toddler Maurita being chased about the yard by a rooster! (I will switch to "first person" now in this narrative.)

Farming was not successful. Mother and Daddy were not satisfied with the rural life, and determined to move to St. Louis. My Estes grandparents still lived in St. Louis with Grandfather, the general Agent with Aetna Life Insurance Co. My father went to work for that agency soon. They found an apartment in North St. Louis. The next-door neighbor in the 4-family apartment became life-long friends and their daughter, Harriet, became my first playmate. The big story in those years was about my doll, nearly life-size. She had a record in her back that allowed her to talk to me. Alas! As the story went, Harriet knocked her off the chair and she could no longer talk. When I was four the folks moved to University City, the first suburb of St. Louis, that was to be my home until 1946 when I was first married.

Now I will continue this life story only with dates and high points as I have written extensive memoirs and journaled every era.

A True Friend

For a long time I looked.
For a while I never booked
What I call a true friend.

But now at least, I think,
Of my chain of friends as a link.
I have a person that's a true friend.

We have fun together when we're
        joyful
And she stands with me when I'm
        sorrowful
She is a true friend.

She gives me lots of slaps;
But, of course, too, "high caps"
Because she's a true friend.

It was at camp I met the one.
We have lots of things in common.
Surely, she's a true friend.

Emmy Jane (Maurita's pseudonym)
July 19, 1937

Fay, Maurita & Betty Estes, 1932

Maurita Estes, Christmas 1922

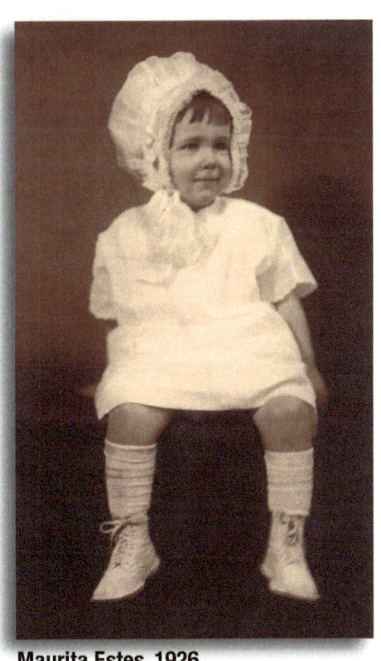
Maurita Estes, 1926

Hillandale

To reflect on experiences that had great impact on the shaping of my life is of great interest to me. Too often it is suggested that we think of people who have influenced us, but it does seem to me that places and activities often have a more enduring stamp on the orchestration of our lives.

My special memories of living in country lands close to the natural world are abundant. Though I have lived entirely in an urban setting (except for my first two and a half years). I was fortunate to have spent many weekends, and maybe a week or two each year, at the "farm".

These 7000 acres near Potosi, Missouri, belonged originally to my grandparents who had moved to California in 1925. Grandmother named it Hillandale, though my family just called it "the farm" for, in fact, from my early childhood we had the Rickner family living on "the place", farming and caretaking the house and yard. It would be called subsistence farming in today's vernacular. What else could be done with the rocky and shallow soil of pine/oak forest lands?

How lucky could two city kids be to have freedom to explore, run, holler, find a "queen's bathtub" in the creek? My sister and I thought we had the best of two worlds. Plus, we knew Ben (Mr. Rickner) and Mrs. Rickner. I am sure Mrs. Rickner had a first name, but Mother called her Mrs. and for me to do otherwise was not condoned.

Ben patiently let us sit on his donkey while he led it around the barnyard. We tried to milk the cow, and best of all, he let me take a piglet home for a week between our visits. Such a cunning pet, rather dark gray except for an ivory girdle around his tummy and a pink nose. Mother must have provided for its needs just as she met my needs for a pet.

Through our girlhood years we did not venture too far from the house that my father had built as a bachelor before he courted my school marm Mother. He had seen her in town and yearned for a proper introduction from the family with whom she was boarding. Daddy was a "city slicker" and therefore had to seek a way to meet her. The "city slickers" and I moved to St. Louis when I was two-and-a-half, but for four or more decades my family, friends and my children enjoyed the house, woods, barn, and creeks as a retreat from the city. My grandparents came back several months in the Fall. The pump for the water, generator for electricity were never operable so we lived as our forebears had b.e. (before electricity). A small stream of water came by gravity flow from a spring up back of the house, an outhouse functioned well, water carried up from the Springhouse was heated on the wood stove. Light from kerosene lamps cast shadows

Hillandale

around the room. One had an Aladdin lamp that made a brighter light on our game table while we played "Flinch". My Grandparents had no cards, as in "playing cards" (hearts, diamonds, spades, clubs). "Flinch" was played with special cards. A wind-up Victrola afforded us old classics, even one of Caruso, the Tenor of note in 1925.

It was in those times I learned about the culture and work of the people in the Ozark foothills. We had a row of houses built of slabs of timber where the "tie-hacks" lived while they timbered our pine forests, carefully managing the cutting to preserve the forest for continued growth. It was this group who gathered on Saturday night for a dance in our attic that gave me my first experience with square dancing. This was their authentic dancing with a fiddler and what came to be called a "hoe down" in later years in the "city". I danced many years in Webster Groves, loving every minute, but never was it so authentic. Our group in the St. Louis suburb did not wear forester boots and stomp so rhythmically and zealously.

Maurita in the fountain at Hillandale

Playing in the creeks provided some of our best fun especially in the summer. "There", exclaimed my sister Betty, "catch that crawdad for me". She was six years younger and not so daring as I. We created small dams and once found a pool so deep we could sit in it, calling it the "queen's bathtub". When I grew up, I could never find that site again. One's perspective does change as years pass.

We had two miles of road from our nearest neighbor and had to ford a large creek. On the county map it was known as *fourche de renault*, the crossing of the fox. This reminds us of our French heritage in Missouri that was rather successfully erased from memory by the British coming into the Mississippi much later. The local folks just call this wide creek "forshanuh", the water in which I first dog-paddled, the crossing where one time the 1930's car stalled and Daddy had to carry Mother and me to land, the water that later became part of the watershed for Sunnen Lake at the YMCA of the Ozarks.

I must finally mention the cave on our property. As children we could only explore with grown-ups. Caves do not change a lot in one's lifetime, only a blip in the life of a cave. The "fatman's pinch" was as far as my grandfather could go. Forty years later it was still the stopping point for some. Daddy gave permission for visitors to the YMCA to come and explore this little cave. When stalactites were broken from the ceiling and visitors left watermelon rinds in our creek, the polite gesture for visits was withdrawn. No doubt this had happened many times, but we were on the site at this time. I learned a lesson in respect for property of others.

Wellborn, Fay & Maurita Estes, 1923

How quiet a summer evening was at Hillandale. How cool to loll on the porch as the moonlight rose through the trees. We waited for the whippoorwill to begin its nighttime lullaby. We listened to the winds through the pines. In 1982 I named our Colorado home "Pine Winds".

So, I ask myself: "How is it that I was happier in pigtails and shorts on camping vacations than in a resort or city shopping?" How is it that I have had travels to many parts of our world but find the most interesting ones discovering varied, sometimes weird landscapes, walking desert trails, rafting rivers, climbing mountains? How is our life designed? And I answer: "Through bundles of experiences, layering one on another".

February 18, 2011

Grandparents Come for Autumn Visits

Memories of climbing up and up onto Fafa's quite ample "tummy" was a joy of my early childhood. Fafa was my own translation of "Foddy" as his daughter, my Aunt Alline, spoke to him. Fafa was my paternal grandfather and Muddee (another name I translated from English) was my paternal grandmother. That was about the time motoring in one's own car across our transcontinental highway became a possibility. Adventurous Americans ventured forth in numbers. My grandparents retired to California to return in the Autumn months to be with us in St. Louis. On these visits they would stay down near Potosi, Missouri, at Hillandale, a home Daddy had built on property about twelve miles from town. I had lived there until I was about three, when Mother and Daddy moved into St. Louis. Therefore, my early memories of my grandparents were there, as we went down to visit every weekend in the Fall when they were visiting from California.

While cuddling with Fafa he told me stories of two boys and their adventures. Bob and Bill lived on the banks of the ocean. I used to remember more and wish that he had written the stories down. I can still hear his voice and feel hugged, so it is probably as well he only told the stories. I recall only one about these boys going down to the beach. They made amazing discoveries…the water in the ocean was MAPLE SYRUP and the pancakes were made of beach sand…how delicious! His telling this tale built incredible suspense, asking me to imagine with him. Of course, these could not be written…Fafa made up the stories as he was telling me. Storytelling is a lost art, perhaps.

I pause and reflect on time spent with my three "great-grands". Usually once or twice a year with Ayla and Milo in West Virginia. I expect little or no recall. Now I have moved to Ohio to be nearer to some family. Iris, the #3 great-grand, is here. What time might she recall from age three or four when she opens her Memory Bank as an adult?

Memories I have of Muddee are, likewise, simply bits and

pieces, although I later did go to California for a visit when I was about eight. Just as I sit here at my desk, I can feel the texture of Muddee's face, a mass of soft wrinkles, delicate and "velvety" to my touch. The large two-story stucco house at Hillandale stood at the top of a hill with a long walk leading up to it flanked with roses and irises. Halfway up was a square concrete basin about 5' x 5' and 3' deep for a fountain that made a very safe wading pool. It was special fun when Daddy turned on the fountain to spray me. A very thin coating of the accumulation of algae made the bottom just slick enough to add another dimension to the wading.

In 1930 and probably forward into the 60's we had only 2-lane highways on our weekend drives from St. Louis to "the farm" (Hillandale). I was fearful of travel, especially when Daddy had to pass into the other lane to avoid farm machines and trucks not traveling at his speed. I can hear Mother now, "Oh Bun, be careful"! Other admonitions followed often and each one made me a bit more fearful. Returning on Sunday nights I can still see the long trail of taillights Daddy would pass. I crouched in the back seat, hardly breathing. I do not recall any other fears from childhood, but to this day I do not relish

Tallula Martha Carroll Estes, Santa Ana CA, 1938

two-lane roads. We have years of "road trips" and I learned not to take my turn driving on "country" roads until Neil was ready for a nap. I said to myself, "I will just drive until he wakes up", because I knew then he would find a time to say, "Pass him, pass him".

2018

Designs for Living

"We haven't moved in yet", my Father said in response to my excitement looking at a new apartment. "Just wait a while to make plans". It did seem that our family visited many apartments for rent. The fact is we did live in four places in my first eight years. As I look back over these homes, I find I recall something of note about each one.

The first was on northeast Kings Highway, now razed for building an interstate highway. The address would be somewhere in my private archives but is of no import to my story. A doll as big as I was at age three is more important. She had real hair, eyes that opened and shut and best of all a record in her back that "talked". Certainly not a doll with which I could play. But I do remember how sad (and maybe angry) I was when Harriet, my one and only playmate, knocked her off the arm of the chair and I could no longer wind her up. The incident, traumatic at the time, did not affect our friendship, as we remained friends through high school.

The other event has been related to me, so I do not have it in my own Memory Bank. It seems I informed my mother one day when I was three, "I am going down to see Daddy at his office". Mother nodded her head and did not further the conversation. Sometime later, so I was told, she frantically started out to find me on NE Kings Highway. Seeing a single woman racing along prompted a passing car to stop, and there I was in the front seat with the driver. Mother relating the story when I was grown up needed to say no more. Even in 1926 kids did get lost.

Before I turned five, we moved to University City, the first suburb of St. Louis. U. City had been founded about 1902, a bit more than 20 years earlier. Having heard innumerable times that Mother wanted to move to Webster Groves, a small town like she had grown up in. She thought that living in apartments would be like "cliff dwellers", though she had never seen the "cliff dwellers" except in the *National Geographic*. Daddy, having grown up in St. Louis, probably countered: "Oh, no Webster Groves is too far out of town, too far out from where I will want to work". I cannot recall ever hearing a conversation specifically, but I have heard variations multiple times. To this day I do not like apartments, though I have lived in several in the last decade. Has Mother's attitude surfaced in my dislike? I am happily living in a cottage, across the drive from the three-story apartment building in a retirement community.

In tribute to my parents, I must say that in my childhood at the time I was living in a neighborhood of 100% apartments and I liked where I lived. Despite some negative feelings Mother harbored, we had a good home wherever we were. The first was at 761 Heman between Eastgate and Westgate in University City. It was from there I walked to kindergarten about 3/4 of a mile, crossing Westgate, going under some tracks in a tunnel, and on up past the Loop to Delmar-Harvard. I remember it taking a long time to cross Westgate, as I was not to cross if I saw a car coming. That school will be closed this year after a long history. We lived on the first floor and there my sister was born. In today's world much is made of the second sibling, how to introduce the new baby, to watch for sibling rivalry. I either have a poor memory, or the folks did a good job of bringing on a sister. Or we just did not make crises out of every normal happening. In any event we did move again.

The big remembrance for me in the next home at 710 Limit was the tornado of 1927. Without any fear I was standing at the window in the sunroom, home from morning kindergarten around noon. I was struck with wonder and awe as it was dark as night. Fear was not an emotion I felt. When I grew up, I realized how anxious my mother must have been until she could have some word re: the whereabouts of Daddy. In the days before instant newscasts, cell phones, sirens, how was she to know where the tornado had hit down or where Daddy was? He was rarely in his office but out around the city "making calls" in his insurance business.

Next move, 6250 Enright, third floor was in the next couple of years when I was in the 2nd or 3rd grade. This apartment, typical of the whole block, had a center walk into the building flanked by lawn with each side having a centered tree. These trees we called "Umbrella trees", as they were pruned to be about 10 feet tall with a crown like an umbrella. Such a fad as it was to have an umbrella tree. I knew nothing more about this species of nature until I was older and much interested in trees. They were catalpa trees, spectacular beautiful showy flowers and long seed pods developed known as "Lady cigars". It is a tree that is considered "messy" by those who want plants to suit one's individual tastes rather than to the natural bent of the tree.

It was from this home that I was able to roller skate every day after school. There was a walk between our apartment and next door with a ramp down to the sidewalk. With practice I could navigate that ramp, make a turn onto the sidewalk. And with my advanced age of eight I could also skate across the back alley over to Delmar where there was a new sidewalk with a "float finish", smooth for skating unlike the brown granitoid on my street.

My sister, Betty, and I slept in a Murphy Bed in the "back room" at times when my Uncle John lived with us. This was a bed, coming back into fashion now, that let down from a wall closet. It was from here that we could see the lighted top of the Park Plaza high up in the sky on Kings Highway. We imagined it to be an ocean liner sailing in the dark sky. We stayed in this apartment until I was ten. Boys came into my life there...my first Valentine, a tiny heart-shaped cake left at my door. The giver ran away, as we were not supposed to know who gave us a Valentine. Of course, I knew. (I still see Eddie now and then around town). And I learned the art of communication before cell phones. We had two tin cans and a long string to talk across our back porches—David at one end, me at the other. And there was David with whom I could walk to school and have big discussions on politics. FDR was in the news.

Memories sometimes become like a cobbler, just cobbled up. History should be exacting, but not necessarily in a story. I was nearing my 10th birthday when Daddy asked me one evening: "Sweetie, will you go down to the garage and bring me my 'rate' book? I left it on the front seat". I complied and jumped down the three flights of back steel steps and ran across the backyard to the alley. I was so excited to see a shiny bicycle in the garage! I picked up the rate book, ran back upstairs and, thinking the bicycle was to be a surprise, said nothing about seeing it. How disappointed Daddy must have been. How silly I was not to know that he expected me to see it. Nevertheless, I remember it well...my first bicycle, a 28" wheel with coaster brakes. I rode miles for the next eight years when I bought a used English bike with gears that was to be my mode of transportation for my first city job.

We moved one last time in my "growing-up" years soon after that birthday. This time into a Dutch Colonial home at 775 Harvard. It had a large yard, the last on the block. A living room was across the front of the house entered into from a porch (screened in the summer) the same length. A dining room and kitchen were across the back of the house. Stairs went up to a landing with a large Bay window and window seat. Turning, we went to the second floor with three bedrooms and a bath. A basement housed a fine new furnace, an "Iron Fireman" that burned coke, rather than coal. That was known to be better for the environment. A washing machine with a hand-turned wringer made Mother feel up to date for 1936!

775 Harvard was Home. The apartments were just like stepping stones to this one where I lived until I went away to College. Those years were big chapters in growing up.

March 3, 2011

Home at Seven Seven Five

Soon after my tenth birthday we moved from the apartment district in the east end of University City to a neighborhood of single-family dwellings at the western end of University City. University City was the first suburb of St. Louis. Missouri. Excitement heightened for me as always with a move. We had moved 3 times in five years. Seven seven five would be my address until I graduated from High School.

Our Dutch Colonial six-room house was the last in a long downhill block of modest homes. It was crowned at the top with an historic landmark, the Magazine Building circa 1903, now our City Hall. Coming down the slight hill, passing Delmar-Harvard grade school and Ward Junior High School, ours had the largest yard curving around the bottom of the hill. All of Harvard seemed like a tunnel with large, overarching Elm trees.

Well do I remember being the "new kid on the block". About the first day after moving one of the boys on the street ran into my brand-new bike and broke a spoke. Eugene, for that was his name, might have done that on purpose to tease me, trying to act like a smart boy all of twelve or thirteen. Never was he nor his brother in our Harvard group. I realize now that they were older than most of us.

This house had many features much to my liking. I delighted especially in having my own room. Tiny as it was, it had room for just a twin bed, a dresser, two windows, a closet and no room for my sister, Betty. The first time in my life I had a room of my own.

As the years passed this old house was able to meet our changing needs. A large, cedar-lined closet in one of the bedrooms afforded me plenty of floor space for a real hide-away, a space always needed for girls of ten with secrets.

Underneath the landing of the basement stairs was the kind of place needed for the "club house" years. Here the GDDC club was organized. The mission had something to do with Good Deeds and was the setting for my first novel written in a brown spiral notebook. I had no marketing experience and, therefore, it was never published.

The best architectural feature any teenage girl would relish was the large Bay window with a window seat on the landing of the stairs. It was a storage for blankets for Mother, but when the lid was down there was ample depth ideal for lolling on while talking endlessly on the telephone. This talking time usually after school was as necessary in the '30's, much as the mobile phone and texting in 2018. The telephone served for the necessary communication with friends. The phone was not portable and therefore, it was an after-school activity, not an ongoing addiction as it seems to be today.

775 Harvard

Our garage, free standing at the top of the drive, filled an especially important niche in Junior High when the girls on the block mounted a drama event. Writing a play based on *Little Women* the garage became the stage; the theater, folding chairs set up on the driveway in front. We were quite serious about our production, costumes and staging. My father captured the "after-party" on the lawn with a 16mm movie camera. This had to be outside as at the time he did not have lights for indoors. Those silly, teasing boys crashed our party just to make goofy faces at the camera. Home movies were very much of a novelty at the time. Wesley Mahan, my grandson, has digitized many reels of these movies and made a DVD "Family Journeys 1930-1970" to pass on to the 3rd generation. It was only a couple of years later that those boys no longer were clowning around but gathered in our homes for co-ed activities. Jack's Dad ** installed a jukebox in their rathskeller and we learned to dance to the tunes of the Big Bands. Bill ** had a ping-pong table and his parents welcomed us to sharpen that skill, as well as learning to play card games and even one with dice called "21". Ray**, the oldest brother in the Pepping household, spent all his time fixing up old cars and on rare occasions took us for a ride around the block. Charlie,** a 10th grader, asked me to go to a dance at high school when I was only a 9th grader. I wore a yellow knit dress I had completed as my first knitting project, feeling quite grown-up! Of course, we walked to and from the high school for the dance. "Unbelievable" my granddaughter, sixteen, commented recently when I related the story. "Grandmother", she asked incredulously, "you walked out to the dance? Unbelievable". I explained that only about two of our classmates had cars. A fellow had to use the family car for dates.

Eighth grade was the year that the crowd gathered for home parties, branching out sometimes beyond our immediate neighborhood. This happened because three elementary schools combined into one Junior High School. One of the boys from another neighborhood joined us in our old crowd. I found I had a tiny feeling that he was someone special. He became my husband about thirteen years later.

Outdoor activities, especially on summer nights, were the highlight of summer. The exceptionally large school yard afforded us the space for "Capture the Flag" and "Prisoner's Base", the smooth concrete space in front of Junior High was perfect for roller-skating, not rough like the granitoid sidewalks. "Kick the Can", most popular on our driveway in the daylight, was converted to "Tag the Lamppost" at night. Lying down on the lawn in the long shadow cast by the lamppost posed a problem for "It".

When "everyone out come in free" was shouted for everyone to hear the game became a race. No one could be identified by name until "It" was close; a race to tag the lamppost ensued at once.

Mid-summer nights were just as hot and muggy as today. Having no air conditioning, many nights we could not sleep upstairs but had a pallet or a cot on the front screen porch. The sound of the night watchman dropping his stick on the sidewalk as he made rounds was always a comfort to us. I can hear it now.

What a "lark" it was for us one year when the River Des Peres overflowed the banks flooding our yard. Some guys came paddling up in their canoe. Our basement had a few feet of water in it. Daddy's adrenaline surely kicked in as he lifted the washing machine up on the table out of the water. Helping cleanup was just part of living in our family. No complaints. I know now it was no adventure for my parents!

775 was home, always a beehive of activity, until I left for College. The folks moved to a duplex at 7104 Amherst while I was away at school. This apartment was never home for me though I lived there my last two years until graduating from Washington University. Moving on, I left for my first job in West Virginia. I returned to St. Louis in 1946 to be married to that new boy from another neighborhood in Junior High.

**indicating one of the neighbors on Harvard
April 2018, revised June 13, 2018

Finding Grandfather

Sometime ago, in our year 2014, Mike, my nephew, received an email from an unknown address. Being one of the Millennial generation wary of unknown addresses on an email, he made no response. A second and a third came from the same woman in Florida and he responded. The sender suggested to Mike that her husband was related to Mike's great-grandfather. Indeed, that piqued the interest of our whole family.

Mike has a strong interest in genealogy, having already generated a volume on his maternal side of the family. No one knew anything at all about the paternal grandfather. Three generations had only oral tradition about this Grandfather named "Mr. Carroll". We pictured him a "swashbuckling young man, swooping into the small town in Mississippi and sweeping a young woman who was to be our grandmother off her feet". He went off to the Civil War, leaving his bride pregnant and never returning. Such a romantic story, more so as we embellished it through retelling it through the years. Baby was born and named Martha Tallulah Carroll, my paternal Grandmother, whose Mother had died while she was an infant. Muddee, my affectionate name for one dearly beloved, was raised by childless Aunt Sal and Uncle Gid. She lived to be 97. She was a delightful raconteur, but there was never any more story of her lost father. That is until 2014.

Mike pursued his correspondence with Florida, and now there is another story all told by email and possible only with the Internet. Now I can tell another story gleaned from Florida, even sending pictures. Because my nephew dabbled in family ancestry, it was known on various websites that he was interested in the Carroll family. In Jackson, MI, where he was living, Carroll is a common name. Hence the initial email was generated.

"Mrs. Florida" wrote: "My husband is the son of Charles Carroll, that I think is your lost Grandfather. We have known that family many years and here is their story. Young, wounded soldier, Charles Carroll did return from the war and did learn that his wife had died, and baby was being well cared for. Surely, he asked himself: 'How can I possibly care for my baby, I, wounded, jobless, homeless veteran?' Or did Uncle Gid insist he leave town? We like to think he made himself known, met Martha, his baby, met Uncle Gid and decided to go on. Fact is that Charles Carroll did settle about 20 miles away and made his home with a 'buddy's' family. Several years later he married the daughter of the family with whom he lived. Subsequently, the new Charles Carroll family went to Belize, a colony then of Britain. Needing a labor force, Americans were given land to farm cotton. That venture failed and the Carrolls moved back to Florida and raised a family."

Thanks to the Internet and a nephew to follow his emails, our family now has a new legend. I will be the storyteller for my immediate family. I will make it romantic for my children, the Grands and the Greats.

October 28, 2015; Revised and updated March 26, 2018

Around the Table

"Six o'clock, time to eat. Wash your hands for dinner". I can hear Mother's voice now, never cross, but authoritative. As long as I can remember we sat down to dinner with Daddy, just four around the table counting my sister, Betty. Daddy said the "blessing", always the same. I can hear his voice over the years. Frustrated Betty, six years younger, said: "Daddy you say the same thing every night and I cannot understand you"! She asked me recently: "What grace did Daddy say? I never could understand". I do not recall that his diction ever improved.

Mother was a good nutritionist in the days when it was not a subject uppermost in minds as it seems to be in 2014. We ate organically, as in 1930's and 40's we did not have the variety of foods brought in from all over the world. Fresh vegetables were on the menu only when they were "home-grown". All our markets were "farmer's markets". No great variety and we all ate what was on our plates. I do not remember any picky eaters and my mother is not here to share her memory.

Monday nights we had Baked Potato, Spinach and Calves Liver. Greenish gray canned spinach I might add, except in the growing season. Not until I was grown and married did I learn that Daddy did not like liver or spinach, and he was never home for dinner on Monday nights as the Poker Club met then. Mother knew we had to have Liver and Spinach for our iron; therefore, it would be served on Monday nights.

No pies, lard in the crust was not "good for us". Cokes were unheard of in our diet. Maybe we had one at a birthday party. Root Beer floats we had only if the temperature was over 100.

Breakfast was a MUST. Corn Flakes and Rice Krispies were the choices for cereal sometimes. Hot cereal was *de rigueur* through the winter and there we had three choices: oatmeal, cream of wheat and Ralston. We heard about the latter every night at 5:45 when we listened to "Jack Armstrong, the All-American Boy". Ralston sponsored that program on the radio until "Dinner at Six".

Sunday "dinner" was at noon when we got home from church. It was the time we sometimes had a roast. Our beef through the week came in the form of meatloaf, sometimes hamburger.

Desserts consisted of fruit, custards, homemade cookies, and cake for special times. "Mother's Delight" we called an Angel Food Cake iced with Droste's Cocoa in whipped cream. I know for certain that was almost only on the menu one or two times a year. It was too costly, too fat, and too caloric. Today it would not be so special, as "Whipped Cream" is commonly artificial and "fat-free". Mother's recipe "Devil's Food Cake with Mocha Icing" has been handed down to at least two of my daughters.

Our family dinners were not hurried and remembered fondly by both my sister and me. Daddy would often pose arithmetic problems to us. For example, he would say "Take seven, take away three, multiply by 10...what is the answer?" He would have six or ten factors for us to follow in our heads, giving the answer when he chose to stop asking. Or we could have spelling bees at the table. But there were rules. Betty could not bring a book to the table for example. We had to make "Hoover" plates (the Shiny Plate club of today) before we could have dessert. I make "shiny plates" to this day. We sat up straight, too. We could chide each other with a special song about not wanting any "camels at our table with a hump". We did not learn to cook as we grew up. but were expected to help in the kitchen some, set the table, do the dishes. As a teenager I did help serve dinner when Mother and Daddy had guests.

The only cooking experience I recall was on Friday night when I was in high school. That night I was responsible for having dinner ready at six when Daddy, having picked Mother up from the Symphony, would arrive home. I liked pounding out a Round steak smothered in Tomatoes and that became my standard fare for Friday.

Though we had no extended family in St. Louis regularly, there were some years when one or another of Mother's relatives lived in St. Louis for a time. It was great fun to have aunts and uncles around for a time. The one-time Daddy's brother-in-law, Uncle Harry, and his sister Aunt Alline came to dinner I enjoyed. Uncle Harry had been a photographer for *National Geographic* which, of course, made him seem special as those magazines were to us. They came from Rochester, New York, a place so exotic. At dinner this memorable evening, Daddy was struggling with the wooden skewers holding a "rolled rib roast" together. "Here", said Uncle Harry, "Let me help you". With that he opened his suit coat, reached around his back where he had a large tool belt, and handed Daddy a pair of pliers. "Here, Wellborn, these will grab hold of that skewer". I was poised and did not laugh. I still can muffle a giggle when I think of that episode.

    I do regret that the "Family Dinner" seems passe today. I think it was a time to have conversation with our parents, to talk about the school day or plans coming up. We did not seem to be always rushing. What has taken that piece of Family Life in today's society?

March 6, 2014

My Crowning Glory

"Be sure to cut just above the tip of her ear, and the bang should be straight across her forehead…" my mother said to Theresa in the beauty parlor as I sat swathed in a white sheet, hiding me completely. Mother was one who doted on manners, looks, and neatness above all. I learned quickly to be very still as I could see those scissors snipping just above my eyebrows.

I behaved because that was my mother's expectation. I think I must have liked the whole setting in the beauty parlor. It had some smells of lotions and shampoos that were different from home. I found the little flames heating up some gadget to curl ladies' hair intriguing as well as those big metal drums ladies put their heads in to dry their hair. Theresa was the barber, and I did like her a lot. I was acquainted with the beauty parlor because I had gone with Mother many times for her hair care.

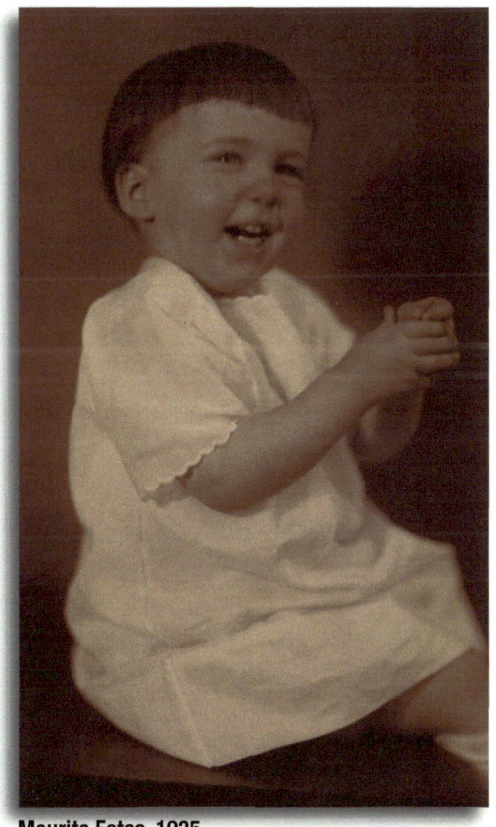
Maurita Estes, 1925

Washing our hair was really a ritual. "Your hair is your crowning glory", Mother said. Oftentimes this weekly hair routine would begin with a hot oil treatment when little dabs of cotton soaked with warm olive oil were rubbed all over my scalp. This was followed by washing with Castile soap that had somehow been melted. (No commercial shampoos were available or else Mother thought Castile was the purest.) A special vinegar rinse followed many water rinses. Being a dark brunette called for the vinegar rinse for me, while my little sister, a blond with Shirley Temple curls, had a lemon juice rinse.

When I was six or seven, we had no shower in our apartment, so the whole shampooing was done with me kneeling in the tub with my head under the faucet. By age 10, I pleaded with Mother, "Please let me wash my hair in the basin. You can watch to be sure I rinse it well". Towel drying in the summer was OK, but in winter to dry our hair we had to sit in front of the open door of the gas oven, with a newspaper tent over our head. Mother was sure we would "catch cold" if we just let it dry naturally. In my house it was always "Mother knows best" and I endured the drying method.

I turned 12 years of age and straight hair was NOT the style, so the same beauty parlor gave me my first of many years of permanents. The process began with a monstrous machine from which dangled curlers around which my hair was wrapped and, like magic, my hair would become curly. I did feel grown up at the beauty parlor, it being a world of ladies "under dryers" or ladies being marcelled and the smells of lotions and shampoos making the place smell so clean. I do not have any recall of dialogue or discussion with mother to curl or not to curl. It was just time to have curls.

Believe me, we really worked hard for me to be in-fashion and keep the curls. The routine became curlers every night, rubber, metal, bristly ones, plastic ones, rag strips, and regular permanents. Always a new kind, none of which really were ever satisfactory. Summers were a blessing because I went to camp and could wear pigtails!

Finally, I "came of age" about age 20 and could wear a chignon, or braids in coronet style around my head or "pigtails" in camp every summer until I was about 24. Those years I was directing camps, and so was OK with such a hairdo.

A few years later, in my early thirties, I naturally came into fashion. Friends would ask: "Who frosts your hair? Or who tips your hair"? Those colorings were the "fad". I would just say "Oh! God is the artist". My hair had been turning white in streaks or tips since about age 19.

Some change became necessary as my family activities and community responsibilities changed. One summer, I was going on a camping vacation. My hair would need care where care was not going to be around. It was time for a haircut! This cut necessitated not one, but two trips to the beauty parlor. I just could not cut my long hair all at once.

I have not had long hair since that time at about age 45. I could go camping, bicycling, swimming without giving my hair a thought. AH! Freedom! I still fuss with my hair a lot to little or no avail. I still have bad hair days. I keep trying different styles and different salons. But straight hair is what I have, and I am grateful to still have some. My crowning glory!

October 14, 2010; rewrite January 1, 2011

Olley, Olley, Outs in Free

"Kick the Can" was probably played around the world, or some game likened to the game we played. We played every day as I recall. My recollection is not correct I am sure because in the same years I was roller-skating, jumping rope, practicing my piano, riding a bicycle. Be that as it may, this game was the most popular with all the neighborhood. I can readily count nine regular players ranging in age from six to twelve, boys and girls.

I did not understand the words of the chant we yelled out. It sounded like "alley, alley oxen free". It was recently, like last week, I read an article titled "Games We Played" that I saw the words in print for the first time. I knew the rules of the game, when to call out and then what to do. If a player could run out of hiding and kick the can before being tagged all players previously caught would be freed.

If a player could climb the small Maple tree near the drive, hide in the leaves, she or he could readily jump down and kick the can when "It" was scouring the bushes or looking around a corner.

It was most fun to play after dark when the game became "Tag the Lamppost". Our street curved all the way around our side yard with the lamppost at the curve, casting a shadow all the way back to the house. A rose bed was in the center of this part of the lawn. Bodies lying down on the grass behind somewhat resembled large towels. Since "It" had to call the name of a player while trying to be the first to reach the lamppost, it became a footrace if a "Towel" could get up fast enough after being identified.

Games varied as we grew up. Early elementary years, "Mother May I?" was played with little sisters. "Drop the Handkerchief" was a standard for birthday parties. "Jacks" was one we could play for years, as we swiftly became more and more proficient. We could scoop up three, four, or all the jacks with one bounce. Mother was a daunting opponent. Hopscotch seems to be played even now. I see remnants of chalk on the sidewalks. I wonder if there are competitions in the schools. I was the champion in third grade. I wonder if that is where I first began to wear out the cartilage in my knee. Standing on one leg, leaning down to pick up the rock where it landed would help my balance today of that I am sure....hmm! Jumping rope, particularly Double-Dutch, was a recess activity. I must think to ask friends if anyone can remember the rhymes and rhythms we had as we jumped. But where is recess in the school day today?

We played many variations of Tag. Two come quickly to mind: 1) keep a hand on your body that had been tagged; 2) stoop tag—stoop to avoid being tagged. We were so fortunate to have our school yard open for playing after school until darkness sent us home. How unfortunate kids in the city without yards do not have this permission now. This enabled us to have wide games like "Capture the Flag", a tag game involving two teams with a mission to capture the "flag" (someone's bandana or an old banner of someone's father). Being co-ed, this was especially popular as we began to take note of those guys who had played "Kick the Can".

"Lemonade" was a fun Junior High game; variations are played today. Two teams huddle apart to think of words, books, movies that have dramatic possibilities. On call, one team marches across the playing field—room, yard, gym, church basement—approaching the adversaries chanting "here we come". Response "Where from?" Answer: New York, New Orleans, Kirkwood, any location chosen. "What's your trade?" "Lemonade" "Well, show us some". And the whole group dramatizes the word, book, previously chosen. When one on the "audience" team shouts out the correct answer the WHOLE acting team turns quickly and runs back to "home base". Those caught stay with the catchers. This is an adaptation of Charades, a "grown-up" game played for several generations. My 75-year-old version I think is more creative-fun-style than my children and grandchildren play. It must be a good activity as it is still played today.

Variations of these games were played by my friend growing up in Poland. It was a cross-cultural "game" we played remembering "things our mothers taught us"..."hold hands when you cross the street" was one that tickled our memories.

November 6, 2013

Just for Fun

Just for fun, in this memoir I will allow my memory this evening simply to flow while I jot down what crosses my mind. This has been a stunning Autumn day. Leaves still dress the trees in clear yellows, the Sour Gum in Blackburn Park is brilliantly clothed in vermillion. As I let my memories drift, the wind tells me that Father Winter may chase Autumn away tonight. I still delight in shuffling through the leaves though I am so happy not to any longer rake great lawns, but only my small patio at Dogwood Cottage in "Pacific Place". I have lived here ten months.

  Looking up at the clouds, scanning to see what airplane is overhead, I remember when Charles Lindbergh returned to St. Louis after his pioneer flight overseas in 1927. It was the first flight over the Atlantic, from St. Louis to Paris. Daddy took me out to see him in his motor cavalcade. I have been told we went out on Warson Road by a Gate House to a large Estate where he was staying. As I have grown up in St. Louis, I do not believe today that was where we went. I do not know and why should I need to find out really where we were when I was five? I cherish my memory and have shared it with some of my children. That is how oral traditions become truths.

  Scarves have always been a part of my wardrobe. Woolen scarves for warmth when ice skating out of doors. Large light-weight wool to wear around our shoulders *in lieu* of a coat. When I first went to France, it was a very European style. Today scarves are an important accessory to an outfit. Folks in Retail or Wardrobe Consultants do demonstrations on clever ways to wear these decorative scarves. Attending one such program recently I had a showing of one of the newest attempts to dramatize a suit or dress. Taking the scarf, folding, tying in a way to encircle one's neck, the saleslady thought she had a most creative and attractive item. She tied a scarf on me for further demonstration. I felt just like I had a rag salved with Vicks Vaporub around my throat. Such was the remedy for sore throats when I was a child.

I seldom have desserts after dinner, but this evening, dining out, I thought the menu item, Beignet with Strawberry Sauce, sounded most delightful. Beignet, of course, reminded me of New Orleans and my honeymoon. In 1946 the Bride's family did all the preparations for the wedding and the groom, as per tradition, made plans for the Honeymoon. Destination weddings were not even in dreams then. Simmering in my mind just now is one dinner we had at a large hotel dining room in New Orleans. Neil, my groom, had very recently returned from overseas serving in WWII. He casually mentioned to the waiter that he sure had missed having salads while in the Army. When his salad was served, I gasped, as I had never seen a salad so large served with dinner. Kindness like this was not infrequent for men serving in the military then. If only we could have received men returning from VietNam in the same way.

What did I wish for as a child? I do not recall many wishes. One remains vivid: a bicycle I did really want when I was ten. That wish came true, my only two-wheeler, coaster brake bike until I bought an English bike for transportation to my first "summer job" at 18. A Party was seldom a part of the birthday celebration, but always an angel food cake. I did not know until after I married that one had a choice of cakes for his/her birthday cake. Mine just was angel cake with a hole in the middle, white seven-minute icing, candles numbering our age plus one to grow on. I wonder if any child or grandchild of mine with "home" parties or at the Zoo or "Chuck E. Cheese" will have any fonder memories after eight decades. I am certain no one will recall helping beat the 7-minute icing with a hand-operated eggbeater. My mother needed our help as seven minutes was too long to stand and beat alone. When I was three or four, I was pleased to share songs from Sunday School or that I learned from my grandfather, Fafa. I sang some ditty learned by rote the end line being: "All good things for children and dogs". (Translation: ...for children we know) Or, from Fafa: "Row, row your boat, gently down the stream, Life is butter dream". I know these anecdotes because Daddy told them to his grandchildren.

Memories ooze around in my head when I lie abed after my alarm awakens me each morning. Just think, dear reader, how many days have dawned and then folded into memory as each night falls!

November 2011

Thirteen in Thirty-five

Mark Twain is quoted as saying: "When I was a boy of fourteen, my father was so ignorant. But when I got to be twenty-one, I was astonished at how much the man had learned in seven years". Parodying, I would say, "When I was a girl of fourteen my father asked me to dance one evening and I thought he was rather dull because he did not 'dip' and 'twirl' like the guys in high school. When I was 21 and had the chance to dance with Daddy, I thought he was a wonderful dancer. How did he learn so fast?" To this day, I cherish having danced with Daddy, one of the best dancers ever to lead me.

It was probably in the Rothwell's basement, two houses up the street, that I really learned to dance. Mr. Rothwell had installed a Jukebox with great bands playing on it and a "slug" to use. Ping-pong was set up there and my first card-playing. It was the "teen" center of the neighborhood before such centers became a part of the cityscapes. No dating was in my life until I entered 10th grade. But the Rothwell's teen center gave me good preparation as that same gang morphed into first dates.

My first high school dance was really the spring of my 9th grade year with a date with Charlie, one of the neighborhood group. We walked out to the dance at school and home again. One

Maurita & Joe Burch, University City High School Classmates

mile each way. Dates for High School dances were most always special dates. We had many dances sponsored by clubs in High School. Student Council, Hi-Y*and Tribe**. Many off-campus dances were sponsored by sororities and fraternities. Barn dances were popular, too. Some formal, but all were dresses and heels except in Barns. Movie dates were popular as today. If we were asked to go downtown to the Ambassador or to Grand Avenue, heels and gloves were *de rigueur*. One of my best friends going back to Grade School was Louis Maull. He transferred to CBC for High School, so all of our dates were with his high school fraternity or movies. Best of all, he liked to go to the Candlelight for cinnamon toast and tea. This was a special place farther west on Clayton Road than Parkmoor where everyone usually went after any date. My first date with the boy driving was with Louie and my mother remembered all her life watching the taillights go up the hill from our home. We dated all through High School with nary a hug nor a kiss and kept our friendship through college and into our early years of marriage. After our respective marriages, we were friends as couples.

    Mother and Daddy had firm boundaries for my social life. One hour after a dance or movie was over, I had to be home. That was ample time for a hamburger or tea. No Sunday nights except League meetings (the Methodist Teen meetings). They knew the closing time of those meetings. No dates on weeknights.

    My High School, University City, had three classes: 1100 students in 1937. Three years later we had 233 students graduating, about 25% headed to college. We had many extra-curricular clubs, sports, and organizations. I was on the swim team, though we did not have a natatorium as they do today. However, Helen Manley was head of all the Physical Education in the school and made arrangements for us to swim downtown at Bishop Tuttle High School in mid-city St. Louis. Miss Manley had arranged this fine experience. We had no busses at this time, no field trips. With such commitment she built a team with a pool in our school.

    An embarrassment in my Junior year is still in the cobwebs in my brain. I was walking home from school (as I did every day) with my long-time friend, John. We were leisurely strolling along, holding hands, when one of our teachers drove by. I could have crawled in any one of the sidewalk cracks as he waved to us.

I was involved in clubs at school as well as in a high school sorority, Psi Beta Sigma. There were three, one of which was mostly Clayton High girls. We met on Sunday afternoons, the only time I could have the car. We had two dances a year. It was here I first learned from the Seniors some of the ways of the world outside of school. These were bits about living as a teen that my mother had not told me. At the time it was important that I "belong" to a group.

I still see several of my classmates from U. City. We agree we had the best of schools. Some teachers stand out in my memory. Ugly Miss Cowan who excited us to read Shakespeare as she dramatized the witches from "Macbeth" while stirring her cauldron. Miss Johnson taught Senior Comp, the first and only writing class I had. Handing in a theme every Monday morning was her assignment. Miss Wofner, French teacher, was so "hippy" she could not waddle down rows between the desks except sideways. She made the culture of France and the sight of Paris come alive for us. If only "Junior year Abroad" had been available in our year, we would not have needed a map to find our way around Paris. Dr. Urch, wrinkly and small, we thought as ancient as the Ancient History he taught. We took notes on his lectures just as we would do in college.

Did any friendships last? My answer is a resounding "Yes"! I married Neil who had been one of the eighth-grade gang I have written about previously. We were married 46 years. Joe Burch, our Senior Class president, became my second husband 61 years after we graduated. We saw each other at the 55th Class Reunion and married six years later.

*Hi-Y sponsored by the YMCA
**Tribe -a club whose members had earned letters in school sports

November 10, 2012

Pin Oak

My father, Welborn Estes, was always self-employed. Hence, we had no vacations like so many corporate employees. Daddy was an agent for Aetna Life Insurance company. He was a top producer with a mid-career change to Occidental Life Insurance company. Only in later years of his career did we take any vacations. However, each year we did have a 10 day "road trip". We went in different directions every year. I did not know any other way for a family to travel with our budget.

I had happy summer activities and found a heap of fun, and Mother approved because I was outdoors and learning new skills every day. From age 11 through college and early marriage years I spent time in camp. My camp years when I was 14 and 15 years old were times of my best learning and were most exceptional in every respect.

My birthday is in mid-August, and therefore I could not go to "Pioneer Hill" the year I was going to be 14 according to

Maurita, Counselor at Cedarledge Resident Camp St. Louis Girl Scout Council, 1940

the St. Louis Girl Scout Council. To camp on "Pioneer Hill" had been my goal since I was 11 years old and attended Camp Cedarledge. To my extreme good fortune, that year St. Louis Senior Scouts had a new opportunity to be in a waterfront unit at Camp Pin Oak on the Lake of the Ozarks. What a lucky day for me that the Council realized that waterfront activities were missing from the St. Louis Council camp program. One unit at Pin Oak was rented from the Jefferson City Girl Scout Council. From that summer, I spent six weeks in a world of my own at Pin Oak—13 going on 14 and 14 going on 15. One unit of 24 girls with our own staff was self-sufficient. We did not have any contact with other girls in camp. Our staff was a cook, Nurse, Leader and Assistant Leader and a Waterfront Director.

Some girls only stayed two weeks or one session. I was one of eight girls who "stayed over" for three sessions. This special opportunity came as an addition to Camp Cedarledge, giving all girls the waterfront experience.

"Christopher and Boots" were the co-leaders. Christopher, Dorothy Taylor, went on to work for Girl Scouts USA. Boots, Estelle Dempke, stayed in St. Louis and I later worked with her as an adult.

We were able to take our canoes and kayaks for three days around the Lake of the Ozarks State Park. Friends I made these years I knew through high school and then on to college. Several pledged my college sorority, Pi Beta Phi. I recalled so much of what we did at Ipesi. This is a gypsy word. Christopher said it meant, "I don't know where we are going but we are having a good time getting there". (She made up many things.) I recall so many activities and programs that we seemed to have. I think Christopher promoted interest in one girl and others followed. The "Stay Over" girls took in new girls each session. My memories just roll out as happening sometime in 1936 and 1937. Some were different ongoing sessions, but all are part of my story.

One session involved world passports. We had maps and went on a cruise. The staff had pre-planned these activities, but they were developed by the unit.

Winnie the Pooh was introduced to us hence the name

Christopher. We read A. A. Milne. I am distressed now that my Great-Grandchildren only know Pooh as a Disney character. The book I made as a craft is still on my bookshelf. It is a treasure of poems that I liked. Reading poems at Ipesi was another activity on a hot Missouri day.

Singing was a big part of camp life, especially evening programs. We could sing by memory with altos even able to come into the song. We did not learn the usual camp song but ones from other countries. Ours was a sophisticated program. Songs learned to celebrate holidays in other countries. We could paddle canoes while singing "If you could go to Venice, you could find a magic town". We started a tradition of putting our little boats afloat on the lake on the last night of camp. Good wishes were written on each boat.

Au Revoir, this boat so small is true to its name,
As it means in foreign call, until we meet again.
My wish this peaceful night is the very same,
At Ipesi camp we all meet again.

September 3, 2019

Christmas at Grandmother's 1937

For the first and only Christmas away from my home during my first twenty-one years, my parents and sister were bound for Little Rock, Arkansas. This most unusual winter road trip was to be a family reunion with my Grandmother Ostner and my mother's extended family. I was a sophomore in High School and, though none of mother's family lived in St. Louis, circumstances arose from time to time over the years to bring my aunts, uncles, and cousins to St. Louis. There had been one or two times even that we got together at my family's home, Hillandale, near Potosi.

This was the first of many reunions of the eight siblings in my mother's Ostner family. Spouses and Grandchildren made for a lively and large family group. I want to write about this family for several reasons:

Grandfather and Mama O Ostner

First, I have only the fondest memories of all the times I have shared with them, even to this day. By now, all the elders have died except for one uncle.

Secondly, I think this family should be known to my Grandchildren and the "greats". My family now have spread across the country from Colorado to West Virginia, and only my immediate family has known any of these Ostners; the next generation, now two generations removed, will never know any of their Great-Great-Great Grandparents unless I tell this story.

Thirdly, I have always found the Ostners unusually refreshing in that they remained quite loyal to one another including all the "outlaws" (as my father referred to all those who married into the family). I have come to know of the many trials, tribulations and complex dynamics in the family, and many disagreements. Still, loyalty and family love abounded even after Grandmother, my Mama-O, passed away. She had been widowed just when I was born and left with five still to raise. She was lovingly respected as the "Queen Bee" by her adult children.

In 1937, I was still relegated to the "children's" table, only because there was not room for everyone at the big table. The highlight for me was to be taken by my next oldest cousin, a freshman in College, to a tea dance. Max Brown was so kind to pay me attention and I, only a Sophomore, felt quite grown up. Movies were taken with all of us marching down the steps from

Mabel, Fay, Max, Helene, John, Doris, Marshall, Sarah Ostner, Charleston, MO, 1917

Mabel Elizabeth Ostner (b.11/2/1893-d.3/12/1976) married Harry Lee Bond (2 children)
Ruth Angelique Ostner (3/15/1895)
Francis Maximillian "Max" Ostner (b.9/15/1896-d.2/13/1970) married Annie Brown (2 children)
Clara Fay Ostner (b.12/23/1899-d.10/10/1975) married Welborn Estes (2 children)
Selma Helen (Helene) Ostner (b.8/20/1902-d.9/24/1977) married Bailey Wilkinson (no children)
Marshall Alexander Ostner (b. 10/9/1905-d.10/13/1984) married Eula Stewart (no children)
Doris Louise Ostner (b.4/2/1909-d.9/25/1947) married Theodore "Ted" Stevens, Jr. (no children)
John Matthew Ostner (b. 7/21/1910-d.married "Dorothy" Poynter (2 children)
Sarah married Francis Walter Heitlage (2 children)

the porch. We could sing while Daddy played his banjo. The grownups had many jokes to tell and stories of their memories. What can I say that you, reader, can glimpse the members of this family?

Aunt Mabel, the eldest, and her husband, Uncle Harry. Aunt Mabel was a fubsy lady, a kindly way of saying, large! Uncle Max said: "There's just that much more to love"! From my 16-year-old viewpoint, I thought they were still sweethearts, though two daughters were older than I by nine or ten years. Mary Elizabeth and Dorothy Frances were too-old-to-play, but we kept in touch for the rest of their lives. Later, Tullis, Mary Elizabeth's husband, would be a pioneer pilot with Braniff, flying to South America. She became our first overseas traveler. How romantic!

Next came Uncle Max and Aunt Annie. They had lived a couple of years in St. Louis, so I did know them. She was so pretty, a red-head, and one with whom Daddy did enjoy visiting. Every conversation he would say: "Tell me about your Grandchildren"! And she would shyly bring him up to date.

My mother was third-born and the first to leave the ancestral home, Charleston, Missouri when she married.

Aunt Helene was the sister closest to Mother. When my sister was born, I went down to stay with my Grandmother. I went to school with Aunt Helene, who was then teaching elementary school. Helene taught until she married. Uncle Bailey. She made me a gorgeous negligee for my trousseau from a parachute that my husband had brought home from WWII. A most talented seamstress, she was costume designer (and producer) for a Theatre company in Oklahoma, City. This Ostner clan had regular reunions through many years, and I came to know Uncle Bailey as a tall, stiff man thin, blond hair that he slicked down. Not much fun!

And fifth came Uncle Marshall. He was not yet married at this first reunion. Uncle Marshall, called Kraut by his peers, was mostly bald as were the Ostner men, rimless glasses and not one of the uncles that paid me any attention. He married at age 37 to a beautiful lady, Aunt Eula, whom we all adored.

Sixth, Aunt Doris who was not married in 1937 either, but was a dental assistant, a profession now called Dental Hygienist. Aunt Doris was tiny, with crinkly, twinkly brown eyes and lived with Mama-O until she married Ted, another "late" one to be married. They were the liveliest couple all through the years of our reunions, especially devoted, enthusiastic square dancers. They traveled the country dancing, she so tiny and he quite a small man. All of us were organized to square dance, especially, to dance the Hokey-Pokey. Movies documented that, too.

Uncle John, our all-time favorite uncle, and his petite sweetheart, Aunt Dorothy, added the seventh pair. Uncle John had lived with my parents as an 18-year-old and had his first job out of high school at the old St. Louis Dairy Company. I really knew him best of all and his two children, my youngest cousins, John Lee and Catherine.

Last to be born, only 8 years before I, was Sarah. I knew her well as she was registrar at Lindenwood College when I was a student there. She married Walter who taught in the Agriculture school at the University of Missouri and in the Extension Service. I gleaned some understanding of farming, agriculture, "dust bowls".

These "thumbnail" sketches serve as an introduction to the characters in the dramas that have unfolded for me through my lifetime. Each one is a treasure. My heart is filled with gratitude for the enrichment in my life from Mama-O's family!

October 6, 2011

Wellborn Estes, Western Military Academy, Alton IL

Wellborn Estes, Cornell University, Ithica, NY

New Athletic Field Named

An additional athletic and recreational field being developed at CMC for use this fall, has been named the Wellborn Estes Athletic Field by the Board of Curators. Wellborn Estes, Class of '18, is currently secretary to the Board of Curators of which he has been a member since 1950.

While a student at CMC Mr. Estes was interested in athletics, starred as an end in football and as catcher in baseball. For many years he has been the donor of the Estes Prize in athletics, a ring awarded annually to the most outstanding athlete recommended by the faculty athletic committee. He received the Distinguished Alumni Plaque from CMC in 1953.

Wellborn Estes at 17

Wellborn Estes

The Wellborn Estes Athletic Field will be used for baseball and other recreational Activities including the large intramural program conducted by CMC.

Wellborn and mother Lulu Estes, 1951

Senior Comp 1939

She was straight, tall, imposing, and serious. It was with anxiety I filed into my first class of "Senior Comp". For those of us college bound, four years of English were required. Miss Johnson was always the teacher. Of course, she had a given name but as students we did not know it.

This was my first and only writing class and we were assigned a theme every Friday, due on Monday morning. These essays were to be short, not more than a page or so expressing emotions, engaging descriptive moments or observations made. Why do I remember only one of these efforts rather specifically?

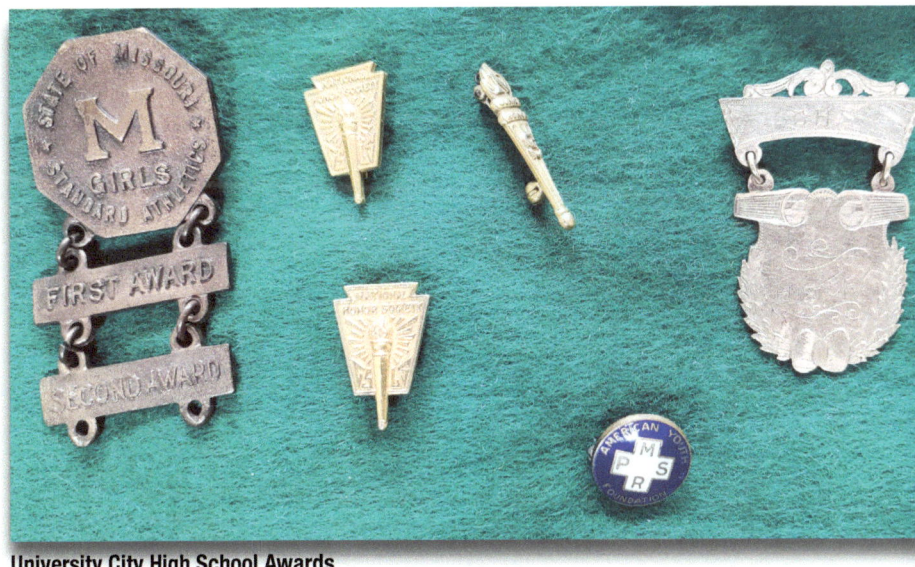

University City High School Awards

I recounted munching on a grass stem, sleekly pulled from its casing and put in my mouth. Pulling it out between my teeth I could extract sweet juice, and then I could tickle my chin with the grass head. I walked home every day ofttimes with a friend, sucking on a grass stem. I have no further recollection of this theme. That was 72 years ago!

However, I still enjoy grass stems and have added leaves to enjoy. Study of botany in all these years I am careful which specimens on which I chew. Sassafras is a favorite. Singing along the way, with a good friend my enjoyment observing the little things along the trail is heightened over these years. Writing skills are not as sharp, but the fun and joy of writing is probably more so. Thank you, Miss Johnson, for Senior Comp.

Singing Along the Way

On the cusp of my tenth decade, I have hundreds of songs in my head that I have learned along life's way. My vocal cords can no longer sing out, but that does not keep me from walking more easily with a tune in my head: "I've got a six-pence, jolly jolly six-pence"* or silently hum the words of "Shadows Creep" when I hear "The New World Symphony".

Singing along the way began for me at an early age when I learned to sing a "round" with my Grandfather and Daddy. "Row, row, row your boat". I heard the words: "Life is butter dream" and Daddy called me his "Butter Dream" for many years. At the same time, I proudly brought home a song from Sunday School ending with "all good things for children and dogs". The song really said: "All good things for children we know". Youngsters still learn by rote and probably sing what he or she hears.

Every summer from age eleven to nineteen, I was in camp two weeks to ten weeks—being a camper or staff. Singing was a rich tradition in each of the three camps I attended in those years. A heritage I cherish that helps me sing along the way.

Campers have always had "Camp Songs". Boy Scouts sing as they hike, maybe "100 bottles of beer" or "I left my wife and 49 kids…" Lots of loud singing and "hoop-la" cheering for "Camp T" in my granddaughter's camp. I was fortunate to amass a repertoire of folk music from around the world, semi-classical music, Venetian songs when we had "Venetian nights", some parodies of the classics. Poor way to learn but did lead me to enjoyment of the Operas when I heard them at the Symphony concerts.

Several Summers we learned special songs with themes of the units in which we were placed. "Border Village" called for "Home on the Range". A quiet cowboy lullaby's images: "Sleepy winks of lightning on the far skyline".* My favorite "It's Up in the Morning", three stanzas reciting the day in a cowboy's life from the early chuck wagon to noon time and "the cool shady creek" to the bedding down of the cattle at night.

Being on the staff in "Gypsy Dell" led me to find folk songs from Romany, "Walking at night along the meadow way, Home from the dance beside my maiden gay", words I can still hear in my head and music to engage my senses as I heard the same rhythms in Eastern Europe in recent years.

In a waterfront unit, of course, sea shanties and sea songs permeated the campfires, water games, and dramatic productions. Sailing the Virgin Isles, I understood the songs I had learned as a young teen as we sang "haul on the bowline" on our yacht *Crista Galli* or *Ceilidh*. Driving from Kansas City just last week, the heavens were filled with "Cloud Ships". All the words of that song from long ago broke into my consciousness.

Maurita Estes, 1939

Our family sang along the way as we took road trips every year crossing the country. Our girls had learned songs from me as they grew up and many of their own in their camps. Our Challenge was to bring Daddy and Brother into our singing. Daddy was not the most glorious tenor or baritone and he was driving so we had to teach him easy parts. "The Orchestra" was a great favorite. We girls could take the lovely parts of the strings and leave the horn to Larry. The drums were always the part Daddy took. There were just two notes: "one, five, five, one, five, five, five one". He sang his part lustily, booming as the drum.

"Grasshoppers Three" was Larry's favorite round. The girls recalled our great fun with that silly song and sang a trio at his wedding with appropriate fiddling gestures as the grasshoppers "a-fiddling went".

Singing as we hiked in camp and as adults in the Rockies was the most fun of all. I often found that a song about 3 p.m. was the only way I would drag back into the trailhead after a long hike. The Field Artillery, the troops in the Boer War, WWI and WWII have always known that singing made marching and hiking go better. I had a whole raft of hiking songs from the Swiss, the South Africans, WWII, gypsies in my repertoire. My daughter, Linda, brought us new ones from overseas, her camp in New Hampshire and her great interest in music.

Walking around Old Orchard for "exercise" in 2012 I have a song in my head encouraging me to walk. This "Foot Traveler" is slow paced now but I "do not pine and sigh"* with a tune and words in my head. I might even try to sing to myself to exercise my vocal cords a bit.

*asterisks each time are quotes from songs we know

April 26, 2012

Sure Enough, A Real Tenderfoot

Going on a week-end camping trip sounded like a great adventure to me, a new Tenderfoot scout, new to the troop and certainly new to camp. When I was not much beyond my eleventh birthday, I joined University City Troop 1 with girls ranging in age from 10-17. I had been in the troop just a few months, learned the Law and Promise, the motto, sign and salute, the pledge of allegiance, respect for the flag and how it should be displayed. I practiced tying five special knots over and over so we could use them when needed.

It was an April weekend, and I was off to Camp Cedarledge to be in a primitive unit, Trail's End. The highlights I remember well and have relived them over and over through the years.

First on arriving was the necessity of putting up hammocks in which we would sleep. The older experienced Scouts helped us two tenderfoot girls. These hammocks were not the lovely "Jungle Hammocks" used in WWII in which I slept many years later, but just flat canvas. One of my knots, the clove hitch, I could use to hang up my night's abode. I was helped to lay out my bedding known as a "klondike" that was carefully made up with blanket, sheets, and a poncho folded a special way. I was to scoot into the middle of the envelope having blankets on top and underneath me.

Next, I was assigned to the patrol to build the latrine. We had to break a trail to where we would construct our latrine. I do not remember what tools I used, just that I was behind my taskmaster. The first botany lesson, learning to recognize poison ivy, was at that point. The skills involved in designing the latrine I cannot recall. Since then, I have built many, each one specific to the particular site.

We explored the creek running by Trail's End and went to Tub Springs. It was from here that we had to get our water and chlorinate it for purification. Needless to say, I drank as little as possible on the weekend. Kool-Aid masked the taste of chlorine.

Fire-building was a skill I did not have, but I quickly learned to gather wood, tinder and bigger fuel. Older and wiser ones could build the fire and do the cooking. Such an advantage to have those older girls helping the leaders. We cut our sticks for Smores. I was a happy camper as I toasted marshmallows over the open fire.

Darkness fell, campfire and singing, and time for bed. Now how does one get up into the hammock, into the Klondike bed? I had no idea of the balancing act necessary for this procedure. Even with willing helpers I fell out, shall I say, more than once or even twice. Did I sleep? Did I move a muscle? I cannot say. It must not have been too traumatic as I slept many comfortable nights in a hammock, but rarely ever again slung a Navy flat canvas one. "Klondikes" were replaced with sleeping bags. I felt so lucky when I had earned enough money to buy one my first year as a counsellor in that camp.

Arriving home late afternoon on Sunday, I was locked out of the house. While waiting for my parents to arrive, I sat on the doorstep happily counting my chigger bites. Chiggers had found me tasty in the past but never in such numbers. They were so numerous, maybe 200. I waged war against them for years afterwards and found many antidotes to repel the microscopic spiders. Having spent most summers in Colorado for the last 25 years, I still relish shuffling through grasslands knowing there are no chiggers!

In my adult years Mother told me how she had inquired around to find a troop I could join. She particularly stressed that she wanted me to have the experience of camping, hiking and other outdoor activities adding: "The closest I ever came to the outdoors when I was a girl was the front-porch swing with my boyfriend". She thought it important and knowing the natural world has been one of the most meaningful aspects of my life. Is it not a wonder that she encouraged me to go back to camp after this first experience? Is it not a wonder that I wanted to go again, and again, and again for life-long adventures out-of-doors?

November 2010

The Premier Transition

Daddy helped me to pack for my first major life transition. There have been many since that Autumn day in September 1939, but none quite like the first. Though I had been away from home many summers before this time, this would be for nine months, my first year away to college.

I had spent much of my senior year in high school, writing to various colleges, perusing catalogues, dreaming of Northwestern University, Sophie Newcomb in Baton Rouge, women's colleges in the East and the south. My mother, a Stephens College graduate, had registered me at that school when I was seven. Its reputation at my High School in University City was not impressive and I did not want to go there! Lindenwood loomed of interest to me when Mother and I went to visit my Aunt Sarah who was registrar at the time. I found the campus most beautiful and the curriculum to my liking. My folks discouraged me, saying: "It is so close" and continuing "You will want to come home every weekend". They even added: "It is hardly going away to college".

I replied: "If you think that, then I will not come home at all until Holiday time". This was probably the first time I did not do just what parents wanted. At least, I had chosen a "woman's college" as that had been part of the programming done for me since I was about seven which read "2 years in a woman's college, 2 years in a university". I never wavered from the part of the program regarding going to college.

Packing the car consisted in carrying the three pieces of luggage, a gift for graduation from high school. One, a so called "two suitor", large with two layers for clothes, a second piece specifically for hats and shoes, and a third designed for "cosmetics". Mother, Daddy and my only sister, ten years old, came along.

Entering Lindenwood's beautiful campus I found my assigned dorm room on the third floor in Niccolls Hall. It was here all Freshmen lived. I had been assigned a roommate named Harriet Thistlewood. That was all I was expected to know...no orientation, no correspondence, no matching up, maybe no common interests. How did we manage this great transition?

Harriet was nowhere to be found, but she had already settled into our small room. Two twin beds, a chest of drawers, two desks, two chairs, two windows, one sink, and one closet furnished where we two would live. In the closet were 20 pairs of shoes neatly lined up. My roommate did have lots of shoes, that much I learned even before we met!

I hung up my few clothes, mostly dresses and skirts Mother had made. I had "school shoes", jodhpur boots, probably black and navy pumps, galoshes (boots for snow and rain in case, dear reader, you do not know about that kind of footwear).

Harriet was petite, blond, with very deep dimples, and contagious laughter. She was an art major, I tended to science. She was tiny; I was the same size (almost) as I am now, 5'6"; she was blonde and curly, I was dark brunette and with very straight hair. She was from a small town, Cairo, Illinois, I was an urban kid from University City. We roomed together happily for two years, she was "T", I was "Ess" and we quickly found a group on our floor, numbering eight, all on the third floor. Friendships flourished, some lasting the rest of our lives.

My world rapidly expanded. It was so easy to become acquainted and develop lots of friends on a 700 student campus. Girls came to Lindenwood, a four-year College, from Texas to Virginia and all points in between. Hailing from varied cultures and backgrounds, I could make acquaintance of girls from farmlands in Iowa to the deep south lands and small towns where cotton, soy, or corn were "kings". Accents I had not heard in St. Louis. New subjects to study-botany, zoology were extensions of high school science. Bible and voice and diction were required for freshman who had never had a voice lesson in their "other" life, let alone sung in Italian!

There has not been much with which to compare it to in my lifetime. That is until I crossed my latest threshold into a Senior Living complex. My son-in-law jokingly observed when visiting here recently, "The apartment building is a Co-ed Sorority house". "True, I agreed, somewhat".

Living in the College dorm, c.1940, had House Rules predicated on our safety, consideration and courtesy, and health. Lights Out, 11 p.m., regular times for meals, three meals a day served to us. Date nights: weekends; home at midnight. Do not cross the Missouri River, do not go down to "Main Street" and be sure to "sign out" and with whom. Yes, the College in those olden days did have oversight as "parents". Ah! yes, there were rebellious girls, girls sneaked out, rules were ignored.

Dinners were planned to be gracious, courteous as young women were expected to be. I probably still have dinner-size white linen napkins with my name-i.d. that we had to send to the College. We "dressed" for dinner with hose and heels. If the stockings had "runs" in them, no matter. No one scolded. A faculty was often seated at each round table. I do remember having to sit at the "French" table from time to time and speak only French. How quiet dinner conversation was these nights.

On occasion we had formal dinners. I only remember that in my wardrobe I did have to have a "Dinner Dress", which was long with covered shoulders. This design as opposed to a "Formal" that would be backless, strapless and sleeveless. My dinner dress was one I well remember as I had it many years after college. It was a bright royal blue velvet with a bodice sheered and puffy with square neck and short sleeves. I felt so pretty when I wore it.

Social life was considerably different from high school. I did have a few dates with a "townie" who worked at the Weldon Springs Ammunition Plant near St. Charles, but "dates" came from St. Louis. This was the one advantage I had being near home and the advantage some of my friends had. It was quite easy for my friend from home to bring several other guys with him and I would match up some of my friends. We mostly danced on campus, went to movies in town watched our time carefully to be back in the dorm by curfew. A few exciting weekends away I remember them well...off to Rolla where my future husband was in school at Missouri School of Mines, or off to Kemper Military School for one of their formal affairs. Those guys really had curfews to be obeyed. When their witching hour was near, they RAN for their dorms after squiring us to our hotels. And most fun of all, perhaps, was when a busload of Lindenwood girls would be driven into St. Louis to the Chase Hotel for a dance with Scott Air Force based G.I.'s. If one of us met one of them and "hit it off", as we would say, the boys could come to St. Charles for future dates or begin a correspondence. Yes, we did write letters and put a stamp on them, even "sealing" it "with a kiss". The letters SWAK would appear on the envelope. On campus, we often just danced with girls. Some could lead as well or better than many fellows. It certainly was not as enjoyable as dancing with a guy, but a good time to learn and practice.

 Girls needed to learn social graces, needed to study and apply ourselves to our classes, but learning new skills for recreation and health was most important, too. I had never had the opportunity to try horseback riding and I found this sport most enjoyable and I became comfortable and did well participating in our horse shows. I so enjoyed riding a "Tennessee Walking horse" and a 5-gaited horse especially. Alas, that was a two-year experience. I have rarely been on horseback since except a few trail rides in the west on vacations.

 I was not on scholarship in College but did have some income from the program of FDR (President Franklin D. Roosevelt) called the National Youth Association. For this pay, I taught swimming, which was a required course for all Freshmen. Each student before graduation had to meet certain requirements. I had already earned my Junior and Senior Life Saving, had had swimming lessons several times since I was eight and felt quite comfortable teaching these skills. It was my first teaching assignment. I taught swimming, lifesaving, and boating until I was about sixty. I enjoyed every minute, teaching boys and girls in the city rec summer programs, mentally-challenged children, and adults in the city and in summer camps as waterfront director. All first begun at Lindenwood.

  I spent two years at this college and transferred to Washington U. I so wished to have finished at the College but came home, probably because of cost. I would not have chosen to return home so I think I must have received an unspoken message from my parents. I have no recollection of discussion though I do recall that Daddy had to ask the President of the College to let me stay to finish the second year even though he did not have the tuition in on time. The course of life might have been different if I had stayed in St. Charles. I might have majored in botany and/or zoo. I say "might". At the time I had the sense that these fields were open to women only in laboratories with few other career opportunities for women. I certainly did not think very carefully then as I had a female zoologist for a teacher who had an international reputation for her study of ants. However, she did not have a prestigious academic appointment, as did E.O. Wilson at the time. (E.O.Wilson was recognized for his study of ants at Harvard.)

The science fields have been the basis of most of my avocations, hobbies, and activities in the Volunteer sector for most of my adult life. Perhaps, I would not have had such exciting volunteer opportunities if I had been "professional".

I have been ever grateful for the opportunity to complete my bachelor's work at Washington University graduating in 1943. The sounds of soldiers training on the campus still ring at times in my ears.

Washington University Mosaic

Maurita Estes, Washington University Graduation, 1943

I left Lindenwood College after two glorious years and returned to complete my undergraduate degree at Washington University in St. Louis. I have no recollection of making this decision. The country was just "coming out" of the Great Depression and economics might have been the deciding factor. I was not unhappy to be coming home to live for two years, thankful I could complete my bachelor's degree. I transferred in as a Junior with all my credits acceptable to Washington, except for a year of "Bible" and a year of "American Civilization". I declared my major Sociology, as I was seriously considering Professional Girl Scouting upon graduation.

Being a transfer student, I did meet with some frustrations. What fraternity invited women to the Tea Dances, designed to be Orientation to Freshmen? Juniors had been oriented as "froshies". I pledged PiPhi and made friends quickly with Juniors and Seniors though I was still a pledge. Social life at school was not my main interest in school, contrary to many students. The University was known as a streetcar College in those early days. As street cars did not come west beyond "the Loop", I walked to school. My good friend, Nancy Jean, was one of a very few who had a car. If our schedules meshed, I rode home with her. Certainly "workouts at the gym" were not necessary for my exercise.

  I gravitated to work with the Campus Y. I liked the director and the activities centered around diverse student groups and some communities off campus with whom we could volunteer. I knew several of the Japanese Neisi students who had come to St. Louis with their families, and not interred in camps on the West Coast following Pearl Harbor and WWII. The diversity of students in the Campus Y lounge made life on campus interesting. It has been important for me to adjust to diversity, repeated many times in my life. As a child I lived in a diverse neighborhood. My schoolmates were Jewish or Catholic. Though there were challenging times, for the most part living with different races, religions, customs, foods, and work has enriched my world. Classes in History, French, many Sociology and Psychology credits and botany and zoology opened many windows and doors for me. I cheer for Liberal Arts education.

Phi Beta Phi pins

  My two years at Washington U. amidst the sounds of

Navy training programs on campus were not "all work and no play". I spent two or three weekends at Rolla School of Mines where Neil was a student. We had "house-parties" with the PiPhi "sisters". I spent Summer weeks on the staff of Camp Cedarledge and made my first trip to New York to attend the Western Hemisphere Encampment of the Girl Scouts.

Neil graduated in January 1943, having completed his Civil engineering degree in 3-1/2 years, ready to leave for Ft. Belvoir. His first order of WWII. I finished May 26, 1943 moving my tassel over my mortar board as graduates do still today. Eleven days later I left for White Sulphur Springs, West Virginia, where I would spend the summer of my new career. I was set to make new friends in another world of diversity. Arriving at 2:30 a.m. on the "C and O" railroad flexibility had to be my middle name.

May 2012

On My Honor, On My Own

May 26, 1943, the big event of my year, graduation from Washington University. Ten days later I boarded a train bound for West Virginia and my professional position as a Field Director in Girl Scouting. I had been programmed from an early age to go to College in order to become independent. Here I was on that very threshold.

To begin my new career, I was to be Program Director in the Council camp near White Sulphur Springs, W. Va. Arriving on the Chesapeake and Ohio train at 2:30 a.m. I was met by the Camp Director and two of her staff. The seven miles to Camp Ann Bailey seemed an eternity. Curvy mountain roads, eerie dark and tall forests would have made me most anxious, save for the jollity of my companions.

Camping in mountains, new songs, new traditions made for a lovely summer and all too soon I faced new prospects of really being "on my own": not at home, not on a college campus, not with longtime friends, and facing new tasks.

A month of professional training at Camp Edith Macy in Pleasantville, N. Y. provided an exciting stimulating program, giving me the confidence to cope with aspects of the job new to me: training leaders, coordinating Day Camps, guiding Council Committees, public relations, supervision of troops throughout the County. My enthusiasm and energy ran high. I believed I had the best Executive Director to be my mentor and the best Girl Scout Council in the U.S. to serve.

The Girl Scout office was downtown, a goodly walk to work. With wartime rationing, the Council had a car for our use with an "A" sticker for gas coupons. Mrs. Reese, the owner of my Boarding House, took my sugar coupons. I used my "shoe stamps". My extra cigarette stamps were appreciated by friends. It went almost without saying that I was not to smoke in public. I had learned at "mother's knee" that ladies did not smoke on the street and seldom in public.

I basked in all aspects of my job, the respect and appreciation by the volunteers with whom I worked and the responsibilities I was given. However, nagging in my heart was the feeling I had of lack of respect from the community and society in general. Teachers, social workers, health care workers, even clergy did not command standing, as professionals though all are especially important to the overall health of our society. Even basketball players seemed more important.

Racial issues were looming on the horizon of our country and in my life. Neil, my fiancé, was a 2nd lieutenant assigned black troops; the army was still segregated. Schools in W. Va. were segregated as they were in Missouri. But Juliette Low had designed a program for girls ahead of her time in 1912. Our Council was to be ahead of our time. The issue of "one or two" Leaders clubs was on the agenda at a Board meeting. Could we combine all leaders to meet in one club? Mrs. Davis, a stunning, talented Black Community leader, wife of the President of West Virginia Institute just stood up at the meeting and with her arms akimbo stated: "We do not need to discuss this, we will just do it". Motion passed. All the leaders came together to struggle to be good leaders of girls in wartime. I, their young professional staff member, did my best to strengthen their commitment.

Not too many years later I found myself working with the Girl Scouts as a Volunteer in St. Louis. The Civil Rights movement had made headlines. Girl Scout leaders and girls—black, white, Asian, and immigrants from all parts of the globe came together in troops and camped together even before schools were desegregated. I continued to be involved in many aspects of Girl Scouting for the next 40+ years. On my honor, I did try:
 to do my best,
 to serve God and my country,
 to help other people at all times
 and to obey the Girl Scout Laws.

January 10, 2013; Revised March 25, 2013

Single Lifestyle of 1943

Don's booming baritone voice filled the kitchen as he sang "Oh what a beautiful morning" from the most popular musical "Oklahoma". It brought a slight smile to sober-faced Mrs. Reese standing at the stove. It gave me a joyous lift every morning as I went in for Breakfast at her Boarding House. She had little time to ever smile as she shopped, planned, and produced two meals each day for about fourteen young working singles who took their meals at her Board. 1943 with World War II still raging I was in Charleston, West Virginia where the economy was based on industry for the war with DuPont, Union Carbide, Monsanto three big players.

We had good meals served "family style" coming for breakfast to fit each one's schedule and assembling for dinner at the same time more or less. The war years brought rationing to the country; therefore, we had to give Mrs. Reese our sugar coupons. My cigarettes were easily given to friends. I was unconcerned about shoes as I never did have but one or two pairs at a time. I had no car, so was unaffected by gas rationing. Mrs. Reese managed to have good meals without any freezer, no plastics, no "boxed" meals or frozen foods. Mr. Reese did help her to a very limited degree. No wonder she was too tired to smile.

Boarding Houses were not uncommon. It served those of us without kitchens, homes, families or many fast-food places in today's world of singles. At the time there was a very popular book titled: *Chicken Every Sunday* that was a story woven around the "Boarding House". Ours was just as the novel developed. Indeed, we did have Chicken Every Sunday. And I did see rolls thrown from one end of the table to the other rather than being passed. It did have a social aspect in addition to meals. We were able to stay after dinner and talk. Some of my best bridge playing was in that living room with three guys, all of whom were the best at the game. I quickly learned their rules: no talking, no bidding until everyone was ready (courtesy, perhaps), no re-hashing of the game. I learned not to bid quickly as that might indicate a poor hand. No facial expressions, as these guys would notice and learn about my hand. Friends were made and afforded us some social life outside of the Boarding House. I was particularly fond of Vincent. I enjoyed his conversations and intellect. He loved to walk, too, as I did. He made it quite clear to me that he wanted no "entangling alliances", as he just was waiting out the war in his War work and then would go back to School on to his PhD. That suited me fine, as I was most interested in Neil who was overseas. Vincent's ego probably motivated him to bring up the subject.

I lived in a private home across the street from Mrs. Reese's house. This was with the Moores, an old family in town that had owned the Book Store for many years. Mr. Moore was somewhat an invalid and Mrs. Moore was our "Mother" for five single women ranging in age from 21 as I was to perhaps 30. I did not know the age of two. My living accommodations had been pre-arranged for me prior to my coming to Charleston to be employed by the Kanawha County Council of Girl Scouts. Board members wanted the assurance that I would be living with a good family in a good neighborhood. It was important to my employer that I would be happy in my new community. No one could have had a better arrangement. Mrs. Moore's son-in-law serving overseas was a St. Louisan with mutual friends. It was serendipity!

I had much to learn about the world beyond the University and home. I graduated from Washington U. eleven days before I boarded the C & O Railroad bound for a place I'd never been, not knowing a soul in the State of West Virginia. I had not had an interview with anyone in this Council nor had I had a visit. As a field director I was out of the office most every day. The Girl Scouts had an "A" gas sticker so we could drive around the county once I had walked to the office downtown or taken a bus. The distance might have been 2-miles.

I had coal-mining towns to visit and there I learned that a miner could be paid on Saturday and not have any left by Monday. I had to cover Institute W. Virginia, the home of the Negro State University. We were below the Mason-Dixon line where I had never lived and long before any Civil Rights Acts and desegregation.

Social activities were simple, unsophisticated and not costly. Long walks on Sundays, sometimes at a nearby State Park. Dinners with friends in their homes was a real treat away from the Boarding House. We danced in a favorite spot across the river that had sawdust floors except on the dance floor. Picnics were popular. We knitted for service men. I volunteered at the USO where guys on leave could come. I enjoyed my friends and did not need a lot of commercial activities. We did not have television, smart phones, iPads, computers. It is difficult to have my grandchildren understand what we did. I do not feel adept at articulating "what we did". I liked the Single Styles at that time.

Maurita Estes, Professional Girl Scout, Serving in Charleston, WV, 1945

Beyond the Workday

Charleston, West Virginia, capital city in the Kanawha River Valley, was my home for nearly four years during World War II. I have written one memoir "On My Honor, On My Own" recalling my position as Field Director of the Girl Scouts; this vignette I could title "Beyond the Workday". I had a southern "belle" for a roommate on the third floor of an old home on Virginia Street, across the street from the back door of the Governor's mansion. Eloise and I had one room; Mary Lee had the other bedroom on the floor. We shared a bath and a square sitting room also known as the upstairs hall. Eloise was a petite brunette, a chemist at the DuPont plant upriver at Belle, W. Virginia. Her prominent dimples and very large brown eyes were accents to her South Carolina speech. On our first meeting she asked me: "Wood y'all like a 'huhshe'"? Puzzled for a moment, I realized she had a Hershey Bar to share. That accent could be thicker than back-strap molasses at appropriate times, times we met a new "fella".

Eloise was a "shift-worker" at DuPont, one of many plants running three 8-hour shifts. It ran six days and many evenings. Times we shared together were rare, always enjoyable, and compatible.

Mrs. Moore, our landlady, hovered around, mothering us. There were two other girls on the second floor and Helene, Mrs. Moore's daughter whose husband was overseas. Mrs. Moore instructed us: "I do not want you girls to make up your bed in the morning because I know you rush out to work and the beds need to be aired".

Home was never like this; happily, I did as I was told.

In the three plus years all of us girls stayed in place and Helene's husband was discharged and home before I left. The Moores took us all in just like family, sheer delight for me being away from home. When Mr. Moore passed (that southern expression was new to me) we girls took up the task attendant with the "wake" held at home. We helped Mrs. Moore make Fruit

Cake in her kitchen. She taught me how to tie a big bow at my neck, one of the "fads" at the time. Mother Moore even had her "say" regarding a young man who came to call on me. She was acquainted with Paul whom I had met at church, her church, likewise. I thought Paul, too old, balding, a bit paunchy. He might have been 28 and I was 21. "Such a fine, young man", she said. "You should go out with him". Well, I did, much to my enjoyment. I enjoyed his passion in photography and fine voice to sing along our way. It was just a new experience to date someone I had not known, who was not in college with me. New experiences outside the office.

We had breakfast and dinner seven days a week, breakfast was flexible for the various offices and labs, dinner more of a set time with some variance for office workers, the chemical plants, downtown banks, brokerage houses and the Girl Scouts. We watched the Charleston Airport take shape by literally scooping off the top of a mountain and filling in the valleys to make a runway. Really high-tech for the time. Today that "scoop and fill" is a big environmental issue in West Virginia as the technique used in strip mining has many unintended consequences.

There were about 16 "boarders" for Mrs. Reese to prepare for with help from her husband. We'd say today that we ate locally (and probably organic) as we had fresh vegetables and fruits only in season or "root" vegetables (beets, carrots, turnips, parsnips) that could be stored over the winter. No plastic, no frozen food, no aluminum foil, no imported strawberries, and blueberries. How did she manage? We did not expect her to be jovial or have any time for "visiting". But at breakfast, when Don came in singing "Oh What a Beautiful Morning" at the top of his rich baritone voice her face flashed a wonderful smile! I get a warm, fuzzy joyful feeling whenever I hear that song from the musical "Oklahoma". I can almost see and hear Don.

The more I write Memoirs, the more I remember. My fellow students in Lifelong Learning are in accord. My memory bank will bulge with portraits of families in Scouting, workers I knew in Monsanto, Du Pont, and other plants in War work. These workers could not even harbor thoughts of quitting their jobs or they would be drafted. I moved my church letter to First Methodist of Charleston leaving my "home" church. I escorted Lady Baden-Powell, widow of Lord Baden-Powell, founder of the Boy Scouts. She was a guest of one of our Girl Scout Board members, Daisey Gordon Lawrence, niece of Juliette Low. And I had my first Mint-Julep made by the neighbor next door. I knew, then, I was in a real southern culture.

May 8, 2013

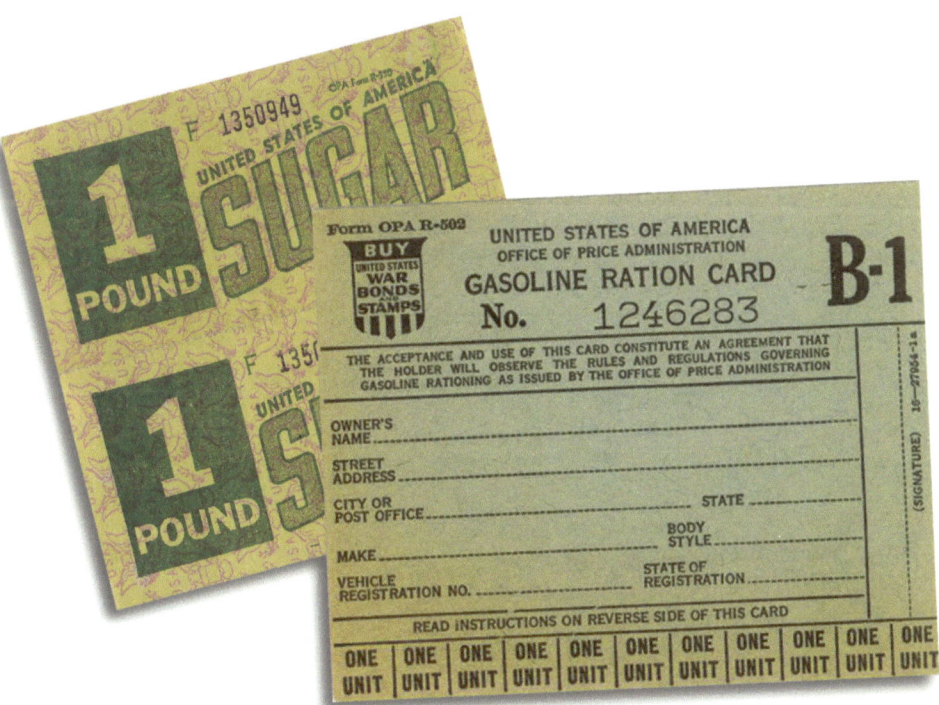

Courtship Unknowingly

It was a soft autumn night in 1938, my Junior year in high school. Just right for a hayride and barn dance held a good way from the urban area in which I lived. What an adventure it was to go way out in the county to Valley Park, a place where barns and hay wagons were nothing very special for those who lived there. As I was dancing with my date, he requested that "Begin the Beguine" be played. It was not what one expected to have at a barn dance, but was, at the time, a new and popular song. That has remained "our" song for me, at least, since that dance in 1939.

I first met that boy with such a sophisticated musical taste in the seventh grade when there was but one Junior High in University City. All three grade schools fed into Ward Junior High. It seemed easy to mix up the students from the three schools.

There was that boy again bringing with him several from Flynn Park School mixing with some of us from Delmar Harvard. We gathered in each others' homes for parties. The entertainment was just what we could devise by ourselves…no TV, no Video, some Board games like Monopoly and games like "Post-Office" and Wink we thought great fun as they involved a little more boy-girl relationships even a kiss if you caught a wink.

Ninth grade graduation was a special time with girls wearing white dresses. A picnic that night was held at Forest Park Highlands, the venue used by many schools throughout the county. No dates just groups. It was memorable for me for many years. I lost fifty cents on the "Flying Turns", most of my allowance. And the special boy rocked on the top of the Ferris Wheel. The more fearful I became the more he teased me by rocking.

We all moved along to our only High School. School dances sponsored by the Student Council, the Hi-Y, the Tribe and even the high school fraternity and sororities became the social events in high school.

A special date might be to go down to Grand Avenue to

the Fox, St Louis, or the Missouri theatre. Here we would see stage show as well as a movie. Because not all boys had a car available for dating, triple dates were planned, most always "double dates". Following parent rules, I had one hour after show time to go to Parkmoor for hamburgers. I felt so sophisticated! But that boy from the Barn Dance only asked me for special dances and events at school, never a "date".

He asked me if I would walk with him on graduation day. My feelings of excitement too soon withered. He had to play his clarinet in the band and could not walk in the procession.

Summer after graduation I went to camp for six weeks; he went on a three-month tour of the west with his family to return just in time to matriculate at Missouri School of Mines in Rolla. I went to Lindenwood College in St. Charles. Our correspondence that was to last six years ensued. Christmas 1939 we were home for Christmas and got together comparing notes about College. I do not remember what we did, but whatever it was I liked being with him still though another one named Bob was really my "first love" as he had been the last year in High School. He was a graduating Senior that year and would go in the Fall to Central Methodist College when I went back to Lindenwood. The clarinet player took 2nd place.

Spring of my Freshman year the boy with whom I played "Wink" and went to Hi-YI dances asked me to come down to Rolla for St. Pat's weekend, the biggest event at Rolla. How exciting that was! I have wondered since then why my parents allowed me this adventure. That is called trust, I think. The weekend was all I expected and more...my first trip to Rolla. We girls stayed in the boys' fraternity house while they went out to the Pennant Hotel. At dawn, the boy turned "froshie" was impressing me with his talent in mimicking the Cardinal's song.

That summer I did not see that boy much as I was counselling in camp many weeks and he did not ask to come down on my "night off". We did have one memorable night I vividly recall. Curfew was relaxed now for College freshman. We were having long conversations. In closing I said, "I only want a buddy, not a sweetheart." It was 4 a.m. when the front door opened by itself. There was my father holding it open for us...Never had he been up when I came home...

Our Sophomore year in College I was obviously off "the boy, now turned man's" list. No communication, few letters but had no regrets; he was abiding by my expressed feeling. We did not revisit the evening at all.

But picked up our Junior year and continued our courtship unknowingly. He was in ROTC, finished his Civil Engineering degree in three-and-a-half-years, graduated, went to OCS. I graduated in the Spring from Washington U. and left in 12 days for West Virginia.

Correspondence picked up again with those "onion skin" sheets to be censored sometimes. Six hundred letters, eighteen months overseas, VJ DAY, man becomes veteran to be married two months after I completed my tasks in West Virginia.

Neil was that boy with whom I first played "Post Office" and danced to "Begin the Beguine". Now you, dear Reader, know why I do not talk about my courtship, where we met, all those questions that are brought up in chatting over a cup of coffee...I really did not have that storybook "falling in love, giddy feelings". I was in love and loved for 46 years. I never rocked on top of a Ferris Wheel.

November 1, 2012

Home for a Special Christmas

Announcing one's engagement had become somewhat of a ritual in St. Louis in 1944, at least in my circle of friends. Though held in different places each had similar vital dimensions. It had to be kept a secret and have an element of surprise. In my case these aspects were a little more probable, as I had been away from home since June and Neil was gone longer from home. Be that as it may, I was home from working in West Virginia and to have a luncheon over the Holidays was not unusual. The third aspect necessary was the specific plan for THE ANNOUNCEMENT.

We girls gathered at Missouri Athletic Club for luncheon. My sister and I had made a recording, she played the piano and I sang with her. We played some of the popular songs of the day as background music during lunch. Interrupting her, I asked: "Say,

John Wesley & Tallulah Carroll Estes, 50th Wedding Anniversary, October 18, 1933

I want to show you what Neil gave me for Christmas. It had to come in the mail since he has been shipped overseas". She exclaimed: "Oh what a gorgeous ring, I'm a hog about that". (Sixty plus years after that bit of slang, I just tell you that expression was the most popular jargon for my fifteen-year-old sister in 1944.) So, the engagement was duly announced.

For the next two and a half years, Neil and I wrote 600 letters back and forth on that blue airline paper with the APO address. The Bomb was dropped, Japan was not invaded, and surrendered; Neil was to spend his days building airstrips with Japanese contractors. They worked together well, apparently from the beginning when the Japanese engineer said: "Lieutenant, you just let us do what has to be done. I know the work needed and we will do it well". Enemies did become friends and the family bestowed a sword from their family to Neil with which we cut our wedding cake.

Martha Wellborn Carroll, married October 18, 1883
(Fay Ostner married October 18, 1921, and
Maurita Estes married October 18, 1946)

June 1946 was the time Neil was coming to Charleston, home from the war. Such excitement and when I asked if I could take the afternoon off, a firm "No! I think you must finish the day". Resigned, I looked forward to Saturday. It was Friday, TGIF was not then in our slang. I had two months to finish my contract. Neil went on a long fishing trip with his Dad. I came home to spend two months being a bride. It was such fun every day to shop, find a wedding dress, choose patterns of crystal, silver, and china. Aunts in Oklahoma, Arkansas, Massachusetts, and Tennessee all helped by shopping in their hometowns. Everything was hard to get as we recovered from the shortages of the war years. I was showered by friends of my mother's, relatives of my other family to be. One shower stands out in my memory, its being co-ed. At the time it was a unique idea. Most of my friends were married or so it seemed, many married before or during the war. This was a shower with men bringing Neil tools, hardware, cocktail shakers, aprons and girls brought me items for the homemaker.

Such glorious days ended abruptly when I woke up on THE day with a severe sinus infection. Off to the doctor I went and of course, waited what seemed like hours. He could give me whatever was helpful to put me on my feet. No miracle antibiotics, usually bed rest, 7-Up and grape juice. Mother had treated me often. The other near calamity of the day was that the driver to pick up Adeline, a bridesmaid, got lost or forgot to get her and someone made an emergency room visit and I was nearly in tears. Daddy seemed calm. Maybe he was a bit teary as this was his first time to have a daughter married. He did establish a precedent after a bit of altercation with the minister. When asked in the service "Who gives this woman to be wed"?

Neil & Maurita's Engagement, 1946

he responded, "Her mother and I do". Daddy had said this at the rehearsal the night before and repeated it at the wedding. The only other mishap: My sister did not make it through a storm from Michigan for the rehearsal dinner the night before. We rehearsed in our living room the next morning…not too difficult to walk, carry a bouquet and the ring.

The date was October 18, the 25th anniversary of my parents' wedding and the 50th of my paternal grandparents'. To be held at the University Methodist Church in which I had grown up, with the same pastor officiating. Dr. Caskey served 26 years in that church, probably the record for any Methodist clergy. I had three bridesmaids, one gowned in green, one in gold and one in rust, each carrying flowers to match their dress. We had six groomsmen…a lovely wedding party of long-time good friends and cousins of Neil's. Looking at the wedding pictures as

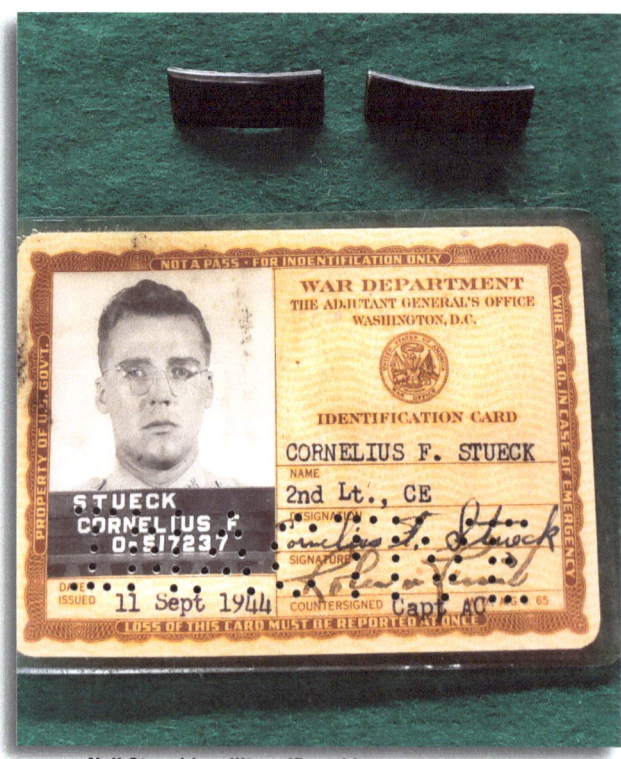

Neil Stueck's military ID and bars

I write I see that all are gone except my sister.

Our reception followed with wedding cake cut with the Japanese sword, friends gathered to wish us well and we left about 10:30 p.m. after my dear friend, Betty Knodel, caught my bouquet. She was home from the Marines and was probably the next one to be married. Catching the bouquet predicted that.

Off to Steelville, Mo. to spend our first night in Uncle

Erwin Stupps' country home there, on to Little Rock, Arkansas to spend with my Aunt Doris and then to New Orleans for the first of numerous trips that Neil and I had together the next forty-six years. We were blessed with four children, and five grandchildren while Neil lived.

It was a good partnership and marriage in the offing for so many years!

May 2, 2016

2nd LT C.F.P. Stueck 1942

CHAPTER TWO
Raising a Family

University Church Wedding, 1946

My purpose of writing is to share my life with others of two or three generations. I have outlived all my family members of the past two generations. The perspective I have of family ties is one that I want to share. Each dawn I receive is a gift that can bring feelings of much gratitude. Some days I have more energy than others. Not every day is very productive. My balance is only fair. I concentrate on pushing away unhappy thoughts. I do not let depression set in.

Marriages

Neil Stueck
October 18, 1946 to his death February 29, 1992, St. Louis, MO

Joseph Burch
October 19, 2000 in Estes Park, CO to his death August 12, 2005 in Redlands, CA

Maurita's and Neil's wedding, October 18, 1946

The Family I Married

The Peter Stupp family lived on Shenandoah in South St. Louis, raising four children two girls, Edna and Lillian, and two boys, Erwin and Norman. The boys were both engineers graduating from Washington University. The girls were sent to National Park Seminary in Washington, D.C. This was a two-year College known in c.1912 as a "finishing school". Edna "finished" and in 1915 married "the boy next door", Arthur Richard Stueck. After a wedding trip to Yosemite National Park (California) the young couple moved to Chanute, Kansas. There they lived with his parents. Arthur worked in his father's smelter company. Their son, Cornelius (Neil) Frederick Peter Stueck, was born in July 24, 1921.

When Neil was about seven his parents were divorced. Edna returned to St. Louis to live with her widowed mother at the Forest Park Hotel, an apartment hotel at that time. Neil recalled playing with Betty Grable* when he lived there. Grandmother Stupp was building a home in the new suburb of University City. 540 Purdue was completed for Grandmother, Edna and Neil, sister Lillian, brother Norman to move in. Norman was soon married and took his bride, Marie, to their own home.

Grandmother lived there only about three years. Edna, Neil, Lillian lived there until 1950. Mother Stueck handled the domestic affairs: cooking, PTA activities, school conferences, Boy Scouts. Aunt Lil enhanced Neil's life introducing the cultural aspects: Art Museum "Treasure hunts" on Saturday mornings, travel, trips to the Zoo and Jefferson Memorial, Day, and summer camps.

I met Mom Stueck when I was in Junior High because Neil was in "our gang" of eighth and ninth graders who gathered in each other's homes from time to time. Pancake suppers at Neil's were fun. Mom made us Apple Pancakes and we could play games in their attic. Aunt Lil had records up there so we could try dancing. I really cannot say I learned to dance up there. My best self-taught dancing sessions were on Harvard with the kids in the neighborhood.

It was many years before I became acquainted with the extended family members in the Stupp-Stueck families. There

Norman, Erwin, Edna & Lillian Stupp

Lillian Laura Stupp

Stueck/Estes Family Tree

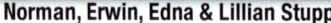

were visits with great-aunts Johanna, Lena, Bessie, Uncles Nor and Er, Aunt Marie and Mildred and many cousins. I met Neil's father, Arthur, my Senior year in High School. He had lived walking distance from Neil in the same elementary school district and had not yet re-married. He made a home with his Aunt Lena all her life and lived the rest of his life in the same apartment on Pershing Avenue in University City.

After four years of college and three years of WWII I married in 1946 at the age of 24. Just as the previous generation we lived about three months with my groom's in-laws. Housing was most difficult even for GI's.

Arthur owned apartment buildings in St. Louis and University City. We had a wait for an apartment to be vacated in which we could live.

I did have a nigh-to-perfect mother-in-law in many respects. Never did she make any suggestions or remarks re: what we did or did not do, no comments on how to raise our kids, and she cheerfully helped us when needed. Sometimes she and Aunt Lil were most "too willing" dropping by to visit more than I thought necessary. The family did have expectations of the new members of the family: Sunday visits to Aunt Johanna, sweeping out the Mausoleum at Bellefontaine Cemetery, Thanksgiving gatherings, Christmas Eve AND Christmas Day. I somehow managed, sometimes with frustrations, to fit these activities into our lives. It took a couple of years for us to wean ourselves away so that there was time to see my family at holiday times. Two Christmas dinners in one day was too much!

Mom was the Queen of "Scrubby Dutch". Seeing her wash my dining table pads sent a message to me that this bride was not a good housekeeper. When she washed Neil's pipes, he quietly suggested that they were NEVER washed.

I do not believe Mom ever had a bad feeling about anyone. She did not gossip. And she thought I was the best girl for her son. I held this position until the birth of our first daughter. Then I took 2nd place.

Mom seldom laughed, seldom played games, and had no sense of humor. Our family just understood this, and no note was made of it. Aunt Lil supplied all the humor Nana (Grandmother's name) lacked. I was so saddened at the cutting, spiteful smirks made by cousins, nieces and nephews and sisters-in-law. Nana did not have the intellect of her siblings, and, sickly as a child, she was not well much of her life. She had a nervous breakdown (now under many medical terms) in c.1930. Somehow, she maintained a cheerful outlook on life, enjoying her days as they came.

Edna & Neil Stueck, 1971

The first several Christmases I labored to make German Lebkuchen, Springerle, as Mom had those. Years later I learned she never baked them but ordered from Germany or bought these treats at the Missouri Bakery on the Hill.

She remained active in her Eastern Star chapter and the Kappa Sigma Mother's Club for many years. For two decades—the 50's and 60's—the "girls"—Edna and Lil—traveled the world. Aunt Lil planned the extensive 6–8-week jaunts, usually overseas, and Nana went along. Her options were to stay home alone or go with "Lil". I never cease to marvel that Nana managed these trips, as she was not very agile. Busses, trains, carriages, rickshaws were modes of transportation she took. Getting into a small plane on a glacier in New Zealand is a challenge for most. I have pictures of her doing that! One night we had a call from Hawaii. "Hi" Aunt Lil's voice rang in our ears. "We are in Hawaii visiting our friends. We have just decided to stay here a few days and then go on to Japan". Nana got on the line, no cell phone in 1960. "Yes, we just think we will do that as we are so close and may never get this way again". Back in St. Louis, we continued to pick up their mail, check their house, pay their bills, etc. We were good "house-sitters".

I could write a book on the family I married!

May 8, 2012

My First Home

I could watch our dinner guest coming up the stairs. He rose taller and bigger with each step up to our Penthouse. I had not met Max but I liked his wife and, as a couple, we had invited them to dinner. It was to be a small, intimate dinner party, as six guests was the maximum to fit in the penthouse. As a bride I had been reading many articles about entertaining. I had read that six was the optimum number for a guest list. I satisfied myself with that rationale rather than the size of our tiny apartment.

We called it "the Penthouse", but it was the attic of a large early 20th century home in the of area of St. Louis-Union Avenue, Soldan High. In my teen years it was a place to live, before the conversion of old mansions into apartments heralded the downfall of the area. In 1946 it was in the control of OPA, controlling the rents. For our attic, converted into two rooms, a hall at the top of the stairs and a bath. If my memory serves me well, we paid $96.00 a month out of a salary of $150.00.

It was our first home and lucky we were to find it only a short while before our planned wedding. Even though my groom was a returning veteran and his father owned two 4-family apartments, there were no vacancies. Because our home was being newly converted, we had the delightful opportunity of choosing "upholstery" for what was to be our bedroom/living area, consisting of two twin beds that would become sofas with coverings and bolsters. With the other provided furnishings, a table and four chairs plus a desk from our family and wedding gifts, we were all set in time to return from our honeymoon. Looking back over these sixty-four years I have mostly happy memories. Mostly I say.

Home from our wedding trip to New Orleans mid-October we had our "best man" come for dinner. Having been given sufficient experiences in the kitchen at home I felt comfortable cooking. I poured over cookbooks and looked forward to dinner guests. Charlie arrived with his sack dinner just in case. We have laughed over that gesture for years. He is the only man from our wedding party still on the planet.

Soon after Ed called to ask my groom, Neil, to go hunting with him. "Oh! No", Neil responded quickly, "I do not want to do that, but bring back a rabbit and Maurita will provide us with dinner". Maurita had NEVER seen a dead rabbit, let alone cooked one. Undaunted, I gave it my best try when Ed returned from his hunting with a rabbit!

As the bride and groom in the family, it was our task to bring our two extended families together. Both of our parents were in St. Louis as well as Neil's extended family of aunts and uncles. He was working for a closely held family corporation started by his Great-Grandfather. I soon learned that I had married into the family corporation as well as the family. This was a new experience for me as I had lived all my life in St. Louis with aunts and uncles coming to work here off and on, but my parents and one sister was really all the local family I had.

The first Christmas I could no longer go Caroling for the Christmas Carolers Association as I had done for many years. We had to deliver some turkeys, gifts from "the plant" and then go to Aunt Mildred's and Uncle Er's home for Christmas Eve with all their kids and another aunt and uncle who had no children. A big change it was from my traditional Christmas Eves.

Christmas Day...back to the other aunt and uncle and we had two Christmas dinners. And for the first time I had a long Christmas list of gifts, to add all this new extended family. Thinking of my budget, I suggested to Neil, "Could I just make some jam or a box of homemade cookies for the aunts and uncles"? "No, that would not be a good gift". This giving was never settled. Always I had to do the shopping with or without the wherewith-all with which to do it.

We had many learning experiences in that first year of marriage as we should have expected, but I do not think we thought ahead too often and that is just as well. Differences must be dealt with as situations arise.

Sometime in that first Advent season, we decided to have both our families to the Penthouse for a gathering. A winter scene for the centerpiece was indicated and I set forth to create one with a mirror, stick figures set around amidst fake snow with whatever material was available at the local dime store, candlelight, of course. Dinner carefully produced and much appreciated by Mother-in-law and maiden aunt Lil, and my parents. Daddy, of course, set his Zippo lighter in front of his place. His twinkling eyes made it a laughable act. And the message was clear. After our celebration, Neil and I amicably agreed that we would enjoy our families separately and each branch of the family would enjoy our gatherings sharing our common interests more. We were fortunate that everyone in the two branches of our family admired, respected each one, bearing no dislikes.

We hosted some of my out-of-town aunts and uncles. Aunt Mabel, the eldest of my mother's seven siblings, came over for dinner one evening as she and Uncle Harry from Little Rock were visiting my folks. Aunt Mabel was "fubsy" as my father said. Uncle Harry said, "that was just more to love". During the evening, Aunt Mabel had to use the bathroom, of course. Lo and behold, this proved to be an hilarious adventure, one that might have been a great embarrassment to one without the ability to laugh a lot. Our bathroom was so small, tucked under the eaves of the old attic, that one had to enter, slip past the basin with one's hips on the basin, then shut the door enabling one to use the commode. Aunt Mabel simply would not slip by the door very easily and became stuck. I do not recall how we helped her to extricate herself. She might have thinned herself laughing.

I was to be the "friend-maker" that first year and for most of time of our marriage. Four couples convened to make "the convention", a dinner-bridge group that continued for the next several decades. We replaced one of the originals when they were transferred from the city. Four couples played together, camped together, bonded together with all eleven of our children. I keep in touch with the original transferred couple. All the rest of The Convention group remained friends until death did us part. Treasured memories remain.

My First-Born, Linda

My first born "Linda" turned 70 on June 2, 2019. Those years from 1949 passed quickly. Happy Years for all the family. I got older, so did she and three siblings. We were married three-and-one-half years and planned for our first child.

Our preparations for a nursery, unlike many couples today, were minimal as we lived in a one-bedroom apartment. The one bedroom was not large enough for a crib, so the back porch off the bedroom became the nursery. It was glassed in, minimally warm and just large enough for a crib and small chest of drawers. It opened into our bedroom and the kitchen—the perfect setup for this newborn baby.

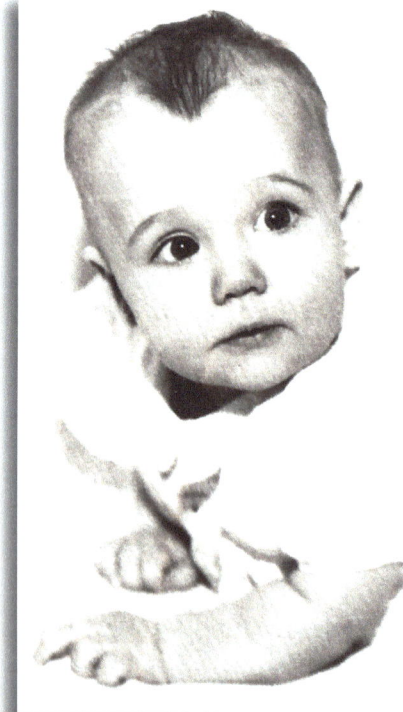

Linda Carroll Stueck, December 1949

Maternity clothes were important. I had a gray suit I thought was quite good looking. The panels over my hump were camouflaging my expanding figure. I had an occasion to wear it to some parties. I was invited to several bridal showers for Jane Schott and attend her wedding while pregnant. (Neil was their best man.) I would like to see the return of maternity wardrobes. There is nothing attractive about women pulling their T-shirts over their large BUMP. In 1950, we were not ashamed to be pregnant or embarrassed but wanted to look our best.

I had regular visits to Dr. Russell Vaughn, son of "old" Dr. Vaughn, who had delivered me 26 years before. The Vaughns and my grandparents had been lifelong friends. I liked Russell Vaughn but hasten to say he had no "bed side manners". I had a routine pregnancy with only monthly visits to the doctor. I did have not have many do's and don'ts for pregnancy. Just to watch salt and not gain too much weight. I asked Dr. Vaughn why he chose such a boring specialty and he responded, "Every birth is a miracle". Because I was pregnant, I could not go to my sister Betty's graduation from University of Michigan. I sent a telegram to her that Linda had been born earlier than the due date. She received it the day of her last final exam.

The scheduled day was approaching. Neil was at a meeting one evening when I had some feeling that perhaps Linda might come before her previously set time. I remember feeling a little embarrassed that perhaps he needed to think about going to St. Luke's Hospital as I was a real beginner to this. Neil came home and I courageously suggested that perhaps I ought to pack my suitcase. I gave no thought to timing contractions. I only had my book learning. I called Dr. Vaughn and he suggested that we go to St. Luke's. Nurses in obstetrics took over immediately and you would think that this baby that I had carried for nine months was the only one they had to care for on the maternity floor. For ten days, I was treated like a queen, although my deliv-

Linda Carroll Stueck, Maurita Estes Stueck, Fay Ostner Estes, Louisa Cavannah Ostner

ery was perfect, and the baby was normal. The schedule was prescribed carefully. The Vaughns were "King of the Hill" doctors at St. Luke's and orders were followed. The ten-day stay was routine for this doctor.

Linda made her exit in four hours and learned to nurse quickly and on schedule. I did not change a diaper until I took Linda home. Then Neil, being the engineer, figured out how to put on the diaper.

Linda was born at 7a.m. and Neil had a quick look and left for work so did not miss a day. He did not hold Linda for five days because of germ concerns. No visitors were permitted to hold the baby. Grandma Stead, my neighbor, became my first advisor on child well-being. My mother came over for a few hours each day, although after such a long stay in the hospital I was ready to go it alone.

Linda was happy and well-fed with my milk supply. We did not nurse babies in public but were advised to be quiet and unhurried and above all to be happy nursing the baby. After four weeks, I pushed Linda in the buggy up the hill to the market to weigh her at the meat counter of the corner grocery. Dr. Vaughn made a house call after a week to see how I was getting along. Imagine that happening in 2019! I was successful weaning her at 9-10 months. Linda became adept at drinking from a cup, which was a 2 oz. silver cup. We did not have sippy cups to use. As a baby, Linda was on a schedule for meals and naps.

Linda and John Mahan, August 5, 1978, St. Louis, MO

At age 70, Linda is still on a routine.

I write this as I am the only one living that can share these bits and pieces.

"Grandmother" My Mother

"I will just let the child give me a name," my mother declared when she learned that I was to give birth to her first grandchild. This baby was christened Linda Carroll and, indeed, she did give my mother her special name. She would be called: "Grandmother". She was not to be called "Nana" or "Me-maw" or Mama-O or Muddee as many grandmothers are called by progeny. Never having any "baby-talk" Linda said "Grandmother" clearly when she heard Mother so addressed. My next-born, Lawrence, who had great difficulty learning English, did likewise.

Mother grew up in Charleston, Missouri the third-born child of Max Lee and Louisa Cavanah Ostner christened Clara Fay. There were eight of these Ostners growing up in what is today one of the "historical" homes, 322 East Commercial Street. The year 1900 was her birth year; so easy to know her age with every birthday. Charleston was the commercial center of southeast Missouri, not in the area known as the "boot-heel" but north of there. Her Father was a banker and an absentee landowner, raising cotton while living in the thriving town. My maternal Grandfather died ten days after I was born. Mother had already married and moved away.

Mother was not a raconteur as storybooks portray grandmothers. Bits and pieces gathered through the year have given me pictures of her girlhood. Floods of the mighty Mississippi must have been most every year. We learned that folks whose homes flooded came into town, as it was the high point, to stay in the high school until waters receded. Kids in her young years did pranks on Halloween we thought hilarious like turning over outhouses. She earned the "History Medal" in high school. She knew all the Kings in the order they reigned throughout the history of England.

Graduating from Stephens College, a two-year woman's college, in Columbia, Missouri, she continued her education at "the University". That was, of course, Missouri University. I have a glimpse of Mother as an independent eighteen-year-old. She pledged Pi Beta Phi Sorority paying little heed to the advice of the "boys from home". "Pledge Kappa" Marion, a favorite "town-lad", advised, "they are the smart ones for you! Those Pi Phis are the "high-steppers" on campus. I quote Mother as she told this story when I pledged Pi Beta Phi at Washington University.

At the end of two years, Mother left school with a teaching certificate and went to Potosi, Missouri, to teach school and live with the Settles, her college roommate's family. Mother was a beautiful young woman I see from the few pictures I have: five foot eight tall, dark brunette, large hazel eyes. She told us she was able to "sit on her hair". Pictures show this hair long and held up somehow until it was cut short in the "bob style" of the 1920's.

She taught High School in Potosi for about three years. In that time a young man from St. Louis was building a home 12 miles out from town on property he hoped to farm. City lad asked Mr. Settle to introduce him to this attractive school marm. Mr. Settle declined as he knew not this "city slicker". There had to be another way to become acquainted with Clara Fay. Ignoring the social codes of the time, he went to a dance, asked her to dance and subsequently took her home.

Hurdling over the 12 miles of barely passable road between them, the "city-slicker", Wellborn Estes the romantic, pursued Fay writing songs to his beloved and speaking in a code over the phone. The phone line was a "party line" and every time a call would be made, everyone on the line could listen in. Wellborn wooed valiantly, convincing his bride to go out to Hillandale to a large newly built home and farm. Daddy was serious about this new career of his and took Extension classes from "the University". Studies at Cornell University were NO preparation for farming in the Ozarks.

They were married in the family home in Charleston and thereafter drove to Bird's Point on the Mississippi, to Ferry across, board a train bound for a Honeymoon to Niagara Falls. That apparently was THE destination for Honeymoons in 1921.

Life at Hillandale must have been a challenge for Mother

like no other she had encountered, as she set up housekeeping in the wilderness twelve miles from town. Electricity was generated on site; water was pumped downhill from the Spring; farming was so little I have heard nothing about it in my whole life. My birth ten months later added another challenge for Mother and Daddy to meet. Often, I have wondered just how they managed. Those were questions I should have asked. I know mother cooked my oatmeal hours on a wood burning stove.

Two-and-a-half years later my little family moved to St. Louis, rented an apartment on Northeast Kingshighway. Mother never did like apartments. She lamented: "It was like living in a Pueblo". Her idea must have been generated in a geography class, as she never was in the Southwest with Pueblos until she was 60. However, thinking back to all I remember of my Mother she always "bloomed where she was planted". At the same time, she read widely, learning all she needed to know to be a good Homemaker, a good parent, an active citizen through her 75 years.

Life in the suburbs of St. Louis was the next adventure in living. The folks moved to University City when I was entering kindergarten. For the next five years we lived in apartments. First, the apartment district just west of Skinker, the western edge of St. Louis, the eastern border of the first suburb in St. Louis, founded c. 1900 by Mr. Lewis. A Woman's Magazine was published in the outstanding architecture of the Magazine Building, now the City Hall. It was widely read and is considered a factor in marketing the St. Louis World's Fair 1904. Women had read about the plans and were encouraged to come to the Fair, the time "all the world came to St. Louis".

It took 5 years for the struggling little family to move out of the apartments. No wonder Mother did not like apartments when she had to pull the baby buggy up those metal stairs after my sister was born a year later. Mother set about to learn all about good nutrition relying I suppose on *The Boston School of Cooking* cookbook and the "Good Housekeeping" magazine.

She belonged to the "Delphian Society" comprising a long shelf of books—a precursor to an encyclopedia. Attendance at study groups. I know she had good grounding on being a

Homemaker from Stephens College. It was there the President proclaimed: "You girls must learn chemistry as most of you will need to learn to cook and chemistry is the basis for much there". Teaching, nursing, secretarial work were the primary occupations for women. Mother and Daddy had many merry times despite what must have been some very hard times. How beautiful she was in her long formals and how handsome he was when they dressed up on Saturday nights to go dancing. My delightful task was to powder Mother's back. They always went "formal" so to not have a shiny back was very important and it was very important for me to do a good job. Five Dollars for an evening at the Missouri Athletic Club was the one extravagance. I say to this day, Daddy was the finest dance partner that I ever had!

Mother, not always calm, developed her plans and expectations for a making a good home, molding the two of us girls in the way she felt right, and taking an active role in her community. Why do I not like apartments to this day? Betty, my only sister, says "that we learned from mother". Why do I know that if the windows are clean on the inside "your whole house will look shinier"? I live in a very dusty part of the city today and I know this statement to be true. Why am I conscious of my "carriage" to this day? My mother is saying, "Stand up straight".

When I was ten Mother sought out the Girl Scouts because she wanted me to know about the natural world as she did not. She recalled: "All I knew was to sit in a swing on the front porch with my boyfriend". She took me on the streetcar downtown to Bishop Tuttle Memorial to learn to swim. She had never had the opportunity and I needed to do so. Many years later I was indeed a Water Safety Instructor, teaching many classes from children with special needs to adults. Mother was in an adult class I had. She was probably 50 and not-so-apt a pupil but lost her fear and became comfortable in the water, though never in a swimming suit. She felt "too skinny".

We had no public library in University City, but used Central Library downtown when needed for any real study, term papers, for example. But when Mother thought I was ready to read for pleasure we went to a lady's home near the Loop who had a "lending library". There I could find the latest Nancy Drew book. This is just another activity "bending the twig as she wished it to grow".

Mother gave me many gifts. Some of these are kitchen utensils and cookware at home in my kitchen today. Some furnishings I treasure from Christmases past: two beautiful lamps. one recently repaired, have brought light to several homes. But the gifts I treasure are not material but values, ethics, and interests that have molded my life that I have not often articulated.

She was disciplined and organized. These were gifts she shared: regular and nutritious meals, good night sleep, habits formed from early age stood with me well into adult-hood and, perhaps, were given to my children. I was programmed and carefully prepared to go to College so that I could "be independent".

Here she was a bit ahead of the woman's movement. Alas! Missouri has yet to pass the ERA. We were firmly anchored in our church and its teachings, respect for one another. To have raised us in an environment rife with prejudice we learned to respect diversity. With reflection I realize how deliberate she (and my father) were in giving me opportunities to experience and care for the natural world, to care for others' needs through volunteer activities in the community. She led by example.

It has been difficult to draw a picture for the next generations of this rather remarkable strongly determined woman who lived to age seventy-five. My skills for writing are unremarkable. I have done my best.

April 26, 2014
(Clara) Fay Ostner Estes   1900-1975

Cupid's Arrow

She should have been named JOY, for that was her gift to our family. Her name was Zora Impson and she came to St Louis from Colorado Springs at the age of 48 to marry my father-in-law, Arthur Stueck. Only one with courage, fine spirit, faith and trust could have done so. Zora had ample supply of all these attributes and changed the dynamics and relationships of our extended family.

Zora was born in Nevada, Missouri but had moved to "The Springs" as a young adult with her parents and an asthmatic brother. The climate in Colorado helped those with respiratory problems. She was the sole bread winner for her family as a piano teacher.

To escape the St. Louis summer heat and humidity, many St. Louisans "summered" in Colorado. My husband's grandfather, Frederick Stueck, was one of these "some-timers" who rented a room in a private home in the Springs before resorts were so numerous. But, dear Reader, you must know more.

Arthur Stueck, my father-in-law, picking up on the custom of his father and mother, likewise went to Colorado Springs in the '30s, rented a room and "cooled off". (He had been divorced from his wife, my husband's mother, in about 1928.) He found space in the Impson home. Zora was still living with her parents.

A romance developed; however, the two did not marry because she provided the sole support for her family. Likewise, Arthur was the sole support of his Aunt Lena and gave some care to Aunt Bertha after she was widowed. Family loyalty and responsibilities prevailed over Cupid's arrow. They had no further contact for the next seventeen years.

I first met Mr. Arthur Stueck when I was a Junior at Washington U. By that time, Neil and I were "pinned" and it was time for me to be introduced to his father. Through all his growing up years Neil was periodically in contact with his father who lived a few blocks from his home. At the time I first met him

Arthur lived in an apartment, dimly lit at all times with closed Venetian blinds. Aunt Lena lived with him until she died a few years later. Aunt Lena only wore black when I was visiting and was the first person I had ever known who wore a wig. Although it was 1940, she seemed to still be living in the first decade of the 20th century, a post-Victorian lady. It appeared that she and Arthur never had more social life than a visit to her sister, Bertha. Arthur did own several rental properties that "Miss Lang" managed for him.

After WWII Neil and I were married. Aunt Lena had died, and we called on Arthur now and then. Arthur had built a home, "Bluebird Hill", in Woodland Park, Colorado. From time to time he would do shopping in Colorado Springs as Woodland Park in the '40's was a tiny settlement.

Katie, Zora & Bridget with Maurita

Fast forward to a lovely Fall evening in 1947 about a year after Neil and I married. We were driving home with Arthur, Neil driving and I in the middle of the front seat. While stopped at an electric signal somewhere on Page Avenue Arthur said: "Well, son, I am getting married soon". I remember it well as it was the one and only time my husband was stunned speechless! Not being one for long pauses, I exclaimed, "Wonderful! Tell us about her"!

He responded, "Recently I nearly knocked Zora down as I was coming out of the drugstore in the Springs. We renewed our friendship after all these years"! They were married soon after that. Only when she arrived in St. Louis following her marriage did she see where he lived. She had a cousin or two in St. Louis whom we met later.

They were only married about 9 years when Arthur passed away, but such joy they shared and that my children shared. The blinds went up, friends came, the honeymooners traveled, Arthur rekindled his delightful sense of humor, sunlight came into their lives. Laughter reined when they came to our house. Zora's bright eyes always twinkling with *joie de vivre*.

At times, our family was invited to their home for dinner. I would often ask Zora about some china piece, a picture, or furniture. Consistently, she would remark, "I do not know about such-and-such as it was here when I came". What it did tell me was that all the "stuff" in Arthur's house had been in his parents' home at one time or another.

Her legal status as Stepmother and Step-grandmother, was never discussed. She was known only to my children as Zora, and she stayed with us as extended family until she died some years later. One Christmas, we all remember her as the lead in a drama, now recorded on film. Santa had brought one of the kids a cardboard house we imagined as a Western cottage. We staged a real hold-up, Western style. Zora, with bandana around her face, of course, was the "hold up" guy... What a good sport! If she recounted the drama to one of her friends, she would have slapped her knee and laughing at herself say: "What a stitch"!

Never was there any lamentation or cries about "growing old". That would have been uncharacteristic. Writing this memoir reminds me to embrace her as a role model for growing old with grace.

Animals Befriended

Recently I have had occasion to observe friends and relations who are being well-trained by their respective pets. My "roof-mate" (not a roommate but one who shares the roof of my cottage in her own cottage) is a delightful Irish woman whom I greatly enjoy, as I do her canine companion, Flake. Flake is a well-behaved, medium size, no descript breed who takes his mistress, Sylvia, for two walks every day. They go only around our complex and a bit up the hill by the University on our boundary. Sylvia stops to chat; Flake waits patiently for a time and then makes it quite clear they must move on. Sylvia moves on.

Katie and TOAGI pet goat 1961

Over Eastertide this year, I spent a week with my son, Lawrence, and my daughter-in-law, Kathleen. A lovely talented daughter-in-law who is beautifully-trained by her Parrot, Gatsby. Gatsby has a small vocabulary but communicates very well without much talking. It has the flying space all around the kitchen and breakfast room, a very large cage in the latter. Gatsby helps herself with never any reprimand to crusts of bread on the table, is often given grapes or bits of chicken even as we are eating at the table. If these morsels are not satisfying to Gatsby, he will whistle to get our attention and more nibbles are immediately forthcoming. All conversation at the table ceases.

Until its recent demise there was a small parakeet caged next to Gatsby. I watched with fascination as Gatsby would pick up a stem of spinach or any other edible and feed it to the little bird. When it died, Gatsby's behavior seemed to indicate mourning.

Gatsby has a large diet to be especially prepared by Kathleen, a large cage to be cleaned each day, toys with which to be amused as one would not want the pet bird to be bored. It takes about one-half hour each day to keep Gatsby well and happy. Gatsby trained me quickly. Since this house is very well-organized, I found that washing dishes was one thing I could do to be helpful. There is a dishwasher used as storage for many kitchen items. Therefore, I found myself standing over the dishpan after Lawrence and Kathleen had gone to work. Gatsby, without saying a word, had landed on my head! Gatsby trained me very quickly to stay out of his territory. I informed Kathleen that I would not continue by dishwashing if she did not leave Gatsby in his cage when she left to work. Ho! Ho! I trained daughter-in-law quickly, too.

With further reflections on pets, I recalled some we had as I was growing up. My mother had patience with pets. One weekend returning home from Hillendale, The Farm, I wanted to take home a piglet being raised by Ben, the caretaker, who did some farming on our family property. I pleaded with Mother. I do not recall how the baby porker trained us, but I am sure there was a way.

I can attest to the fact that parents in every generation must have patience. Our daughter, Katie, yearned for a goat after we had visited "The North Pole" one summer in Colorado with many endearing baby goats to pet. As luck would have it, Daddy had a friend with a goat farm near Pevely, MO. After a bit of negotiation, we were able to have a goat from the farm providing we could return it when the kid became a goat with horns. Our kitchen was an eat-in kitchen c. 1950, not large, but with patience, I managed to have the kid in the kitchen while being bottle-fed. Having the goat go to kindergarten with our youngest daughter, Sara, was a big event for five-year-old urban kids. "Toagi" it was named, and we kept her until my neighbor, Mrs. Schumacher, suggested her roses ought not to be on Toagi's diet. "Does the city allow goats in residence?" she asked one day. As per our agreement, Toagi went back with big goats in Pevely.

I can only list all the other animals that have come to live with us, and our Grandchildren and no doubt the Great-Grandchildren. As yet, there is only a cat in that household. This is just a list of ones I recall quickly off hand: Tuppy, our cocker for 14 years, mice (2 females bought for some science fair experiment) but we did not know one was pregnant, two Abyssinian Guinea Pigs lived several years in Katie's bedroom, a cat given to us by our Hungarian custodian at church. Katie brought in a lizard one time. Just a casual visitor. Granddaughter Bridget had a tarantula. She has agreed that was not much of a pet, but it did live a long while in a terrarium and only needed feeding once a week.

Pets are very important to Senior adults, serving sometimes as service dogs, but more often really are companions. My long-time friend bought his first dog several years ago and I know "Missy" is as important a companion for George as any dog ever was for a boy. Unfortunately, George has noticed Missy does not like any men. Nevertheless, Missy has a home for life even if she does not jump up on his lap. A little Pekinese requires not much care and won't pull her master down. Hopefully, I will not fall over her when I visit there. She insists on my lap when I do not even ask her to jump up.

April 14, 2005

Animals with Special Needs

Some animals I have known and loved do have special needs I feel sure. These have lived with us as "pets" for a period of time and some who have been "wild", have entertained us or been a nuisance.

I will not recount much about the neurotic grand-dog who lives in north Georgia. Abbey is a high-strung, totally undisciplined, beautiful English Cocker. She runs to the point of exhaustion around the fence of their yard, and must be kept on a leash in the house to keep her from running wildly around the five rooms. She is not welcome to travel to any family gathering. Enough said about Abbey, one of my four grand-dogs.

I have had two wild visitors as friends. One is a beautiful Downy Woodpecker, native to Colorado, and a frequent visitor to the bird feeder just off my deck. Downy furnished entertainment most every day last summer as I watched from my dining area. He did have exclusive use of the feeder when he came, as all other feathered friends took to the nearby tree or waited a turn on the railing. Downy would tuck his tail under the feeder to be able to hold on while he strived to get a seed. One at a time was all he could retrieve. Sometimes he fell off several times before any success. Now any amateur birder knows, of course, that woodpeckers are designed to have a diet of insects from trees. We live in a forest; all trees have insects in their fissures. There is one long-dead tree standing near the house left specifically for the woodpeckers. There are even one or two holes already in the trunk. I think Downy is entertaining, but surely is mentally challenged to attempt to eat seeds designed for songbirds.

Now back in Webster Groves on my little patio I am challenged by a squirrel. I sense this squirrel, as yet unnamed (unless it would be "Nuisance") has difficulties adjusting to being a squirrel on my turf. First, he knocked down the bird feeder and ate up the seeds. Tiny, as they are meant for little songbirds, what frustrations it must have been to get that food. Such a diet is not so unusual for a squirrel. I moved the feeder, trying to foil Fluffy

Tail. I have a pot of pansies he has been into several times; pansies repotted. What kind of brain does it have? Pansies are not food for squirrels normally.

    I was in the process of decorating a "grapevine wreath" with wine corks and artificial grapes. Unfinished, I left it out overnight and the next day found several of my artificial grapes on the ground and one partially buried in my pot of pansies. Hmm, does the squirrel of little brain think that grape was a nut he was saving for Winter? He might think Winter is here as it turned so chilly. Whatever the answer here is just more proof that there are domestic and wild animals who seem to deviate from the proper way of their particular species. This is adaptation necessary for their survival in an urban environment. Still, they provide chuckles and sometimes frustrations for me.

May 5, 2011

There's Always Room for One More

In my twenty-seven years of Active Parenting, pets came into our family from time to time. Katie, the third child born in our family, seemed destined to have pets. Her first, I remember, was a lizard proudly presented to me when she was three. Not being wise in Lizard Lore at the time I did not realize this was a sick lizard or Katie could not have caught it. Lizard was not long with us. No tears were lost.

Katie's next loves were small caged pets kept in her room and cared for. This was the hamster and guinea-pig era, not just ordinary guinea-pigs, but Abyssinian breed, white, long-haired and rather attractive pets. Katie was responsible for their care and feeding; that she did happily. Petting its long silky hair was pleasurable, keeping track of it out of the cage challenging. We all did participate in trying to find the errant hamster. Perhaps it was lost somewhere in the heating ducts. No tears were shed.

In sixth grade Katie was assigned a Science project. At this time, science projects were important as our principal at Clark School had been a dearly beloved Science teacher at the high school. Clark School Science Fair was a big event for our school, but not competitive for the entire St. Louis community as "Science Fairs" later became. Katie designed a science project in which she would prove that diet of mice was important to their development. With great care we purchased two female mice to be fed two diets, one only chocolate, the other good nutrition for mice. Charting their weight gain it could be proven that the good diet would grow better; the chocolate diet would not grow as well. The experiment was approved and charts were prepared. The days passed, the weights determined, the poor diet gained more than the good diet! Only a day or so before the fair there was a litter (if that is the correct term) of mice! The experiment had failed; obviously, we had purchased two females, one pregnant at the time. Katie was crest-fallen, but Principal Mr. Barnett, undaunted, turned Katie and her Glass-fish aquarium full of mice, into one of the star attractions of the Fair. Watching the care Mother

Mouse gave to her babies was of most interest. Students insisted on pulling the cover off the babies to see the tiny, pink naked ones. Mother insisted covering the babies time after time! A lesson learned about mothers and their young. We kept Martha and George a long while after giving the babies away to many willing takers!

Our family Cocker Spaniel, Tuppy (short for Tuppence) lived with us fourteen years and truly was the family pet. (She was named Tuppy, as we did have a Penny first who, unfortunately, was hit by a car when little more than a puppy.) Curiously, Tuppy seemed to love us all equally. She went to Obedience School only for two sessions (as I recall). This was at the time she was to appear in the Boy Scout Merit Badge Show held at the Arena each year. Our son, Larry, and his Cub Scout buddy, Larry Keller, were the two to "show" their pets. Tuppy learned to sit, come, and to stop at the curbs, lessons she never forgot. She went to the basement every night but would NEVER go until she was sure we all were to bed down. She seemed to know if I was going to bed, but not my husband. On those nights he had to open the door for her to go downstairs.

One early morning even before Daybreak, her barking awakened me. She continued furious barking even after I let her come upstairs, even after I let her outside. Barking, running all around the yard; it was the night our back-yard neighbor was burglarized! I am certain each of my family could write some incident about Tuppy. She responded to me when I spoke French, telling her to go around to the back door. I would not let her in the front door.

One morning she was not awaiting at the top of the basement stairs when I arose from my bed. She had a stroke apparently and could not get up. My youngest daughter still berates me for not awakening her before Daddy took Tuppy to the Vet, never suspecting he would not return with her.

January 24, 2013

Building Family Friendships

I jump each time the phone rings and run swiftly, just as if it was a vitality important call. I expect sometime I will trip and fall. If only a caller would leave a message, I would not have to move so fast. As I picked up the phone a joyful voice "Hi Maurita" greeted my "hello". "This is Rich Nellums, your Godchild". Rich, the third born of the Nellums family, our dearest friends since we were "30 something". That would be about sixty years. I find it to be unusual, as family friendships are usually based on common interests, sports, employment, church involvement. Usually, friendship is not with the whole family, but only between individuals.

Bob & Betty Nellums

I first met Betty when I attended a meeting at the College Club of St. Louis. We were both newlyweds. She was a newcomer to St. Louis, coming here from California as Bob, her husband, had a position with Monsanto. This was 1946 and companies were noted for transferring employees around the country. Betty soon suggested to me that we visit a book discussion of *A Gift from the Sea* by Anne Lindbergh. This was an interest group of AAUW. Her mother had a long abiding interest in shells. Hence, Betty's interest. We decided that the group were "too old" (probably 50) and that we might start another book group with the eight "recent grads" we knew now in the St. Louis College Club. Soon enough this group "morphed" into a separate branch composed of girls from Webster Groves and Kirkwood. The KW Branch that I chaired and became know as "the founder" but Betty was the instrument of the founder.

While Betty and I developed our common interest in AAUW and the book group, the others in our growing families had activities in their respective churches, sports, Scouts, and other friends. Our families celebrated many holidays, picnics, visited the circus when it came to town. Betty became a friend I could talk with about our family goals and plans for our children.

Friends at Pine Winds Nellums, Harolds, Furmeisters, Rogers, Stuecks

We had weekends together at Hillandale, our family home near Potosi, Missouri. New Year's Eve together became a new tradition. When only one child needed to be bundled up, we did not spend the night. In later years, we celebrated New Years about nine or ten o'clock. Games we played, often devised by Betty, are still recalled by the grown-up kids. Have you, dear reader, ever had two teams blowing ping-pong balls across the finish line on the table? I regret that I did not reach out more to Betty as a newcomer to St. Louis. Never once did she mention being lonesome, needing any help in navigating about St. Louis. Monsanto employees did have a lot of social interaction that helped settle families in new communities.

Each summer the Nellums returned to Yosemite National

park in California. They asked us to join their families in 1958. I was the real reluctant dragon for my own reasons. Neil, ever the adventurer traveler, was ready to go. I rested my case and prepared to go. My memoir "Westward Ho" details this trip, my first trip west to the Sierra Mountains.

Weddings brought several more into our families. The Nellums with four in-laws and we had three scattered about the United States. Rich's high school sweetheart, Karen, is the only "hometown" girl.

Bob and Betty have orphaned their grownup and married progeny. I know each of the family and have met each of the "out-laws" and keep in touch. I do so miss Bob and Betty and treasured them as one of my "gifts" in life. I do believe our "whole family" friendship a rare relationship.

Soggy Scene

Some weekend all the troops the Church sponsored ought to have a Progressive Dinner was a suggestion someone at some time mentioned. The three troops that pursued such a plan were the older scouts: a Cadette troop (7-9 grades), a Sea Scout Ship (Jr. and Sr. High) and a Senior Girl Scout troop (High School). The idea percolated a bit; no problem getting the green light from the young folks.

It developed into a weekend with these three units. No younger Boy Scouts. An active parent (with a boy and girl involved) owned a place on Table Rock Lake and they recommended the public campground. My troop, the Cadettes, had done over-nights and some of the ninth graders had been on a 10-day troop trip the summer before. The Senior Girl Scouts had been Cadettes and were experienced campers likewise. We had access to the District camping equipment: tents, cook equipment, stove. The Sea Scouts had to fend for themselves. One key that made planning fairly simple was that all the leaders knew each other. The kids knew some in every unit, too, either in school or in church. Many of the Senior Girls had been in my Cadette troop. Only a few were members of our church.

We would have one night a Cooperative Dinner. My Cadettes would do the main dish as we had the largest number; the Sea Scouts would do salad. That seemed easier than dessert that the Senior Scouts would plan. Today this seems a little sexist, but women still do most of the cooking in a family I wager. Never mind, the boys delegated two to shop for the salad ingredients. They had no idea of quantity and bought; many heads of cabbage, not lettuce that was on the list. "Gee, I didn't know the difference between lettuce and cabbage", Barry apologized. We said little about the incident. (That boy went on to the US Naval Academy in Annapolis.) Evening activities ensued, each with his/her troop. We girls had to pitch our tents, organize our gear. I have no recollection of the boys' campsites. They were out of earshot wisely we thought. I learned later that the male leaders slept in the vans or cars.

Night became very stormy, the kind of weather that often seemed to follow my troop. My mother remarked one time: "I never plan any outdoor activity when you take your troop camping as I know it will rain". Be that as it may, this was the BIGGEST storm we ever had encountered. Wind was the "devil", making the rain seem even worse. We had many small 2-man tents. One blew down, the one, of course, with one of our youngest girls, Melissa. She appeared somewhat hysterical with no tent and a large Wolf spider in the light of her flashlight. That is a large spider, not harmful, but when I shined my light on him, it looked ENORMOUS! "Course I had to give it not much thought to help Melissa calm down. But what to do with this little seventh grader"?

Putting the tent up was easy enough but settling her down was my challenge! Melissa's tentmate had found shelter in the bathhouse—the only structure on site. Melissa and I headed for that warm, dry shelter. On this very dark, stormy night I could not even spot our car, but I did knock on the window of a friend's car and as luck would have it, he could put Melissa into the car. I said I would be back.

I went back to put the tent up for those two girls. Never before had I tied a taut line hitch with a flashlight, but my luck was holding out. The rain and wind slacked, and I was able to get the girls back in their tent. It was a soggy scene, and I went back to my sleeping bag.

Leisure Time

My offspring from time-to-time ask: "What did you do when we were all in school? What did you do with your time when we were all away from home"? And now I am writing in answer to a question on page 101 of "Writing Your Life", our text for the Life-Long Learning Institute. The question under the title "Leisure Time" is: What religious, social, or other organization have you been active in? (Poor grammar, I think.)

I cannot say any of the following did I consider leisure, but a challenge of active citizenship, some social life, activities of an involved parent who in 2012 is dubbed a "stay-at-home Mom". 'Tis only a myth that we were stay at home Moms. As community volunteers we kept many aspects of our community running.

First, a listing of some of the activities in which I was involved in the years from 1947-2000 with a one-liner describing involvement:

Board member of:

* Girl Scout Council of Greater St. Louis, Trainer, chair of Camp Committee and Program Committee

CASA - Art Council (no longer in existence)

Gifted Resource Council

*AAUW - Treasurer, Chair of International Relations, chair of Recent Grads and president of newly formed Kirkwood Webster Groves branch

White House Conference on Education morphed into Focus St. Louis,

Pi Beta Phi Alumnae Club

*United Methodist Women, District director of Children's Ministries,

Chair of St. Louis Scene, a fund-raising arm of the St Louis Symphony. Guiding Convention groups visiting St. Louis I became most interested in St. Louis history as well as managing a "small company" while planning the details of the group tours.

*Missouri Botanical Garden - Guide chairman, Instructor

Investment Syndicates (I have been active in three)

PTA Clark School- Secretary, work on Bond Issues, etc. etc.

Epworth Family and Children's Services - development of Volunteer Program.

Book groups so very popular in the last decade was a highlight for me in AAUW in 1958. Though I have been involved in four or five since then that was the richest program by far.

* denotes involvement over 50 years

Girl Scouting has shaped my values, abiding interests and skills taken to other facets of my life...travel, hobbies, leadership skills, and furthered interest in Botany, camping, other races and cultures, all life-long joys.

I married an Eagle Scout and, with two exceptions, every male in my family for two generations is an Eagle Scout. Needless to add, I had been a den mother for three years, as well as a Cadette Girl Scout leader for twelve.

The other deep involvement I have had is nearly 30 years as a Guide and Instructor at the Botanical Garden. I have had my interest in Botany dating back to college and several courses as an adult at Washington University enhanced through study of plants worldwide and further through travel with the Garden (and other groups) to every continent (except Antarctica).

My most interesting trips were focused on the natural world.

With this overview of my adult life, thus far, have I answered the question: "What did you do as a 'stay-at-home Mom' and then as an "empty nester"? I was not lounging around eating Bonbons. Probably cutting the grass in my leisure time!

First Flight

I was about to step over another threshold in my life and into the unknown. Four children were now ranging in age from 5-12 and I was planning to leave my "stay-at-home" mother's tasks and fly away. I was to "fly" away to New York. At this writing some forty-seven years later I have no memory of how I planned for my family to manage without me.

I had been invited by the Girl Scout Council of Greater St. Louis to attend training for a new Girl Scout program called Cadettes. This was to be introduced to all Junior High scouts in this year and I would become a leader of a Cadette Troop and a volunteer trainer of other new Cadette leaders. I relished the opportunity to attend this week-long session at Camp Edith Macy, the national adult training camp, in Pleasantville, N.Y.

This was my first flight. I was alone. TWA was my carrier early one morning from Lambert Saint Louis Airport. There were no crowds, in fact, there were maybe six or seven passengers on my plane. I was seated near the rear in a seat alone. Behind me was another lone woman on her first flight. We did not need to exchange much more than "Good Morning" before I realized she was indeed most anxious. I assumed the role of a veteran flier, giving her assurance that this would be a smooth trip. She did relax at least enough that we did not need to have much more conversation. I walked off with her, retrieved some luggage and we parted. I felt I had done my "good deed for the day", as per my Girl Scout motto. As I put such a good show, my anxiety was relieved.

The trip to Pleasantville and a warm welcome by our mentor, Judy Cook, the developer of the Cadette handbook for leaders, completed my first flight.

This was my second trip to Pleasantville, the first being to Camp Andre Clark, the National Girl Scout camp for girls adjacent to the Adult Camp, Edith Macy. In 1940 I attended the first Western Hemisphere Camp. I traveled with another Scout from St. Louis. This was an even bigger adventure for me than the "first flight".

Patty Dunbar, my companion, and I were put on a bus for this trip, (a "tour "bus I realize now) with a load of teachers. Our parents arranged all this, and we just hopped on. We journeyed to New York, stopping along the way for some sight-seeing. Arriving in New York, Patty and I headed for the hotel Mr. Dunbar had reserved for us. He, also, arranged for us to meet one of his

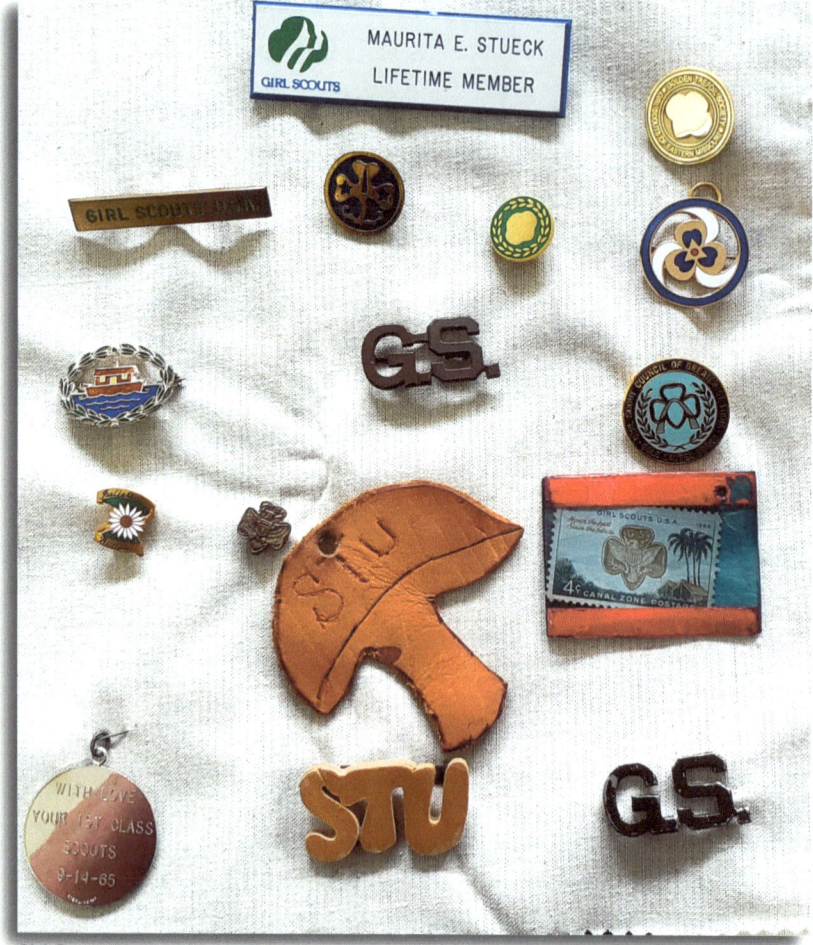

Girl Scout Pins

business partners for dinner our one night in New York before going into camp. "Mr. Business Partner" met us at the designated subway station and we went to a fine restaurant. "Mr. Business Partner" suggested he order a cocktail for us. I had never had any liquor and we were probably under age. After my first cocktail, a frozen daiquiri, the turtle in my soup seemed to be swimming around. Following dinner, "Mr. Business Partner" and his girlfriend took us to the Subway for our ride back to the hotel.

Times Square stop, we clamored up the stairs from the subway. "Wait!" I said to Patty, "this is not where our hotel is". We conferred with each other as to where we were and realized after a few moments of panic that we came up around the other side of Times Square. Such a relief!

Next day we bussed the short ride to Pleasantville, were welcomed into our "new" Girl Scout group and shortly felt "a sister to every other Girl Scout", as part of our Girl Scout Promise and Law.

Soon it was our turn to welcome Girl Guides and Girl Scouts from every country in the western Hemisphere. My tentmate was a Girl Guide, Olga Thistle from Newfoundland. We were to live in a primitive unit in a 2-girl tent. Fortunately, she was from an English-speaking country, as I had no knowledge of Spanish or Portuguese, the dominant tongues of most of the western Hemisphere. In the Encampment, there were 24 Girl Scouts from the USA, two from each of the designated regions at that time. I do not recall how many from other countries. Our unit was somewhat away from the main camp so that we had less interface with other campers except those in our unit. I recall nothing about assignments. If I had had a choice, I would have opted for a primitive unit as such was much to my liking. In New York I relished the idea of sleeping on the ground. as I had not the opportunity in Missouri. We had copperheads and rattlers and chiggers; New York State had no such creatures.

I had skills to teach the Guides who had not cooked over open fires, made "smores" or "Ring Tum Diddy". I so wish I had kept in touch with the Guide from Costa Rica, as I have been there three times in recent years. I did keep in close touch with Olga for about four years. The last letter I had from her she told me she was joining the Royal Women's Air Force and leaving for England. Never again did I have word. It was so easy to lose track of friends moving about during WWII as we did not have any means of communication except letters. We all were on the move a lot. Olga is just one of many treasures of friendship I have stored in my memory.

The highlight of this camp was certainly the day Eleanor Roosevelt came to visit. She, the First Lady, was Honorary President of the "Girl Scouts of the USA"; hence, her visit. Lucky Maurita and Olga were two representing our unit to meet and greet Mrs. Roosevelt and escort her back to our unit. She was dressed for the out-of-doors as well as possible in 1940: "walking shoes" with square Cuban heels, lisle stockings (with darns!), and a full skirt. I noticed the darns in her hose as I walked behind her up a little path through the woods. Darns were in all our socks and stockings  and hers, too. She was one of the most charming women I had ever met. The "Press" talked about her not being so pretty, even homely, not elegant, or good looking. Once she said "Hello" she became radiant. I felt honored in her presence; she seemed genuinely charmed to be with us.

My 18th birthday passed with no fanfare. Memory somehow fades over details of an adventure; one experience to grow on and to be folded into the collage of my life. I started my second year of college several weeks later.

Story of Our Creche

A creche has been set up for Advent/Christmas since the beginnings of our family, 1946. Our first Christmas Neil and I did our shopping at the local "dime" store. Still packed here are some of our purchases on a very limited budget; easily recognized as plaster cow, black wiseman mentioned in Scripture as Balthazar, the lambs, et al. The small wooden Ass was carved by Neil in some by-gone year and added to the creche, as was the black lamb and the "leather" animal. There is a plaster angel from some other year.

The ceramic figures were all handcrafted by Louise Ackerman, our dear neighbor at 75 Webster Woods for many years. We treasured her artistry since the main characters of the Creche arrived c. 1960. In some year thereabouts, Neil, now Daddy to all of us, built the stable. It has moved as have all the figures from Webster Woods to Cloister Walk in Kirkwood and now has come to Pacific Place. The creche historically has been set up by Sara. In 2013 I kept it boxed so she could again set it up when she arrived from Georgia. First, as a six-year-old, she applied her talents to set it up to perfection. The Wise Men and the camels stood aside until some days after Christmas, as they did at the Birth of Baby Jesus according to Scripture. The string of camels are a recent acquisition brought back from some trip...my memory is not sharp on this detail. Needless to add that this creche has just grown over many years.

I hope the tradition continues somewhere in my family. I have enjoyed having it. In Webster Woods it was arranged on the bookshelf next to the fireplace; here it was built to fit on the top of the Server.

January 1, 2014 it is packed away for another year.

Now Why Didn't I think of That?

Playing games at family gatherings has been a long tradition in my family. Growing up a special time was playing "Double Solitaire" with my grandmother, Mama-O, when she visited us for a couple of months in the winter times. Jig-saw puzzles were brought out when aunts and uncles came to visit. In the years after I was married our family played many games for potluck dinners or when we went camping with other families. Gatherings meant games were played.

I recall several that were most popular. The first that comes to mind is the Dictionary Game. Linda, our eldest daughter and the most passionate of all for fun and games, brought it home to us from her summer camp for Seniors. A word was given to us by our "designated chair of the first round". This was a carefully researched word that would be totally unknown to all participants, hence, the name we gave to this entertainment. The room was silent as each one of us constructed a definition that had a tone of authenticity, that would sound like a likely one for the word we were given. Our aim was to convince the group that "ours" was the right definition of the word. The game continued when each one had submitted an imagined word meaning that would be read aloud so each one could vote on the one believed to be the correct one. The dictionary definition was submitted by the "chair" and introduced along with all the hypothetical ones. As years passed our family and friends matured, went to college, married and we had botanists, physicians, professors, and chemists come into play this family game. Clever definitions were written and hilarity reigned as each tried to write a definition that could be plausible, thereby winning some votes over the actual definition imbedded in the readings. A decade later I came across the same game marketed as "Balderdash". Now why didn't my family think of that?

When I was about age ten or twelve, kids (and grown-ups) played a game we called "Battleship". All we needed was just paper and pencil. It revolved around making a grid with squares lettered A to H across the top and 1-10 vertically. On this grid we would mark a battleship (4 squares), a destroyer (3 squares) and two submarines (1 square each). The game progressed by the players taking turns "shooting" at a target (we hoped), calling out the shot with the number and letter to identify the square being targeted. Any hit was acknowledged. When any ship was totally destroyed that had to be announced. The big challenge was to remember all the squares "hit" so that next turn another volley could be sent to a surrounding square. A few years later one could purchase "Battleship" with the grids printed on paper and accessories to make the game more sophisticated. Now it can be purchased as an electronic game! Now why didn't I think of that?

Grandchildren with matching shorts made by Maurita, 1986

Birthday celebrations in the kid's world today are affairs held in public places...pizza parlors, Chuck E. Cheese, the Zoo, and other venues know by Moms. Kids come and often parents attend, too. Not so, I did not have a party so elaborate. With several friends to eat ice cream and angel food cake, my party was complete. Hats, balloons, and games were the program. I can recall one that was fast and frenetic. Each was given a piece of paper and a pencil. (Mother was the organizer and chair of the games and the refreshments.) We raced to complete a list of all the words we could think of beginning with a prescribed letter. Time was of the essence; the one with the most words when "time" was called was the winner of that round. A new letter was given. Adaptations were easy…birds, geographical places, etc. Now the game of Scattergories comes in a big red box with words, pads of paper, pencils, attractive illustrations, and rules by which to play. Now why didn't Mother think of marketing the game?

Christmas 2010 and a new game was brought by 15-year-old Hannah, my youngest granddaughter. She seems to have caught on to family games. This time a slick deck of cards called "Phase 10". The faces of the cards looked like any other deck of playing cards. And there were 10 phases to play through a game, each one different and increasingly hard to implement. Hmm! It was not too challenging (as card games go), easy to "catch on" and that is important in family playtime now with kids being "wired up for the instant" play. I caught on almost instantly because it was "Liverpool Rummy", with some minor changes that I had played 40 years ago with my grandmother!

One game continues to be a "winner" for four generations in my family and that is Parcheesi! Never a variation, electronic version, or new design!

Wheels Across the USA

August 1946, World War II had been over for a year or more, but my fiancé was posted in Japan rebuilding air strips and occupying the country with whom we had fought. Now it was homecoming and back to civilian life, a position with Stupp Brothers Bridge and Iron Company, a family held company in its fourth generation in St. Louis. I was to "marry" the company as well as a nephew of the Stupp bothers. The family legends, other than many stories of building bridges, concerned a "gene" passed down several generations already. I could trace it to Grandmother Stupp who traveled extensively in the 1920's, in the days when one took steamer trunks across the ocean, when she would spend in two consecutive years nine months one trip, more the second year. The "gene" to which I refer is one passionate for travel. This deep desire to see the world was passed on Aunt Lillian, the maiden aunt with whom my husband-to-be had lived with his "single Mom". So here I am planning my wedding in October 1946, not realizing that my groom had inherited that "travel-bug" gene.

When I had completed my contract with Girl Scout council of Kanawha County, Charleston, WV, I returned to St. Louis to be married in two months. Neil planned a lovely wedding trip to New Orleans. This was the first of at least twenty-five more road trips. The term road trip has come into fashion with the newer generations to distinguish "trips" on airplanes I presume. We simply called them "our vacation"—two weeks and bracketed weekends. Daddy worked 6 days a week with Saturdays being until only noon.

I cannot count the miles but know that we covered 47 of the lower 48 states. Having had a great 5-star honeymoon, the next year, we went camping, the kind of vacation we had most of the ensuing 25 years. The Great Smokey mountains beckoned us. We packed the car easily: two cots, two sleeping bags, a fly for shelter, a tiny cooler, our "Ditty" bags left over from my Girl Scouting days, a newly purchased nest of kettles, provision for food. Both experienced campers, we asked for a unit away from crowds of people. Crowds were not like they are now in the Smokies but more than we wanted.

"We only need restrooms and water in our campsite", I told the ranger at the National Park headquarters. "Perhaps, you can direct us to a site not so popular". Following his directions, we found the assigned site and there on a full-sized billboard in full-sized letters: "This water is not potable. It must be boiled before drinking"!!! Restroom? An open pit latrine. We had just what we needed—a restroom and drinking water once we built a fire to boil the water! We made camp—fly and cots, boiled our water, enjoyed our fire (something one cannot do much in National Parks now) and prepared to snuggle on our cots. It was crowded. But newlyweds never mind being crowded.

Sleep was disturbed sometime later. I seemed to feel a bit of dripping from our fly. Sure enough, it was raining, and the fly was not quite waterproof! A good Girl Scout and her Eagle Scout husband were undaunted. I sang an old song, one I had sung on many an overnight or hike: "we weather the weather, whatever the weather, whether we like it or not"! It was not to be the last rainy night. There were tornados, thunder and lightning, flooding and even snow we weathered whether we liked it or not!

We camped with our children, first just one. Then we took two and left baby at home. Then we took three and left the youngest home and finally we were six with a big tent (waterproof), stove, footlocker converted to our "Summer Kitchen". More to load up, but the first trip we always remembered as we explored the Smokies for the first time.

We camped from California to Maine most always with six. Only the last, when eldest daughter was graduated from High School, did we fly…completing a "million-mile road trip".

February 27, 2015

Crossroads of the Generations

In January 2012 the last remaining member of the older generation in my maternal and paternal ancestral families passed away. I consider the "out-laws", as my father referred to those in the family by marriage, as family. Indeed, the last one to whom I refer was Uncle Walter, married to my mother's youngest sister. It was my task to pass this word along to the extended family. I called my dearest first cousin, saying: "Now, John Lee, I want you to know I am the matriarch of the family and I do expect proper respect. Next, I must tell you that you are the third in line to become the patriarch as my sister will follow me". So here I am one who remembers three grandparents, all the aunts, uncles, first and second cousins on both sides of the family and Grandchildren, at least, those of my only sister. Beyond those I do not know Grandchildren. And as far as I know, I have the only Great-Grandchildren. In our very mobile society, I am incredulous as to how in just two generations families cease to be known to one another, as we are spread from the northwest to North Carolina, New Hampshire to Georgia.

    My paternal grandfather I dubbed Fafa. Climbing up on his rotund tummy I curled up to listen to another story of Bob and Bill, his fictional characters, who lived on the banks of the ocean. Many adventures were told to me, but I only recall those associated with the beach, island, and sea. The beach Bob and Bill discovered were stacks of pancakes, the sea maple syrup. Fafa and my Daddy talked together about ventures they dreamed of doing...having apple orchards down on property owned in the Ozarks, about building a lake and having a fishing resort on the same property. From what I have learned of Fafa's life, I would say he was a visionary, and a risk taker. In fact, he did take his family, at the time two children and my grandmother, out to California in 1894 to invest in a gold mine. My father was born in California, while his older siblings were natives of St. Louis. Grandmother (I called Muddee) told the story of getting the gun down from its rack in the cabin when she heard scuffling at the door. Opening the door there was a bear, not a human intruder. She was the best raconteur of the whole family.

The gold mine failed and the family returned to St. Louis. Again in 1926 Fafa set forth for California, this time part of the great Exodus to the West when first cars could travel on Route 66. This was the genesis of highway travel and the next westward expansion, and surprisingly the first fast food restaurant, on the highway to Palm Springs, the birthplace of McDonald's.

That entrepreneurial spirit I see again in my father and into one of my daughters. Musical and artistic talent I can trace, likewise, through three generations. Aunt Alline an artist and publisher of poetry, my son an artist and sculptor. My sister, a professional pianist and choir director. Academicians come into three generations, likewise, as teachers from kindergarten to secondary institutions to research scientists and university professors. In every generation I know a spirit of community activism was present- school board members, symphony Board members.

They were active Methodist church members for three generations. Perhaps, even five as my Great-Grandfather was the first to be named John Wesley with two more to follow. I assume that Great- Grandfather must have been in the family of Methodists. Why else would a baby be named John Wesley Estes? My maternal grandparents were Methodists I know, too. Reunion of the family in the ancestral

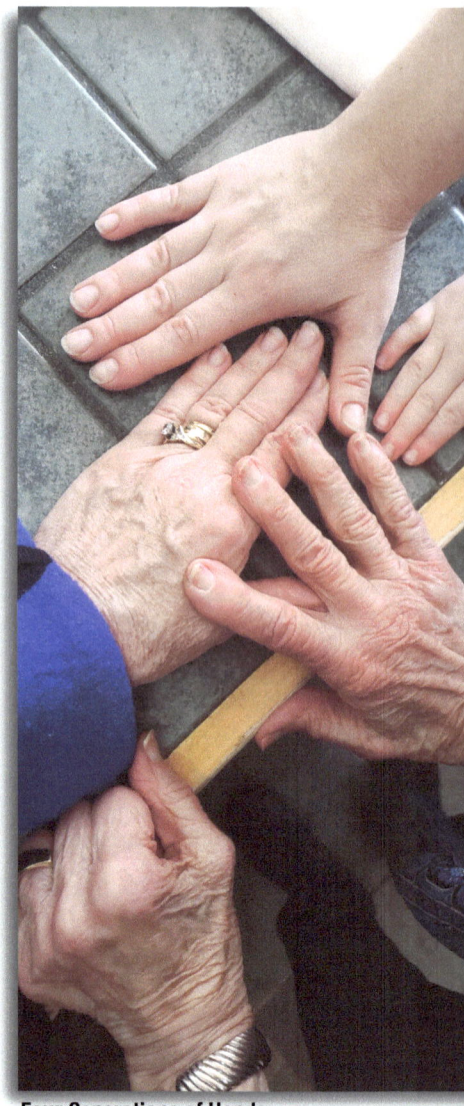

Four Generations of Hands

home, Charleston, Missouri filled up several pews of the Methodist church on Sunday morning. Alas, the fifth generation has changed the course of church-going and much of what I have held so dear.

Joining seems to have been a part of several generations in my family on both sides. Perhaps, it was the times in which we lived as well as where we lived. For the most part we were not farmers or folks who lived in rural areas. Rather, we were urban or from the larger "small towns" of the 20th century. Our males were Lions, Rotarians, fraternities, Masons. Our women were in Missionary Societies, Delphian group, DAR, (daughters of the American Revolution) UDC (United Daughters of the Confederacy), Girl Scouts, 4-H, Extension Services and sororities. and professional organizations associated with music and art.

Both "sides" of the family seem to have been businessmen until the generation of my children and grandchildren. There have been no doctors, no lawyers to my knowledge. Females were teachers, one dental assistant, one university administrator. Women in succeeding generations now are lawyers, university professors and administrators as women have moved into those careers.

We do have a couple of "wayward" folks...a Great Grandfather of whom we have only just recently learned about through the genealogical studies of my nephew. Ah, a mystery unveiled. One cousin just disappeared at about age 20, never to be heard of again...unsolved mystery!

Family members have been fun loving, rather loyal to one another, and a delightful romantic spirit flourished through several generations like a golden thread adding joy to my memories.

Guising on Halloween

No sooner had Daddy come home from work he busied himself outside securing everything that was movable...hoses, cans, lawn furniture and the glider. It was last year that we found that last item on the banks of the River des Peres across the street. We knew the windows in the garage door would be soaped, but, hopefully, with such careful preparation no other mischief. Soon the "trick or treaters" would arrive. Only last year, about 1932, my family had moved from living in apartments to a home where I would live until I left for college. My home was at the bottom of a hill a long block from my grade school and Junior High. That October was the first Halloween I remember when I joined in the ritual of "trick or treat" with ten other street players ten to fourteen years old plus several tag-alongs, our little brothers, and sisters. There were two homes we did not "beg", having learned well that that they did not appreciate street players. Mr. and Mrs. Reese were the favorites on the block. Older than the other neighbors, they welcomed us into their dining room set with a tablecloth and decorations. So many goodies and Lucious steaming cups of cocoa. How comfortable I was sitting with them. My sister, 6 years younger, concurs in my remembrances.

One year I was disconcerted when one of my friends changed her costume so she could return to some of the houses for "seconds". Several years later in Junior High I did not go around with the kids on the block as my social circle had broadened to include those who had come from another elementary school into our "one and only Junior High". A group of 6 or 8 walked from home to home, dropping into each to see what the mothers had prepared. When I drive these distances now it seems in credulous that we meandered several miles. We moved a few garbage cans around that someone had failed to put away. How daring of Wayne to spank Ina Lee as he perched on one!

Years later my husband confessed to our kids some mischief in which he had participated in the 7th grade. He and several other boys picked up all the newly-laid bricks on a terrace and restacked them on a nearby vacant lot. No sooner discovered in the morning and the boys moved them all back! Oh that we could have such innocuous pranks nowadays!

More than a decade later another "night for spooks" I well remember. It was just a week after we had moved into our newly built home with a newly-seeded lawn. Nary one spook could set a muddy foot onto our new carpet. What to do? We shepherded all the costumed street players around into our garage where two large tubs had floating apples. "Bobbing" was introduced to all for a splashy good time. Our treat for their trick!

My husband (the boy who had moved bricks) and his zany brother-in-law, Uncle Connie, donned masks and "tried trick or treating" after all the little kids had gone home. Their "trick" did not generate but a drink or two for "treat". Being unrecognized by many of the close neighbors, no admittance was granted to the big kids.

Another generation came along, and a haunted house was created by our two oldest daughters in our playroom/basement. Younger spooks were escorted downstairs for another trick on our part.

Kirkwood and Estes Park, Colorado, two towns that share my love, have established new customs. No "trick or treaters" door-to-door, but the hordes of kids come into town costumed with their parent chaperones to be greeted by merchants with treats. Youth groups in church and home parties provide further celebrations. As has happened around the world for centuries new rituals and customs evolve for this centuries old festival.

I hold dear memories of those few years when we were free to put on a mask, if we chose to do so, create a costume to our liking, take a flashlight and unafraid move about with our gang.

Crossing Another Threshold

I deem July 2012 as Reunion Month. I cross another threshold as I close the ninth decade composing my life. For the 29th summer I am at home in Estes Park, Colorado at Pine Winds.

Hannah, my youngest granddaughter, was the first of the family to arrive with plans to spend a week with Grandmother before going to Camp Timberline for her "shift" year. She had been alerted by other campers that washing camp dishes was to be the primary task of her position; she announced she would do all our dishes while visiting. I accepted the offer graciously, not suspecting she had an undercover motive.

Hannah needed some training for mountain hikes and happily joined in with my Rambler hiking group. At seventeen she has a charming talent for conversing with any one she meets, teens or octogenarians, and soon knew each walker by name. When she encountered several at the "Page-Turner's" meeting later in the week she said: "Hi! I'm Hannah and I met you on our hike", or punching me, she whispered: "There's Emerson and Dorothy. And there's Pat". They all remembered her, too. I did feel I needed to tell her, as gently as I could that her demeanor during the book discussion was unsatisfactory.

She had curled up working on her Sudoku puzzles the entire time. She haughtily informed me: "Grandmother I can multi-task easily and, furthermore, I don't like books". I heard that period almost as if she had stamped her foot.

The highlight of our week was compiling the "first edition" of my memoirs, written over the last five terms at the Life-Long Learning Institute as Washington U. I suggested she design the cover for each of the four books we were assembling. Here was her chance to have a purpose for her Art. She concentrated, giving thought to personalizing designs. Cocking her head, chewing on her pen, she mused: "I wonder what colors Aunt Linda would like"?

Her social schedule included a day or two in Fort Collins

with Aunt Linda and Uncle John. She is a rising senior and here was an opportunity to visit her first colleges. Colorado State University, Northern Colorado State, and Front Range were on the list. Of course, she knew which one she liked best, giving no thought whatsoever to cost, admission requirements, etc. She will be learning more soon, we hope.

I took Hannah to camp on her return. The gambol from my car to her cabin took a long while with hugs, screams of joy, jumps up and down as each friend from the last years of camp appeared on our trail. At last, duffel was downed. As a mountain storm was brewing, I bid my good-bye, hurriedly driving through a tunnel of waves created by two rows of camp staff cheering me on my way.

90th birthday at Pine Winds with gift of Passages to children

Katie and Michael came on June 28th to celebrate her birthday. They were with me just overnight on their way to Tabernash on the western slope of the Rockies. Katie had requested a Chocolate birthday cake. I thought I would deviate slightly by baking a Red Velvet cake. Having never had one I did not realize it really has no resemblance to a chocolate cake in flavor or looks. It is RED, most unappealing. It was a learning experience; never do a Red Velvet cake, not even a cupcake.

Kathleen and Lawrence came up early afternoon July 3. Being the first in, they chose to settle into the Loft. Having not seen son and daughter since last Thanksgiving, we had "catch-up" time, dinner and then awaited Sara's arrival about 9 p.m. Alas, the shower in the Loft leaked. Of course, leaks never occur until the plumbing in question is used. First order of business July fifth: Call the plumber. Meanwhile, all showers will be taken on the first floor.

July fourth: no fireworks, as there is a statewide ban on outdoor fires and fireworks. We have had a rash of fires, the one in High Park, fifteen miles northwest of Ft. Collins will be down in history as the largest in Colorado's history. 300 homes were lost there and nearly as many in Colorado Springs where the entire Air Force Academy, personnel and planes were evacuated. Estes Park had its own fire in the High Drive area. Even there 23 homes were lost. God was surely watching over all he could; the wind turned and went up the hill instead of across Highway 36 to the National Park Service headquarters and two or three motorhome parks.

After hanging out our new Flag, having breakfast specials, Lawrence and Kathleen and I decided to go down to the Coolest Car Show in Colorado, a new experience for each of us. The most aged car was a 1918 Ford from Tucson in good running condition. Surprising to me was that the classic cars, at least twenty-five years old, were all updated: new transmissions, new upholstery, sunroofs, designed paint jobs. Collecting Classic cars is an expensive hobby, and the owners stand proudly by their cars just as canine owners at a Dog Show or the owners on Cub Scout Derby Day.

July 5 was the first day of the Reunion/Birthday celebration. The rest of the family had been arriving on the West side of the divide as we had been assembling on the East side. All were to gather at Pine Winds by 11:30. The three in residence here had the food ready and waiting. Sara had deviled 18 eggs. Kathleen had created a luscious Pasta Salad. I had thawed and baked the Pulled Pork, created by the chef at Safeway. Linda arrived from Ft. Collins with dessert and veggie dips. Lawrence did the "man's work": tables, umbrellas, chairs, dusted the deck. Seventeen assembled, 100% minus one, son-in-law away in Africa. Elsi Dodge (her father and Neil had been cousins) came up from Boulder as the only "kissin' cousin". We tried to become acquainted with the Great-Grands, Ayla and Milo. Both toddlers only wanted a parent.

Digital cameras came from every pocket. Original song by Elsi was sung lustily to the tune of "Puff the Magic Dragon", my contribution was a poem sent to me by a St. Louis friend. The title tells the story: "I am drinking from my saucer because my cup has overflowed". The expression was most *apropos* for the first Family Reunion in 17 years. We all missed dearly our Paternal Head. Michael, the eldest of the next generation, must take this responsibility. Singing the Doxology expressed our praise and thanksgiving for our multitude of blessings.

Hannah was the surprise package at the Birthday party. Lawrence and Sara had just made up an excuse to go to town, and retrieved Hannah from camp. She could receive, in person, the kudos for her Art when I presented the first edition of *Passages* to Linda, Lawrence, Katie and Sara.

This party ended at 5:30 p.m. Hannah went back to camp, Elsi and Wes off to Boulder, all the others over the Trail Ridge Road to their home in Tabernash. beyond. And we, of course, did the clean-up and played "Bananagrams". Kathleen had to keep her crown as the "Bananagram Queen".

Two days later the East side gang went "over the Hill" to Tabernash to give Katie and Michael a "housewarming". After a Pontoon Boat ride on Grand Lake, beach-combing on the lake side, and dinner at Grand Lake Lodge we caravanned to Tabernash. It is beautifully situated in a small community around a little lake. The Continental Divide is the horizon. We can see Indian Peaks Wilderness area, a favorite hiking area for us on the east side. I do look forward to hiking with the west-side folk next year.

Opening my eyes in the morning, I beheld a pastoral scene, breathtaking with the sun shining over the Divide, a stunningly different scene from the mountains, forest and distant meadow I have at Pine Winds. Our piece of the planet diverse and peaceable—if only the whole planet could rest in peace.

Our next days were filled with whatever anyone wanted to do: visits on short walks around the lake, attending Milo, napping. Ayla and Sara entertained each other for a very long time (for a 3-year-old) having an imaginative dramatic trip from Colorado to West Virginia by train. Such adventures! Too soon it was "going home time" again. Back to Denver, West Virginia, Ohio, Georgia and "over the hill".

There was yet more to the Month of Celebration...a party for fourteen friends on August 18. I only had to take a Salad to that affair. Here there were four honored "birthday girls" ranging in age from 70 to 90. With many candles and a script of icing, there was only a crust of cake.

The upstairs shower is still not in operation. When that is finished there will be another celebration. It has been over a month of plumbers, carpenters, tile setters, glass installers, and bills.

October 5, 2012; Revised January 31, 2013

Maurita & Children at Athens Academy

Grandmother Maurita reading with Bridget and Brenden McNeil, Christmas 1980

Katie and Maurita, August 5, 2006; Grandson Brenden McNeil and Karen Culcasi wedding in Massachusetts. Maurita also attended the weddings of 3 granddaughters.

Katie Stueck McNeil, March 16, 1974

73 Webster Woods, built in 1949 by Neil and Maurita Stueck

Webster Woods

Raising a family: Linda, Larry, Katie, Sara, at 73 Webster Woods

Gnaegy family: Sister Betty Gnaegy with Connie, Suzanne, David and Mike

Betty Jane Estes Gnaegy
March 22, 1928 – January 11, 2017

CHAPTER THREE
Places I Have Lived

Happy in Estes Park at Pine Winds

Women have broken many barriers in the latter half of the 20th century for which I am grateful. An old Chinese proverb, now attributed to Mao, wisely states: "Women hold up half the sky". I do trust that my daughters, Granddaughters, and now a Great-Granddaughter will believe this and continue to help "break barriers" for women in our country and around the world.

My Gathering Places

"Meet you at the Quad Shop", I called to Ann as we left each other to go to our respective 8 o'clock classes. There was no need to say more as we met with Jane and Betty every Tuesday and Thursdays during our Junior year at Washington University. I was a "transfer" student, a Pi Phi pledge, and spending this hour at the Quad Shop between classes had become a kind of "getting acquainted" ritual. It was here that I first smoked, first drank coffee, first just visited for an hour in our student center.

When I drop in the Danforth Student Center, the new Gathering Place for students at Washington U. I feel I really am a relic of the past. Computer center, reading lounges, food marts, two cafes, TV...most anything a student could need or want. It is not cozy/crowded as in 1941. But kids are still just "hanging out" not gathered around a small table often lounging alone, slumped over a "lap-top" computer or talking on the cell phone. Some groups seem to be conversing, gossiping, or studying with another.

As I write another bit of this "Memoir" in 2012, I am again dropping into a "Coffee House". Most Friday mornings I meet with four other girls, just forty or fifty years older than girls I joined with at the University. After our exercise class at the Recreation Center in Webster Groves, we visit Starbucks! Historian Brian Cowan described English coffee houses as "places where people gathered to drink coffee and learn the news of the day, and perhaps, meet other local residents and discuss matters of mutual concern".

From Wikipedia, the free encyclopedia (on the Internet) I read, "Historians define English coffee houses as public social houses in which patrons would assemble for conversation and social interaction, while taking part in newly emerging coffee consumption habit for the time. Coffee houses acted as an alternate sphere for intellectual thought, supplementary to the university". That does somewhat define my 1940's Quad Shop. It defines very well the 21st century coffee house. Ours is "Starbuck's", but could be "In Kind", "Seattle's Best" or one not "franchised" but locally owned like "The Boardwalk " around the corner from Starbuck's.

Here is a diverse demographic of customers. "Goodmorning" I say to a fellow I know only because he is a "regular", a bald one. "Mr. Baldy" works all the tables attired in an oversized sweat shirt wearing his good nature convivial smile. He chats with us like an old friend and then moves on. He does lean over to converse more seriously with another "Mr. Young One" who seems more interested in his coffee than conversation.

No more can we get a coffee for the price of a penny as in merry old England. Plain small coffee can be bought for under $2.00, fancy ones like Latte, Espresso, Caramel Frappuccino, will be three to four or more dollars. If economy and calories are not an issue, we can have biscotti, a myriad of choices of muffins, coffee cakes, cookies, scones. Strolling around the counter while waiting in line for my coffee, the small coffee house resembles a boutique retail shop...mugs, tumblers of all sizes, coffee containers for the road, pounds of their special coffees to buy. Baseball hats with STARBUCK'S embroidered on the bill, and beach balls for the kids.

It is ten o'clock on Friday morning. Some days we get the last chairs. Barb, one of our group and a regular customer at other times, often sidles up to one of the other regulars and gets chairs for us. A young girl at the end of a long table cuddles into the corner, engrossed in her computer assures us we will not disturb her. Jim stops by to say hello to Barb. He knows her only in this place as I do. Every Friday I observe his bracelet and necklace, his jauntily worn scarf, glasses pushed up on his head. I glance at "Mr. Dry", expressionless as he scans his morning paper. "Mr. Orange Jacket with Bicycle Shorts" comes in, orders his coffee and goes outside to sit with his girl and bicycles. All smokers are outside, seemingly the only regulation of the coffee-house.

We are only a block from Webster University. Back-packing students are often catching some study-time between classes. To round out a three-generation morning, I usually encounter a young mother with her "young'un" in a stroller having a morning "coffee break".

I can't say that the four or five of us have any deep discussions, but we do share news of the day, the latest on aging, exercise, diet and especially where to go in town. We encourage Barb to write a column on "things to do and where to eat". Maybe we talk about a new book, or the latest in gardening (Claire is our resident expert) or some new aspect with our doctor (Kay is a retired nurse). Most interesting is just looking around at the folks gathered in the 21st century "Coffee-House". It is a new slice of life, a diversity in my week. Those with more wit in writing will surely portray the Coffee House in the 21st century as a distinctive part of the culture of the city.

Secrets

Sunday evenings I often listen to the reruns of "The Lawrence Welk Show". The costumes for his singing girls are from days long gone. The gowns then perhaps circa 1950's were made to be beautiful as the dancers' feet moved swiftly into turns. No acrobatics that seem part of dancing in 2015 or 2020.

As I tuned in this week, the Big Bands were featured—Ah! my time. "Begin the Beguine" just happened to be the "first up". Whatever my heart was doing at that moment it switched pronto back to a Barn Dance c.1937—I was a junior in High School. Neil was one of the classmates. And he asked me to go with him to the dance. No one went steady. We enjoyed different classmates. The "order of dancing" began with the "date" having the first dance, last before intermissions and last of the evening. "Cut-ins" took care of the remaining dances. If we danced a whole number without a "cut-in" I felt "stuck". The Barn Dance was sponsored by the HI-Y.

Neil requested the band to play "Begin the Beguine", which was an unusual request. I had observed Neil often did the unusual! After that first dance, that song became our song for me. Sixty plus years later, my heart remembers and switches back to the Barn Dance and Neil's unusual request.

We had other secrets. We shared in 46 years of marriage. Two squeezes in a "hand hold" coded "know what?" Two squeezes in return coded "No what?" Three squeezes back "I love you". This holding hands was code begun in college. Today, the code would still be used except I have no hand to hold.

At My Window on a Winter Day

This day it had been misting snow for several hours. I perched near the window in the sunroom of the White Garden Inn with the sunshine on my shoulders. I was not but two or three feet from two bird feeders that have been well placed to afford a view for "bird watching" but giving the bird much protection with higher shrubs shielding them.

Beyond this area of great activity, I looked over our meadow to the forest that borders the property of the Inn. The tree trunks and branches appeared to be frosted with powdered sugar. Snow mist still coming down. It was a quiet world.

But not so at my window, where perhaps fifteen birds would come and go quickly to take a turn at the feeding stations. The Cardinal seemed to be the largest, males and females. The Cardinal is the State bird of Ohio. Reading in a book on birds, I found it interesting that the origin of the name was because red was the color of the high-ranking officials in the Catholic church. Hence, the name of this bird. Indeed, the Cardinal does dominate the bird world in Ohio. Both males and females sing, which is not true of many bird species.

The Nuthatch came to my feeder. It is known as the "upside down" bird. Indeed, it is the bird that does walk down tree trunks. All other birds go up. The toes of the nuthatch are unusual. Maybe it is unique, at least in the birds in the United States. The feet of the Nuthatch have a different structure than other birds. Most birds have three toes that point forward and one pointing back. The nuthatch still has four toes, but two point forward and two back thus allowing it to go down headfirst. It is a little bird and gives me joy to watch.

A Hydrangea shrub stands to one side of my window. All summer long we enjoyed its beautiful blossoms. My daughter, Katie, the owner of the B&B, the White Garden Inn, says they look like "popcorn balls". I see them now dried for the winter as large Muffins with white icing. Water droplets have collected on the underside of some of the sturdier twigs on another nearby shrub. Perhaps collecting at each node of the twig it resembles a crystal necklace hanging on the winter twig.

    A large book on the table nearby was my help in identifying some of the birds at my feeder. There were several kinds of sparrows moving so quickly in and out, back and forth that even at my close encounter I found it difficult to identify. I must return to my window again soon. With that book in hand, I can make some new friends in the World of Birds. If only they would not move so quickly!

The Centerpiece a Stack of Teddy-Bears

May 17, 2013 only nine of my classmates Washington University Class of 1943 attended our 70th Reunion this year. The first gathering of the weekend was a luncheon at the Ritz-Carlton Restaurant celebrating with the class five years later. Our centerpieces were stacks of bears-some in red vests, some in green ones, familiar colors of our Washington University. A large, scrolled number "Seventy" designated our class. I did not know any of those attending except Don Essen who had been our chair of the last several reunions. Pat, his wife, had been a good friend of mine when in College had passed away within the past year. Don came, frail and quiet, escorted by his daughter and the professional care-giver. The others were all mobile, several having traveled from Florida and Georgia. We thought we were in better shape than some at the "Sixty-five" table.

My friend of long-standing from High School and the University whom I have seen off and on all through the years was the only person I knew at the table. The widower of another friend was there. I remembered meeting him only one time in 1982 at a Beach-house in North Carolina in a group of six couples. We did recall that fun week, regretting that only 4 of us are still traveling on the planet. Surprisingly, the conversation at this table and in several sessions the next day there was little talk about "the good old days". We heard plans for the future from Chancellor Wightman. We marveled at the expansion of the University, and its stature as a "first tier" University now. We had gone to what was called a "street-car" college in 1940. I walked to school and hoped I could "cage" a ride home now and then with one of the two sorority sisters who had a car.

One of our guys today kept insisting he would live to be 100 and then go on welfare. This was just his "dream", but I really enjoyed his upbeat outlook on our world. Too often I am around only elders mooning about growing old. This is a fact of which we are all keenly aware. We do not need to dwell on this fact known to all. Mel is still active in his own accounting firm founded with a partner many years ago. He has just finished doing the taxes for a few friends.

Robert drove up to St. Louis from Athens, Georgia with a student for company. He enjoyed a career as a geographer teaching at University of Georgia. He chooses not to fly any more like a lot of my friends. "It is just too much hassle", Bob expressed, saying he is setting forth on a long road trip this summer, driving out to Oregon and back to Denver visiting family he knows in several generations. We elders in our nineties do not just sit in rocking chairs as younger folks seem to believe.

Through the weekend I was quite surprised at the comments many younger than I made. A friend I have known a long while read my name tag hanging on a lanyard with my graduation year emblazoned. "My", she exclaimed, "am I 15 years older than you"? "It would appear that way", I responded. The comment that brought chuckles was from a total stranger at the Friday evening Garden Party. Noticing my nametag, he said: "1943. You are well preserved"!

Washington U. has been important in my life-long learning. In our very early marriage Neil and I audited Econ 101. Those were the days when the University allowed auditing at little or no cost. As it grew, our income grew, and I took a semester (no credit, no tests, high motivation) in Botany. This underscored my knowledge in being a Guide at the Botanical Garden and my first love. I did not pursue science as an undergraduate. Women in science found themselves mostly in labs peering into a microscope in 1943. At least that was my perception; I did not seek any guidance as I was quite timid and not at all assertive. I simply took paths that I felt I could manage successfully. But some years later I delighted in the study of natural sciences; my community activities in outdoor education, travel, instructing at the Botanical Garden were my "hobbies". Maybe it was just as well that I did not take the science-route in the University.

Washington U. has afforded me many lectures, events, opportunities that have enriched my life especially in those middle years between 50 and 70. I discovered Lifelong Learning first a few years ago, but not until recent years did I delve a little more as I really "retired" from many community responsibilities. How do I envision the years to come? Where will I live? With whom will I spend my time? How will the world be different in 5 years? Or 10? I cannot imagine the world my sixth grandchild, just turned 18, will find even when she is 28! And what world will my 3-year-old great-grandchild find when she is 18? Geographers talk about the world "spinning". That is true of the earth, as well as time. Problems seem insurmountable in our country and the world. I have faith that our young people can find solutions—ways for peace. I can only do what little I can to be peaceable where I am, to find tasks where I am needed and that I can physically do. I am not asked often to do anything. Rarely do I volunteer and when I do folks, busy people, do not hear me.

It was pleasant to be at the reunion. The classmates of '43, although not moving so fast, did listen to each other.

Dreamy Nights

Long dreamy nights can reveal so much, maybe even some writing that would be of interest to the PENs group. Or, maybe, it would be the making of yet another essay to leave to the family.

I'm not sure. At times that direction is not necessarily the best. At least not valid for me. But my family is concerned always for my "safety". Translate that to mean "my need to stay upright and healthy for my age". This later expression is sometimes not understood by the "younger". 'Tis an eternal problem I know because the "care" of us "oldsters" by young'uns is the concern of many of our children.

Except for one son-in-law it seems my lot to "pitch" for every day of independence. I have fought the move and I'm on the losing side, standing alone.

"Only 40 minute" drive seems to be avoidable. Ah! There is the first point to consider. How often will the "caregiver branch" be called on, how often really needed? Such questions were never deeply considered. Some questions went without discussion, never around content of this background move and Oxford. It was just assumed.

I'm to move in a few days to the Knolls at Oxford, a community within a community designed for seniors with the corporation "Maple Knolls", the umbrella ruling the "Knolls" apartments. Their reputation is excellent. One 2-bedroom apartment is available, but I said I would not live in a corner apartment.

From my first visit I found the layout, architecture, and activity of no interest to me. It is designed for all levels of aging adults "with help and a check" added at each level.

My apartment is the only available now and to wait for an available one was not considered as the move to Oxford is a *fait accompli*. This apartment is in a large building a complete circle around a very attractive garden. The complex contains apartments, dining room, nurse station, and art studio. Each apartment has access to the garden, but to get out in the world on must exit one of six doors.

Dinner Clubs, writing groups, quilting, luncheon speakers, and activities are offered in the auditorium. Like, Mt. Pleasant getting involved is still my responsibility.

In dreamland last night I was planning a dinner party as I used to do. How fun it would be to dress up, have a candlelight dinner - "DLOT". Dinner Like Old Times. Never did I give a thought to guess how many table linens, china, my finest crystal, wine/champagnes. Then I thought Kroger could provide and serve the whole meal for me.

My apartment is 214 at the Knolls. There are 3 rooms which front on the garden. One will house my table and 4 chairs. One will be my bedroom for a chest, dresser, and a bed. The third is my sitting room with the TV, loveseat, desk, reading chair and curio cabinet. I will miss seeing the hills, forest, clouds that have given me such pleasure.

But back to my plans for a dinner party. To get acquainted with my new friends as I find them.

As I continue dreaming, I realized I would need two tables, each for 4 or 5, if I am to have more than 4 people. I realize I could not have plated dinners popular in 2019. Before dinner I could have drinks and appetizers served in two front rooms. Solutions are found.

January 2020

Stepping Over a New Threshold

Here I am poised to step over a new threshold in my life, one of many I have navigated. Being born was a big crossing for tiny me. Then there was Childhood, followed by the Teen years, not traumatic as they seem to be for the teens now. Graduation from High School and College brought many more crossings: young adult single, married, child-rearing, working for financial rewards and even better rewards as a volunteer and twice "on my own" after the death of two husbands. Living for fifty-two years in one home and moving three times in the last decade gave me experience in "down-sizing". This word is not on the list of fifty new words entered into the dictionary in 2010, but it aptly describes the prologue and preparation I did in six weeks of 2010. My tasks often were suggested or completed by Committee, a committee of grown siblings and their spouses, with additions being made by accountants, lawyers, coin dealers, landlords, and even, the Goodwill. Three items the latter could not take from me: a student desk, a metal step stool, a long-handled ax. I was told: "We can't sell an ax, the step stool needs painting, and the student 'kneehole' desk won't sell in our store". Four carloads to "Goodwill", one truck from the Salvation Army and innumerable trips to church, Scholarship, and other sources were necessary preludes to moving day.

I tried to keep my days happy and not solely devoted to packing. Still had a semblance of social life, attending the Symphony, Wash. U. LLI, the Rep. And the Holidays brought wonderful Advent programs, two branches from my family tree came home for Christmas, the first time in ten years. Because I could use their help in the game of "down-sizing" each was able to share their respective talents. In delegating to Sara I asked: "Can you tear off my social from this stack of paper, shred the pieces and trash the rest"? To Kathleen I suggested: "Can you pack all the items in the server and label the boxes for us to take in the Subaru"? Lawrence was to use his strength to load the truck headed for Public Storage. I coordinated hundreds of items into three primary piles: Keep and store, move into place of next residence, trash. Each pile had sub-designations.

It was a 7-hour move on a Monday in January 2011, remembered as arising at six a.m. with breakfast at seven. On our feet until three-thirty when a resident and friend in Pacific Place hosted a tea for my daughter, Linda, and me. At bedtime, Linda and I spoke of "finding" our beds, each one still piled with boxes. My bed was so damaged in the move that it had to be taken away; I slept on a mattress and box spring; I could not have been more comfortable had it been "Grandma's Feather Bed".

Here on a new threshold of life I already feel a sense of freedom having sorted through more than eight decades of memorabilia, stored many scrapbooks, photograph albums and memories, now free to live forward. For several years I have enjoyed the company of John O'Donohue reading in his book of Blessings, "Bless the Space Between Us". For my reader I want to share some of his words I find appropriate as I cross the threshold of a retirement community.

> *"May the light of your soul mind you....*
> *May you be given wisdom for the eyes of your soul*
> *To see this as a time of gracious harvesting...*
> *Above all, may you be given the wonderful gift*
> *Of meeting the eternal light that is within you*
> *May you be blessed,*
> *And may you find a wonderful love*
> *In yourself for yourself"*

I say to myself: "Have I made a right decision? Should I move closer to one of the children? Will I really enjoy this new world into which I have moved"? Life will take me somewhere interesting. Where will be revealed as past mysteries of life have been. Meanwhile, just where can all those books be put? How about a shelf above the door with a fern for accent?

January 26, 2011

Making Mountain Memories

As my family set forth to climb Chapin, Chiquita and Ypsilon, the shining mountains seemed to call to me "come out, come out, the wind in fair, come out and join me in the open air". These three mountains seem to stand shoulder to shoulder on the ridge of the Front Range of the Rockies.

Local hiking groups dubbed the three "C, C, and Y". Ypsilon has a couloir shaped like th Greek letter for Y that is a near-permanent snow field; hence, its name. Linda, John, Peter and Wes were taking Grandmother to new heights; perhaps, higher for Peter and Wes, too. They were grandkids about eight and ten.

With water, lunch, and the ever-present poncho in our day packs, we loaded into the VW van to drive up the Fall River road to Chapin Pass, the trailhead from whence we would walk.

Parking at the trailhead, we hopped out, tied up our boots and began to walk sprightly on a soft forested pathway with not too much elevation gain as we headed for the saddle between Chapin and Chiquita. I hummed the tune "I go to the hills…" from the "Sound of Music" musical so well known. In only a short while we broke out of the forest into a sunny Alpine meadow, loitering along by a small pond. Dragonflies were dancing over the water. Insects do not live at this altitude but are blown up. Seeing them living above the tree line was a nice surprise. A little grassy valley was our trailside lunch counter.

Then we began to climb up the shoulder of Chiquita, walking for a ways on the ridge where we could look down on the town of Estes Park and Moraine Park, stretching our eyes to the east along the mountain range. Soon it was easier to walk on the back side of the mountain, angling slowly over rock "streams" washed down the mountainside. These are not streams of water but of rocks that have settles into gashes eroded into the landscape. Better to be called "ribbons of rock", usually not difficult to cross as these are not boulders; only small obstacles hikers must navigate.

Suddenly we became aware of an approaching storm.

Such is to be expected in the mountains; fair warning to take cover. But there is no cover. We are way above tree line, as we have been since popping out of the forest. I saw my companions way up from me take cover under a rock out-cropping. Not wanting to go up to where they were, I walked rapidly down to where I might find some shelter. Rain soon pelted down. Peeking out from under my poncho hood, I could see a small copse of trees to make my destination. When I lifted my head again I had nearly bumped into a congregation of elk in the same shelter. I had to believe they would ignore my intrusion.

I knew where I was. Where was the trailhead? I had no concern about the kids as John is the best mountaineer man I know. With a topographic map in his back pocket he can find his way always.

I could not panic. I had to make a plan. I had my compass and trusted "hiking" book with little maps of the trails. Turning to the page "Chapin Trail", I oriented my compass and waited for the rain to abate. Then said "ta-ta" to the elk, and with a prayer for a safe *rendezvous*, set my course. It was just luck I stumbled shortly to the trailhead. There the boys and Linda were waiting for me. But where was John? Anxiously he had set forth to find me. Relieved when he returned, we rejoiced. We packed into the van, vowing to return to the top another day.

It was the second time I had been turned back because of weather. We had captured another mountain memory.

April 23, 2013

Light Show in Estes Morning

Hello world, 1:13 a.m. this morning, I was awakened suddenly by the sound of clanging chains and slashing of sharp sheets of ice just outside of my bedroom, seemingly outside the corner of the room. The sounds were a real mystery. I thought it would be wise to further investigate. I put on my robe and proceeded to go outside. At the back door, snow had fallen. I put on the outside lights and proceeded to go to the other doors. White blobs of ice and what seemed like patches of snow and ice were spread round the house. I continued padding round the whole first floor while from time-to-time lightning would flash illuminating the entire valley. There seemed to be no thunder preceding the enormous lightning flashes still not producing sound, only illuminating vast areas, but lasting only a very short while, hardly long enough for me to have more than a momentary glimpse of the landscape. By 1:18 a.m., Wesley had come upstairs from his bed in the undercroft. The light show continued now moving up onto the mountains surrounding Estes Park, even extending to the top of the hills over Estes Park. We stood in awe. Continuing to glide around the house, Wesley realized it was great hail that was now covering the deck. The hail stones larger than most seemed to have fused together to form large mats of white snow. Strange we had not seen it snowing at all. The light show was over and we each crawled back to bed. Weird storm!

1:32 a.m. July 26, 2018

Loafing with Lawrence

Indeed, it was a week of loafing with my only son, Lawrence. This in my memory, a "first"…We have shared years of family "road trips", camping vacations, and sailing many years in our beloved BVI, British Virgin Islands. Every one of these summer vacations and countless holiday gatherings with various members of the family and friends were joyous times shared with Lawrence. The week this summer in the "Celebration Month" of July was the absolute first time that just the two of us could loaf through the week. I should have Journaled every night as our days were full of visiting, pouring over a genealogy book from Mike Gnaegy, remembering High School days…so many topics for our conversations plus many activities as I shared my days in Estes Park.

My "housemate" this week discharged my long-standing "to do" list. This is an ongoing list of items to which I give little thought. Chores I cannot do any longer just stay on the list: light bulbs too high for me to reach, woodpecker holes in the house too high, weeds I do not want to pull, screws I cannot screw. It is a litany, and it delighted me to have them eliminated.

Walking together was another delight. I know I should walk every day, briskly, just for my good health. "Briskly" means to me "try to pick up my pace". Walk and briskly are two activities more fun with a companion. No one disputes this. Lawrence and I walked some every day, strolling along Lake Estes, circumnavigating Lily Lake. Exploring the Riverwalk through town was a study of fashions of tourists, play of children on the playground, computer and reading time of townsfolk in the two coffee shops we passed, window shopping. We meandered around Husted Heights with my running commentary on the neighbors, the condition of the road, and poking around the mansionized home under construction on Hillcrest. With a price listed for the unfinished home at one million, three hundred thousand dollars, I felt I was certainly in an upscale neighborhood. The property has not been sold yet. It may be a "white elephant" neighborhood.

We attended a most lovely musical program at the Y one evening. Here was a quartet that has performed year after year, and rightly so. A zither, a double bass, a violin, and piano comprised the quartet playing some folk music, some old melodies new to the two of us, some classical. This diversity provided a soothing evening of good listening. Afterwards, we went to Cori's home with her St. Louis visitors, Cathy and Carl, my friends from Kirkwood. Ice cream and brownies and chit-chat until nearly eleven climaxed our evening in town. Lawrence makes a delightful visitor, able to be comfortable with most any age no matter the background of folks.

I was proud to introduce Lawrence at the Summer-Resident dinner one evening at Lake Shore Lodge and again at one of the Wednesday breakfasts at the Y. He is gracious and can make anyone feel at ease. I enjoy his conversations with strangers. Several have asked if he is still in town.

He enjoyed the time he had getting acquainted with his iPhone (I think that is his newest toy). This palm-sized new wave of technology can take pictures, be a cell phone, and find answers to most any questions that come into one's head. We asked it queries about a recent book, about Go's particle, the newest physics discovery, and distances to the nearest planet. He was able to show me pictures of their recent jaunt up to New England. Most impressive was a beautiful picture showing the several ranges of mountains, in varying shades of gray, that we enjoyed one night at twilight. Technology is coming at me from all directions ever so quickly. I am lagging further and further behind as I spin around on the planet.

We went to Boulder one day, picked up Wes, met Linda and John out on I-25 and headed to Denver to see the exhibit of DaVinci works coming to Denver from St. Louis which George and I had witnessed with excitement. It was at my instigation that we all met here. Lawrence and I had gone to Fort Collins the day before to visit Linda and John. Their yard is so lovely now and is, indeed, a work in progress for John. Gardens are dynamic, never finished, always changing, or bringing change. Linda had two museums that she thought we would find interesting. Sure enough, the "bead and baskets" exhibit in the Global Village museum was another uncommon experience. Beads, bead works, baskets having been gathered from all over the world by one or two collectors made a most interesting experience in this "homegrown" attractions. We did not spend the night, as Lawrence said he had been in five beds in the last five nights, and another had no appeal. Our loft as Pine Winds was THE best. Lawrence observed that Linda organized us well.

Some diversions surfaced unplanned. An afternoon perusing the book of my ancestors compiled by Mike Gnaegy afforded much interest. Tracing the Estes line back to a bit before 1500 was of interest, especially since we only were back to England and not Italy as I had always heard from my father. However, I also remember seeing a long chart of the ancestors that he had and a book, neither of which I have here. We did find a "skeleton" in the Espinase family, my line through my maternal Grandmother. Elizabeth Espinase, according to the computer-generated ancestral chart was my Great-Great-Grandmother, noted as born just 5 months after her parents were married. Hmm! It has been happening for many generations or someone miscopied or did not speak accurately. Memories have often failed I am sure. Nevertheless, it was a fact to find while enjoying reflecting on our ancestors. It strengthened my resolve to find out more about the Stueck ancestors, as husband Neil is the last of that line and had asked me several times to find out more. This seems like a good thing to work on next Winter.

Too soon my week with Lawrence came to a close. Though he disliked the thought of leaving our cool climate, I am sure he was glad to get home to his own Kathleen. It seems only a short while ago that Dr. Vaughn, the doctor who delivered Lawrence, stood at the foot of my bed on the next day's hospital "round" and told me I was now blessed to have a son and daughter. Little did I know then how very blessed I would be all the years we have shared, now numbering 61, nearly 62 and "counting" as we say.

We were ready and waiting for the shuttle that arrived at 6:45 a.m.

I have already had a note, always a lovely invitation, from Kathleen inviting me down for a visit this Winter. I will look forward to that, as my visits in Watkinsville are always fun.

Lawrence Stueck and Kathleen McQuiston

Ralph Spends the Night

"Oh! Grandmother, that bird is in the house", Hannah shrieked as only an exuberant dramatic 18-year-old can shriek. Hannah, my granddaughter from Georgia, was visiting me in Colorado. I ofttimes jump as she startles me. I glanced over to the window, disagreed with her. "I think it is hovering outside the window". But with a quick second look I saw that the little hummingbird was, indeed, inside the house. Hannah was too excited to even think. We did have a problem. How to encourage this fragile, frightened tiny bird to go back outside? Doors to the deck were wide open but it was frantically flying into the uppermost stationary window, in the peak of the very steep A-frame, probably eighteen feet from the floor.

One does not call the "fish and wildlife" agency to retrieve a hummingbird. They are reserved for wild turkeys, at least. "Hannah", I said, "Please get the little milking stool to stand on and I will get my long-handled duster. Perhaps, you can entice this hummer down to the open door"!

She did my bidding quickly. The duster handle was too short. The bird only flew higher! We did shut all doors out of the main room so that it was trapped with two open doors. I suggested we ought to name this winged "jewel on wings".

A phone call for Hannah interrupted our swishing operation. She babbled with sheer high-soprano voice to Jud, the current boyfriend calling from Georgia, excitedly passing on my suggestion that we give this multi-colored house guest a name. Immediately, Jud said: "Name him Ralph". That was it...was our brilliantly colored guest male or female? Hannah certainly did not give sex a thought; Jud said: "Ralph". That was it.

My next ploy was to make some sugar water as we had fed the hummingbirds earlier in the summer. I had not done this for a month or so as the feeder tends to attract bears, but I knew that hummers liked it. But not this one. The smell from the boiling water was of no interest.

Soon Ralph settled down a bit and flew up to sit on a

blade of the ceiling fan. From there he darted around the loft but returned to the same fan blade. It was so quiet in the house. We could hear the "whirr" of his wings as he flew from resting place to resting place. We relaxed knowing that Ralph would spend the night. It was our bedtime. Hannah had always been rather squeamish about Daddy Long Legs, mice, June Bugs, moths and crickets around the house in the mountains. Somehow, she did have trust as I told her Ralph would not bother her up in the loft. We all bedded down. Ralph on the fan blade, Hannah on her bed and I back in my bedroom. "Sleep with the angels", I called to Hannah as I always did.

    Morning came and I started breakfast. Ralph flew down to the front window where he had been when he first arrived. He was calm flying to the middle window now and then up to a light on the beak of a duck decoy placed on a beam across the room, and back up to the same window and back to the same beak. As I measured the coffee, poured orange juice I thought seriously how I could entice Ralph to leave.

    Hummingbirds had fed at all my geraniums. I carried a pink one full of blossoms swollen with nectar to the open door. Ralph was too busy following the morning flight pattern to stop for a sip. I recalled a shirt with red flowers I had years ago that always attracted hummingbirds to me. I carried my largest red geranium around from the back to the front and placed it right in the open door. In a matter of maybe three minutes Ralph altered his flight pattern, stopped off for a sip from the red geranium as he flew out into fresh morning air swooping around the billowing drapery. He flew out so quickly I did not have time to alert Hannah that her houseguest was gone.

    For several weeks I saw Ralph back at the red geranium. I have no way of knowing the sex of this bird. Perhaps, it was Ralphine and not Ralph. As September came, I missed the visitations. It was time for the long flight to southern climes. I like to think it will be in the line-up at the feeders in Costa Rica when I am there. The hummingbird's visit was one of many delightful experiences with wildlife in the mountains.

October 10, 2013; Revised May 12, 2016

Grandmother and Hannah in Colorado

**Maurita with Hannah and Mitchell Brannon
May 2018 in Georgia**

Shades of Grey

There it was, a tiny patch of light "baby" blue sky with two small cloud ships sailing through. Billowing massive puffs of clouds in shades of gray buttoned down six mountains arranged along the horizon. Had this day been the usual clear Colorado Blue sky with bright sunshine we would only have counted one or two mountains. Bright days seem to blend the range of mountains together.

This day on Dry Gulch, I paused to reflect on another morning in the Cascade Mountains of Washington state where we had been camping one summer holiday. We were camping with another family, a total of four adults and six children now in high school and college. As we were planning, "they", the natives, said: "It never rains in August in these mountains". I was a gloomy Mom as I sloshed through rain for the third morning.

It was hard not to be gloomy when shoes did not dry out and ponchos were steamy. But not for son, Lawrence. "Just look, Mom", he cheerily said, pointing toward the distant mountain, "just look at all those shades of gray in the landscape". Many times since I have recalled that walk through forests deep and tall, needles of the spruce glistening in the rain. The day I first appreciated shades of gray in a landscape. seen mystical beauty through the another's eyes.

September 18, 2012

Sunsets

Some sunsets are particularly beautiful. Some seem to last five to ten minutes. Some have beauty for only a few moments. With so many factors, one never knows which sunset will be breathtaking and which ones will make changes while being observed.

August 8, 2019 is one worth remembering. The clouds seem to be layered across the low Western sky with bright shadings of apricot on the upper layers and shading into lighter grayer tones and some bright reaching to the NW. To have layers, thin clouds were brilliantly colored to make an unusual sunset. One could even see dynamics when time was taken to watch.

Dozing and Dreaming

Lately, I have been in some other state than awaking in the night or morning. I have a clock with a lighted dial so no matter when I open my eyes and am conscious of being in some state of consciousness, I know the time. This is a dozing perhaps. By definitions to doze is to have a light sleep.

But what is the time of a semi-consciousness when I am not asleep? I am interested because of matters I consider during those times. Usually, I term the thoughts I have as remembering parts of days I have lived, experiences I have had and do recall. Sometimes I would deem them just dreams. Some may have an explanation, others the bad ones I know "not to tell until after breakfast", a quote from my mother. Now and then I jot down notes to help remember later that day when I might want to tell some one or write a bit of an essay as I am doing now.

Recently, I was really perplexed thinking about a dream. In my dream, I was opening a letter, a nearly everyday occurrence but this letter was dated "8-18-22". That is my birthday, but a letter received in 2017 dated 8-18-22 is perplexing. This letter was in a beautiful Spencerian script clearly addressed "Dear Maurita". The writing continued as if the heading of the body of the page held in my hand. I awakened. I could not read or see any of the body of the letter.

There are times that I can have some logic to analyze why I dream about someone or some past experience. I have no talent for "analyzing" dreams, finding logic or rationale for the dream. Though I know there are those who believe in such logic. One in my family claims red wine will cause her to dream. But that cannot account for the content of the dream.

The dream of last night is one that stimulated my writing this evening. I feel guilty about not keeping any of my journal in the last three months of transition in my life. I can take some action when I have sufficient motivation. That does not account for last night's dreams.

Two dreams in succession were, in fact, quite recognizable

as real happenings in my earlier life, totally unrelated, but not dreams, simply remembering events. What causes my brain to recall some isolated incidents in my young life? Incidents I have not thought of in many years, talked about or even had similar experiences with my own children.

Flash back to ninth grade, c. 1936. Springtime. Charlie French, a boy with whom I had grown up, just one of the many kids on my block-long street. Charlie was one of the older guys a year ahead of me in school. The range of kids up and down the block was only about four years at the most. Charlie asked me to go to the high school dance with him. We had not dated at all and he may not have dated anyone. It did not matter. No one paired off, no one went "steady" even in high school. No one ever had to "break up". At least the group with whom I spent time did not. I did not question Charlie's motives.

I thought it would be fun to go to the high school as that is where I was headed the next Fall. We walked, yes, dear reader in 2017, we walked out to school and we walked home. Charlie was not old enough to drive and folks did not readily "tote" kids around. Besides, we knew the route, we walked it every day! There were no school busses, and no one had two cars. I recall only two guys with cars in the years I was in high school. So much for that remembrance. It was a big night for me to go to the dance with Charlie. As I write sixty-one years later, I suspect he wanted to go to the dance, and he knew no one else to ask except the girl with whom he had been friends for some years.

The same night (back to 2017) I had another musing about a time that was quite special for me. I was asked to be a "maid for the UDC Ball". This was extended to me through some friends of mother's to the UDC, the United Daughters of the Confederacy. To my knowledge, she was never a member of the UDC, although family legend has it that my Grandmother was eligible. Be that as it may, this was an event not like any other I had had at the time.

It involved a white formal gown, as escort for the evening, a real Ball with a procession of all the "maids". Indeed, quite special for a Junior in high school or thereabouts. I do not recall the year exactly. First, a strapless bouffant gown was special and easy to adapt. Finding an escort was a bit more difficult. He had to be able to escort and the boys I knew best did not seem to fit in the picture of the UDC Ball. I was not quite sure what the picture was. After some discussion with Mother, she and I decided to ask another of those guys on the block with whom I had grown up. She must have spoken with his mother. After all, he would need a tux. I very much wanted to attend this Ball. I feel at this writing that the whole event was managed with the help of Mr. Buckles (Bill to be my escort) and my mother.

Dozing and dreaming

Bill accepted. He was a very good dancer. One of the other neighbors had a Juke Box in the Rathskeller where we all learned to dance when that was more important than playing "kick the can". Bill had really taught me, so the Ball did appeal to him. And the UDC Ball event took place downtown in the City Hall of St. Louis. This was and still is a magnificent grey granite building, a showplace in St. Louis. I had never been in the City Hall, having lived always in a suburb of St. Louis. Indeed, it was a large ball room, quite fitting for the Ball.

Neither of these events, as important as they were at the time, have been in my thoughts or even remembered in conjunction with anything remotely related. Why did my brain, my memory conjure them into my early morning resting time before the alarm awakens me? Just another fact of many many happy days. I have had a good life!

Twelve Year Odyssey

Books on writing memoirs suggest it could be important to make floor plans and descriptions of places we lived. I attempt to focus on the aspects of where I lived that helped to shape my life through the years rather than focus on the particularities of the many places I have called home.

In my journey from age four to twelve, I lived in four "home places". The first being on Northeast Kingshighway in north St. Louis, now a part of I-55. Being only four I do not really remember being there, but stories have become a part of family legends, richly embellished with time. The first involves a doll. My doll that I do remember "as nearly my size", had a record in her back that allowed her to talk. Such sadness fell on our little family when she was knocked off the arm of the chair by my playmate, Harriet. No more could she talk. This tragedy was recounted through the years as our families remained friends the rest of our lives.

Even more traumatic was the day I informed Mother: "I am going down to Daddy's office…Bye". Mother, realizing I was not in the apartment, recalled some time later what I had said to her and she frantically ran down Kingshighway, hoping to catch me I suppose. A car stopped and there I was safe in the passenger seat of a stranger. It was an event long remembered.

When I was nearing five and ready for kindergarten, we moved to University City. This was the first suburb established only about 25 years earlier and was the best choice for schools, transportation, and good "walkability" (though not a well-used word then). My mother, having been raised in a small-town, preferred Webster Groves but that was way out of the city. In 1930, folks commuted into St. Louis on the train.

In the next three years we moved three times, three apartments, each time gaining more space. Space really meant more bedrooms, one to two to three. My sister, Betty, required us to have two and the third move provided a fenced in large backyard and garage off an alley.

710 Limit was home when a big tornado of 1927 tore through St. Louis. I was, if not fearful, alarmed by it falling dark at noon when I was just home from kindergarten. I have thought often of Mother with no cell phone, no news 24/7, possibly no phone service, no knowledge of where the storm set down. Where was Daddy? He usually was not in the office but "on the street" selling Life Insurance. Though frantic as she must have been, she did not alarm me.

6250 Enright, now demolished to be a part of Washington University's four-story Student housing apartment. This was the last apartment of my elementary school years. I continued to walk to the same school, Delmar-Harvard, the first public school in the new suburb. On the walks home from school we discussed the coming election of FDR against Hoover for his second term. My, how much we thought we knew about the election gleaned only from our parents.

Roller skating was after school every day. Such a delight when we had a smooth "float finish" sidewalk on Delmar rather than only the brown grainy sidewalk on our street. There I skated by a tea-room with ruffled curtains tied back at the windows. We could see the room filled with ladies at tables playing what I later learned was Mahjong. The game, originating in China, was popular then as it is again in this country.

My sister and I slept in the sunroom where we had a "Murphy" bed that pulled down out of the wall. Today this is "new" in some furniture houses. From here we could see the lighted top of the Park Plaza Apartment Hotel on Kingshighway. Looking out from our third-floor look-out made it easy to imagine an ocean liner cruising on the dark ocean sky.

One night before dinner my father asked me to run down to the car and get his "rate" book. I had not the slightest idea what his rate book was, but we knew it was very important to him and always with him. Down the iron steps and out to the garage I bounced and there I saw a shiny new bike, a 28'. It was to be my birthday surprise the next day. I just knew Daddy had forgotten it was in the garage, so I said nothing when I go back upstairs. That's how to spoil a surprise!

It was experiences in these years that I see now were the nuggets of further learning, even throughout decades of my life journey. Landscaping was not an art in those times, yet we had thorny hedges on the lot lines and along the sidewalks always the same plant. The "fad" in landscaping then were "so-called" Umbrella trees, small about 8 feet tall, single bole with the crown tightly pruned to be like an umbrella. Many years later I learned this was a catalpa pruned to fit small yards of apartments, never to interfere with wires or need much pruning. The wildlife were pigeons found the world over in urban areas. They cooed on the window ledge of the apartment next door, about eight feet. My first "big game" hunt was down near Potosi on the property where Mother and Daddy had lived before moving to St. Louis. We would go down there for weekends that I relished. Freedom, forest, creeks, and whip-o-wills gave me endless joys. I stoned a snake to death hurling rock from the bank of a dry creek bed down on this creature. (I was not yet a conservationist.) Holding it on a stick I proudly showed my catch…known later as a copperhead.

I came home from my first overnight with my Scout troop, sitting on the front steps I waited for my folks to come home while counting my chigger bites. I dealt with chiggers for years after until I finally found ways to have the arachnids avoid me. We moved from the Catholic-Judeo apartment district just as I entered Junior High. 775 Harvard was a Dutch-Colonial six-room house just one long block down from school. No more than 2/3 of a mile with streets to cross. This was to be home for me until I went to College. Here I had my own room for the first time and the last until I was widowed fifty-nine years later.

February 16, 2015

Variations, Transformations and Conversions

By whatever name, change is dynamic in our days. Blessed we are in the Midwest that we have four seasons of change. Our winters have been known as "hard winters", mild winters, long or short winters. With some pride we in St. Louis just say: "If you don't like the weather just now, wait a spell".

I am not certain how long a "spell" is that I wait for a change in the weather, but I can attest to the variations, transformations and conversions of winter.

Sledding was a beloved winter activity for me. Elementary school years my family took me sledding on Art Hill, certainly the most popular place in 1930. Our home movies on a documentary of our local Public Television Channel, show my friend, Patty, and I on a sled with steel runners that we could guide with our feet. Mother in her galoshes and fur-rimmed Sunday coat was caught on film frantically running down the hill to pick my sister and me up when we tumbled off the sled.

By middle-school age, sledding became a group activity, boys and girls, without parents. Our hill was in Lewis Park, walking distance from home. Alas, there were more kids than sleds. Change became inevitable. When flattened large boxes in which refrigerators were shipped in when flattened became our sleds. A creative variation of the "Flyer" with steel runners that could be steered. We still could fly down the hill. Instead of my Chinchilla Sunday coat worn in early years I now sported a "snow suit", the latest winter sport attire. Dark brown wool pants topped with an orange jacket topped with orange and brown hat kept me warm and fashionable. Galoshes were *de rigueur*.

Ice skating was really my favorite winter sport. My skates as well as my abilities had variations and conversions. Daddy brought home my first pair of ice skates, cast-offs from a grown-up friend. They were tall, light brown leather figure skates. With that type of blade I somehow learned how to skate and make circles and go backwards. I learned I was to be no more graceful on figure skates than I would be in ballet slippers. I managed to convert to Hockey skates (another cast-off pair) but Racers were my third conversion. Racers in high school were just what I needed, not that I ever raced. I used these kinds of skates until I was about 65, with anxiety-attacks about speeders at the Webster Groves outdoor rink when I hung up my beloved skates.

I can recall more about outdoor skating in high school. The city would not allow us to skate on lakes in Forest Park until the ice was very thick and the weather had been very cold for many days. By High School we had some wonderful activity in Forest Park. Only two or three cars were available to us, depending on whose parents were homebound and could loan a car to one of us. Bonfires were built by park employees whose presence furnished a kind of supervision. Only one accident do I remember...my best friend, Adeline, was at the end of the line playing "Crack the Whip" when she was flung off the line, crashing on the ice. A concussion resulted. That we knew was a bad accident, but it seemed to have no repercussion. In 2014 we would give such an accident more attention. Fun times ice-skating out-of-doors only happened several times a winter.

I do recall one other "accident" in winter. In my Junior High years, Bill, one of the neighbors on Harvard, threw a snowball at me. Not an unusual occurrence as boys at 14 like to tease girls any time. This snowball was thrown on school property, right at the top of our hill but just inside the school boundary. It just happened to hit me in the eye. It did not *just happen* that Bill was expelled from school. Throwing snowballs on school property was not to be tolerated. I feel my embarrassment just remembering this incident 79 years later. We both had to go to Mr. King's office with our mothers too!

Were our winters milder in the mid-thirties? Or was I just unable to get out to the places to skate and sled? Only two or three friends had cars in high school. We did not "go out" on school nights. We could not avail ourselves of out-door skating until a "cold-spell" had lasted several days.

The Winter Garden, an indoor skating rink, was built on DeBalivere sometime in the 1930's and the streetcar could take us there after school or on Saturday mornings. A whole new wonderful world opened for me. With my new racers, transportation, co-ed friends and even a "Moonlight" session when a "he" might ask me to skate I felt related to Sonja Heine!* No more snow-suits, frozen feet and fingers, or cardboard "sleds". Variations, transformations, and conversions had changed my views of winter.

January 7, 2014

* Norwegian ice skater and film star

In Times Past

"Here it is Monday morning and raining", Mother stated as she was in the kitchen getting breakfast. "You know, they say that if it rains on Monday it rains every day in the week". She admonished my daddy saying: "Bun, be sure to put on your rubbers". He would wear spats in the cold of winter. These were wool coverings snapped over his shoes and ankles.

Of course, we had oatmeal as oatmeal was always served on winter mornings as she assured us, we needed to have something hot in our "tummies" before we set out for school. Galoshes were our footwear for snow and rain. No beautiful "Ughs" then.

We set forth to walk to school—rain or shine. If we forget something and returned Mother always reminded us: "Now be sure to sit down before you go back out or you will have bad luck". We did not believe Mother; it was just a "saying", probably leftover from her childhood. We always sat down though. And my children recall me saying that, too. The tradition carries on. There were other rather common superstitions generally known by everyone. Lots of actions could bring bad luck: black cats crossing your path, walking under a ladder. Some things brought good luck: finding a four-leaf clover, seeing a penny, and picking it up.

I was caught up in conversation this week with several friends, one a young one of 96, another my godson age 60. We brainstormed on some "old fashioned" words; words common when I was growing up that are no longer used. Rich could verify those not used by his generation. Young men do not any longer wear trousers, young women do not go to beauty parlors. Now the Spa is the gathering place that still has the same function to pass along "news of the day", gossip of the neighborhood.

Young men do not have jalopies much anymore but drive used cars; the maintenance being done in many cases by a garage mechanic, not the owner. Teens need cars to drive to school as walking seems to have become not a "cool" thing to do. No longer do we have rumble seats where two of us could sit at the back of the car in a seat that was opened in the space of a modern trunk.

One of my quirky memories is the time my date and I were inveigled into taking my little sister and his younger brother to the movie with us. His family car had a rumble seat; at least, we could stack the kids back there. This was probably a deal worked out with his dad to have the car.

Now "cool" is a word that has changed meanings during my lifetime. Clever articles, columnists and comedians have written so much about words that have changed meanings. I am thinking about words that are just not used in the 21st century that were much a part of the vernacular 50 years ago.

We had to wind up our Victrola to play thick platters with a very scratchy sound. These preceded phonographs, those we could stack several records on so that music could play more than one record at a time. Huddling around the radio to hear 15-minute programs before dinner was the electric "baby-sitter" of the 30's and 40's before TV. I think that parents needed radio just as much as TV for the hour before dinner. "Little Orphan Annie" and "Jack Armstrong, the All-American boy" were the two we listened to from 5:30 to 6:00 p.m. IF we had our practicing done.

"Golly Moses" there is a whole lot more: phosphates at the Soda Fountain, shopping in the Dry Goods store, getting ice from the Iceman in the Alley, and stopping at the Filling Stations for gas. Probably paid "two bits" for a gallon.

Words today that are commonly used in texting and in the newspaper will be old-fashioned in the latter part of this century. I sometimes wonder if we will be talking with each other or if all our communication will be by email, texts. New I-toys are imagined every month now. There will be more creative and innovative devices. But will we be any more efficient, have more time to be loving and peaceable?

Journal entry, January 2, 2008

2008 arrived while I slept. Cori Thomas and I went to see the movie "National Treasure", came back for dinner and managed to stay up until 11 p.m. when "the Ball" in Times Square, New York City, came down.

Reflecting on our family Christmas, I am full of pride for the gifting "from the heart" that my grandchildren and children demonstrated. My former colleague, Dr. Spainhower, president of Lindenwood College wrote about gifting from the heart. Neil and I have done that through the years to various institutions, churches, colleges as we were able through the years.

This year adult children and grandchildren gifted from the heart to charities around the world to each other and "in my honor". So, vicariously, I have a flock of chickens with a family in China (through Heifer International), a family in Pakistan has food for a month, a villager in Nepal has income from a shawl, a U.S. child has a backpack with food supplies (World Vision), a girl has a bicycle in Cambodia for her to get to school more easily (No doubt, a 3-speed w/ a tinkle bell like I saw by the hundreds in Vietnam).

This year I funded the Endowment in our names at the University of Mo-Rolla. This was established soon after Neil died and now it is of a sum (I hope) that the income will be sufficient to bring a lecturer to the campus to enrich Civil Engineers. It has been named the "Distinguished Lecture Series". It is the same concept as "Pathways" at Webster Hills church and the same idea suggested many years ago by Jerry Bayless, acting chair of the Civil Department.

I, also, joyfully gave partial funding for an intern at Washington University in "Women and Gender Studies". I am proud of my family members who remember many around the world who have less than we do. I appreciate them remembering me in their various ways, too.

Two trips added new dimensions to my world understanding, too. Several wiser than I have said: "The world is like a book. If one does not travel, it is like reading only one chapter". Vietnam and the spring blossoms of Holland and Belgium opened two more chapters for me. I am blessed with wealth, good health, and a family, all of whom are fine productive citizens. Some will be furthering careers and moving, some still finding their respective careers, some teaching younger citizens or working to better the communities in which each lives. Laura launched into a new position today at age 23!

February 7, 2013

Snow Days Remembered

This past Tuesday I found the quiet of the early morning a beautiful time. The ice gently coated each winter bud of the dogwood tree outside my window. Tiny icicles were spaced along the top rail of the fence. A robin was in the adjoining tree with maximum puffing to keep warm. No cars were out, no train noises. The world was silent. Memories began to gather in my head, memories of snow times long past.

  I have no recollection of ever being out of school because of snow. I do remember one time Daddy took me to high school because it was 6 degrees; more times I remember walking the route to school. Until 5th grade I had eight or ten blocks to walk and gave that no thought. School busses, family cars were unavailable. There were no long lines of parents picking up their kids.

  As an older elementary student and in Junior High, we lived just a long block uphill from school. High School was only a mile or so, within "walking distance". All distances in the 1930's were "walking distances", as there was no other means of transportation. Kids in St. Louis had street cars, but University City had only two lines, neither of which went to High School.

  My outerwear in Junior High I will call a "snow suit" for lack of any more fashionable name. It consisted of dark brown baggy pants, an over the head orange top with a hat to match, topped with a brown topknot. Boots on my feet, mittens on my hands and I was decked out for school or any after school activity. Weathermen this week have told us we did have more snow in those years. Yet I have no recollection of school being closed for snow. Nor did the morning *Globe-Democrat* advertise fashions for outerwear that everyone must buy.

  Making angels in the snow still are done, though it seems only preschoolers do this in today's world. Sledding was the best winter sport for Grade School and even into High School. Sunday was the day Daddy could take our family to Art Hill, the most popular place in the city. We had a sled on which several of us could hold tenaciously onto each other in the hope we would coast all the way down without rolling off! It was the latest in sled design which gave us the ability to steer by turning the front handlebar.

Some years ago, KETC incorporated some of Daddy's 16mm home movies in a documentary titled "Memories". There we saw Mother frantically running down the hill in her long fur-collared coat, Sunday hat and galoshes to gather us up from a "roll over" and my father in his black overcoat and derby hat on the sled with us. Fleece, nylon, down, thermal socks, thermal gloves had not been invented yet.

The most fun snow times came in Junior High and High School when we had the freedom to walk to neighborhood hills and ponds for sledding and skating. No need to have adults take us, supervise us, organize us except on the school grounds. No snowballs were to be thrown, on the threat of expulsion. We were on our own to resolve conflicts, make our rules, help each other when needed and most of all, deal with the boys who always found a way to tease us girls. At Lewis Park on Delmar, I remember a time I had no sled, but made do with a large, corrugated box. That was a good pond on which to skate, too. Alas, no sledding there any longer because many light posts around the Park now pose too many hazards.

High School brought some organized sledding and skating in Forest Park. Then we had the youth group from church when adults could furnish transportation. The city determined when the ice was thick enough for safe skating and the lagoons afforded us many little tributaries to skate down. I felt like Hans Brinker and his Silver Skates, a character from one of my favorite childhood stories. We played "Crack the Whip" in a long line of kids zigging and zagging crazily trying to break the line. One time we learned the risk of the game when Adeline, my very best friend from 4th grade, flew off the end too fast and fell, giving her a concussion. How dreadful that night was for us all.

My stash of snow-time memories continues to grow. With the advent of lighter warmer clothing and life in a drier climate I have had more enjoyable times in the snow recently. I remember being miserable while ice skating as my feet and hands always seemed to be frostbitten.

While writing I am reminded of a quote from Frank Lloyd Wright, "The longer I live the more beautiful Life becomes". There are times I certainly can agree. Snow-shoeing several years ago in Park City, Utah, takes first place over times from early years. Being there with a crowd from Santa Monica Ski Club, not being a skier, I was left on my own. I located a company that led Snowshoe hikes and signed on. Two of us were taken by a guide on a morning, bright and clear as the mountains often are, to walk on a groomed trail through thick aspen forests and across rolling meadows. Though the temperature was 15, I was warm just with a heavy sweater, hat, and mittens. The air is dry and that lack of moisture that we call humidity makes the difference. As always, landscapes of snow are quiet, be they in Webster Groves a Tuesday morning or Utah in a wilderness area. Snowshoes make no noise, and never have I been in such a dense forest of aspens, their smooth pewter-colored bark glistening in sunlight. I was in a place where my husband, passionate skier that he was, could never see on his skis. Walking on my snowshoes I had no fear of falling. If I did it would be soft and fluffy. Hot cocoa for a rest stop and we continued. Looking up through the bare tree branches to the azure cloudless sky, I stored an image in my mind's eye I can open any time.

Great Grandmother and Arlo, December 2019

My small ice-coated dogwood on my patio at the threshold I crossed just two weeks ago is stored now in my mind to be recalled in springtime as the buds blossom.

February 2, 2011

Down Memory Lane

Decorating for Christmas was just not on the list of "To Do Today". Katie had brought me one of her surplus trees, even wound with a necklace of Ornaments. I just looked at it for a day, dreamed about it at night and this morning said to myself: "I must get out the box of ornaments".

Once that was accomplished, the next step was easy. Unwrapping the first wad of newspaper, I beheld an angel with foil skirt, the last remaining from a whole choir of angels given to me by a dear friend from Lindenwood days c. 1940. I began my walk down "Memory Lane" as I unwrapped the few remaining ornaments saved to move to Ohio.

I did become more enthusiastic about decorating a tree by myself as my memory was jogged with each unwrapping. How simply ugly those purchased at the Dime Store the first Christmas Neil and I were married. It was Christmas Eve and the local "dime" had some ornaments to add to the ones we had made with sparkles on lids of cans and twisted pieces of the cans cut with "tin snips" from Neil's tool box.

Several "plastic ones looking like crystal" etched with a greeting from Lindenwood c. 1986 and other long-ago dates. A little engine, a jolly little Santa, other gaudy angels, cherubs glittering from their pop-cultures past. Finally, a velvet gold bead trimmed skirt. My! I had never had such a stunning skirt on a tree. We had only one all handmade with felt letters: "the Stuecks". This one, like the tree, is the gift for my new home. Last year's tree in Pacific Place was too small now that I have up-sized rather than down-sized like we usually do with aging.

I wound the necklace again around the tree, not as lavishly as it had been naked. My last task I first thought I could not do. It was something I had to think about as it involved kneeling, peering under the curio cabinet, finding the plug for the lights. I assessed where I was and how I would get up if I knelt. The floors seem to be further away than they used to be. I carefully proceeded with my plan to plug in the lights of the tree by first pushing a chair to be near in case of need. This aging Girl Scout must always "Be Prepared". Voila! All worked well, then there was light! Decorating the tree was fun and enjoyable. Now I must have Miss Iris and her team of support for dinner and maybe even have some neighbors in for Egg Nog.

December 3, 2016

Two Spring Awakenings

Living in a temperate climate, we learn in our Picture Books that we have four seasons in any given year: Spring, Summer, Autumn, and Winter. These four seasons are somewhat erratic, some we call "Late Spring" or "Early Winter". Come whatever we weather the weather, whether we like it or not, is what it is. Native plants seem to do the same, flowering earlier and managing to live if the plant is native to an area.

I planned to visit two of my "out-of-town" families living about four hours one from another in Georgia. Georgia is about as long North to South as Missouri is East to West. Hence, by flying to Atlanta and with careful planning around schedules, I managed to visit all family living in Georgia. I did have to traverse many miles of highway and much traffic to do this. Perhaps I will plan two trips to Atlanta another time.

Happy to be a Garden Guide

Arriving in Atlanta only four hours late via United Airlines, my son met me at the jetway. Since all computers were out of commission and not a single United plane flew East of the

Mississippi, all regulations about "meeting passengers" were relaxed, hence my surprise when Lawrence was at the end of the jetway as I stepped off. Waiting several hours because computers were down was a new experience for me, even though I have flown to all but one continent on our planet.

The next morning, I was ecstatic to see the Redbud tree at my window awakening to Spring. The pale ruby flowers were just peeking out of their buds. I was on the threshold of Spring 2015. There was no hint of spring in Webster Groves when I left only yesterday.

Kathleen, the Mistress of the Manor and my delightful daughter-in-law, is a Landscape Designer. The grounds around the old church in which they make their home have been beautifully designed, often with some used plants Kathleen might find in the grounds of her clients. When one knows design, plants take on a special beauty. Here on Spring awakening, hellebores were already in bloom edging the back brick walk.

By the third day that I was there, Redbud trees were all in bloom, the pale ruby color becoming full and vibrant. Large deciduous trees now had buds swelling only a bit, giving a green gauzy feel to their shapes. But not all. The old pecan trees had no blush of green. Still "sleeping".

As I walked around the yards in the next few days, I noticed buds first on one species and then another began to open, oh so slowly. But, by mid-week, the Dogwoods showed their rich creamy bracts, creamy color like the cream on the top of our milk before homogenization. It only took one day for the buds to open and bracts to begin to grow. First marred by rusty edges, the bract unfolded and another day, the blossoms flattened as we know Dogwoods to be.

But watching the fig tree join the spring show was of particular interest, as we do not have that tree in Missouri. In California, I ate my first fresh figs, but I had never seen a Spring fig leaf. It was not until after the Dogwood show that I first noted the tiniest green bud on the fig. It was 1/8 inch but by the next day it was 1/2 inch. Could I see it grow? By the time I left, the leaves were probably over one inch. Maybe two. I knew what to expect as I had seen mature leaves. The latest report from the family there: "The fig leaves are as big as your palm".

I stayed a little over a week, enjoying life in this very small-town dating back way before the Civil War. To enjoy another next year, I would just have to be lucky. The plants will cycle again in their own time.

Returning to St. Louis, I had my Second Spring. I checked my own dogwood tree that always gives me such joy each year. Buds looked just like they did all winter. Hmm! This tree could not just die over Winter. After all it is a Native. I was puzzled...but impatient I found.

I do not have to recount the next few days here in St. Louis. I have no Hellebores, but the Redbuds came out in all their glory, the Dogwood was very creamy and soon became snow white. Same timing as Georgia. Each in its own time.

I had two Springs in 2015. But the Landscape Designer (owner of my complex) put in Red Maples and these flowers and fruits have put on a show not seen in the home in Georgia. A Billion tiny mauve colored winged seeds are strewn in my driveway. Each is a variant of mauve, lavender and/or purple, nearly translucent. These tiny seeds add still another dimension tinting the asphalt drive with a light pink wash. My Second Spring will soon have further awakening. Peony buds are ready to open soon.

Reflections on the 40th Anniversary of Kirkwood Webster Groves AAUW Branch

I have been called, sweetly I hope, the Founding Mother of the Kirkwood Webster Groves AAUW Branch. If that is so, Theresa Mayer was the Grandmother. Theresa was a "mover and shaker" in AAUW, the United Nations UNICEF, and many other community activities in the 50's and 60's. It was she who asked me to spearhead the organization of a new Branch of the American Association of University Women. The Association had only then approved of such organization, thinking that additional Branches would weaken the existing Branches. Ferguson-Florissant is older than this Branch, having been organized prior to real permission by the Association.

Starting this Branch took about a year from beginnings of organization to the Charter Banquet, May 1971. In that time, we considered our programming and organization development very carefully. We planned monthly programs so that in the year we addressed each of the facets and interests of AAUW...literature, civics, international relations, history, etc. Our mentors, Theresa, Miss Lillian Stupp, former State President, Ella Bettinger to name several, helped guide us in tasks for officers.

Many of the Chartering group had been members of the St. Louis Branch and could orient us to the Association and its Mission. There were 53 charter members. There are three of us here tonight. I know of four in town still. If only I had found my list sooner maybe I could have pulled them into this party.

Knowing the KWG Branch is still alive and doing well is a Blessing for me. I ask myself just why has this Association held my interest for all my adult life? It all began when I just happen to marry the nephew of Miss Lillian Stupp. Aunt Lil had been enamored and passionate about AAUW, serving as State President and particularly deeply involved in the International Federation of University Women and the Fellowships Program, forerunner of the Educational Foundation today. I have sometimes said "I married AAUW". She gave me an Association Membership for graduation, and I went to West Virginia about 2 weeks later with it in hand. Not knowing one single soul in Charleston, W. Va. where I had my first "real job" I quickly found a Branch of AAUW that gave me contacts and friendships almost immediately with women of common interests, programs to open many windows on my world that otherwise might be narrow. I came back to St. Louis and transferred my membership to St. Louis Branch. A recent-grads group was organized about three years later and that group was the basis of my friendships and social life as a couple for many years. I do not have to tell you we did not stay recent grads all those years, but the friendships lasted long after the "ten-year" decade of being a recent grad.

    I chatted today with Betty Nellums to find out what she recalled...again it was mostly friends and the Book Group that we started. I say it was she who prevailed upon me to attend the existing book group in South St. Louis reading *Gift from the Sea*. Her mother was a shell collector as was the author, Anne Morrow Lindbergh. After that meeting she said: "Let's start a book group in KWG". That group, somehow, morphed into the Peripatetics. The present evening group just sprung up alone.

May 11, 2011

Remember When????

It goes without saying that everything, every incident, is past. Though I do endeavor not to "live in the past" sometimes I do reflect on what has happened in the world. In the U.S. with big events most of us do know what happened, but some of us who lived these events do remember rather clearly.

1937—I was a sophomore in high school when Jackie Robinson played his first game with the Brooklyn Dodgers, becoming the first black athlete to play in Major League Baseball.

1947—The first captive giant panda in the US was brought from China to be on view at the Chicago Brookfield Zoo. An explorer, Ruth Harkness, brought it saying, "this is something very cute". Daffy Duck made his debut for the "Looney Tunes" series.

1957—*The Cat in the Hat* by Dr. Seuss was first published. So now I am mentioning events, dear reader, that you remember. And that same year "Cinderella" was telecast by Rodgers and Hammerstein with Julie Andrews in the title role.

1967—Television was no longer a luxury item. "Mr. Rogers's Neighborhood" became #1 on the Parade for preschoolers or early primary watchers. "Gilligan's Island", popular for so many years, aired its last episode.

1977—Barbara Streisand won an Oscar for the song "Evergreen" from the hit film "A Star Is Born".

1987—Ah, The first televangelist, Jim Bakker, to break the news with a sex scandal. Many more would follow. I think now only a few years later such affairs make news most every day from the President through Congress and government elected officials. On a pleasant note, the popular animated TV show "The Simpsons" made its debut.

1997—The age of the computer is now highly developed and entrenched in our society. The Palm Pilot personal, the second generation of Palm personal digital assistant (PDA), were released, becoming a precursor to smart phones.

2007—"Planet Earth" was broadcast five weeks on Sunday evenings, perhaps, the first of many series and in particular Ken Burns has become America's storyteller with his documentary productions like the "Civil War", WWI, National Parks, etc.

And there's more. A nationwide strike in March 1967 interrupted TV for 13 days. The strike was for an increase in pay for newsmen working on the major networks. Some stayed on but others we knew, like Walter Cronkite and Peter Jennings, joined the picket lines. Disc jockeys, program managers, and after two weeks the strike ended just in time for the Academy Awards.

"The Angels of the Battlefields", the American Red Cross have been one of the many important institutions since 1881.

I must give credit for the foregoing information, even most of the wording to Issue 2 of *American Senior* March/April 2017.

Some other events I remember, events that only I remember vividly.

1930—I was eight and in those distant days the Porter on each sleeping (Pullman) car would be "tipped" to meet my needs, making sure I was fed and had my bed pulled down. Daddy took care of the tip at the start of the trip as I was traveling with a family who were friends of my father. These cars, the sleeping cars, were named "Pullmans" after the designer of this special car with seats for the day trip that converted to beds, one lower bunk, one upper bunk. Meals were prepared and were very good in the dining car. Train rides were luxury travel. Flying had yet to come for pleasure/business travel.

1934—My first time to go to Cedaredge, the St. Louis Girl Scout camp. I was in Woody Glen. There I learned to make my bed with square corners. All of us had a session for this. We cooked our lunch every day over an open fire, so it was there I learned some basics like fire building, wood gathering, etc. All my life I have used those skills and shared with many.

My first travel-by-bus to New York was to the first western Hemisphere Encampment at the Camp Andre Clark in Pleasantville, NY. Patty Dunbar and I were the only Scouts from St. Louis and our folks sent us by bus with a group of teachers. This was my first traveling without my family. It seems I remember all the "firsts", as I presume most of us do. First days at school, first time in Junior High graduations, etc.

And I remember my first kiss from the Freshman in College that I married about ten years later. It was on the top step just at the landing by the front door of the apartment I was living in at the time with my folks, 7104 Amherst. Now there is something no one else knows. It was an important event for me.

Only a few days ago I became the adoptive "parent" of a racoon-size Giant Hero Rat named Ikemba. He is about 4-years-old and is trained to sniff out old landmines in battlefields. He currently is working in Angola. The hero rats have located thousands of old mines across the Middle East and Africa by sniffing and then a person can quickly detonate the landmine. Interesting NGO that John Mahan invested in for me. Finding new events is not hard in my life here at Mt. Pleasant, Ohio Living, Monroe, Ohio. I have been here since September 2016, almost 10 months.

June 11, 2017

November Night and Day

Leaves–red, yellow, bronzed–swirling in flurries
Wind, unseen, was passing by my window.
Darkness fell, all was quiet through the moonlit night.

Morning dawned; the sun shot arrows of light through the tall Maple
dazzling the vermillion leaves still clinging
But little Dogwood, so misshapen under the tall tree
Was left with only nine weathered leaves.

Naked was this tree with so few leaves
Checked gray bark stark contrast with twigs and branch
So smooth and pale the color of pewter.
Sturdy limbs held flower buds upright on a stalk
A four-part covering for protection

Dogwood is now prepared for winter.
Leaves dropped; spring buds protected.
This year's cycle is complete
Snow, ice and cold will come again.

Flood of 2013

It was Wednesday, September 16, 2013. I opened my eyes at the usual seven a.m. and mused: "This is an unusual morning in Estes Park, a town that prides itself on the sun shining 253 days a year". I had scheduled a meeting with Renata Fernandez and the Hahn sisters to monitor property for the Estes Valley Land Trust early because it is always so beautiful in early mornings. But thoughts of traipsing through meadows on a cloudy day did not urge me to throw off the covers and jump out of bed.

"Oh well, someone will surely call off this schedule", I thought as I snuggled down for a bit of "shut-eye". I was not called; I kept the *rendezvous* and no one came. I went back home facing what became an all-day and all-night rain. Two full days of rain. Flood stages were passed; ten inches of rain in some areas. Water seeped through the foundation in our furnace room. Seepage was not too unusual; but flowing water across the carpeted "undercroft" of our house was! A mini waterfall over the furnace room threshold was hitherto unknown.

Thursday morning, I called Briggs Carpet Cleaners, who do Restoration work following fires and floods. An answering service took my telephone number. From early morning news I learned that the business area of Estes Park at the confluence of two rivers was already under water, that Lyons, CO, a small town of 2000 down a few miles from us had become an island with no highways open in any direction. We were in a disaster area. With excessive rain mere creeks had become raging torrents of brown waters roily agitated with white caps.

On awaking Friday morning I gasped in awe the pre-dawn sky, a brilliant apricot huge cloud, a stunningly beautiful soft cast as if seen through tissue paper. In only a matter of seconds a rainbow with fairly strong colors rose straight up out of the valley of Estes Park arching gracefully over to Lumpy Ridge. "Red sky in the morning, sailors take warning". I have repeated this many many times being an old sailor. Would that prove true yet again? All this beauty faded oh so quickly. Yes, the sky turned a slate color streaked with light silvery horizontal slices of cloud.

The last line of an old camp song kept running through my head: "If it gets much wetter I'm gonna be a fish"!

Two federal highways leading out of Estes Park were closed by Friday having had bridges and even 4-lanes of concrete buckled or washed away. Highway 7, a third egress, was closed at certain points. The Trail Ridge Road through Rocky Mountain National Park would be a way out of town over the Continental Divide if one wanted to go west, not to Denver, Loveland, Boulder or Fort Collins. Ah! The "Beaver" at the top of Long's Peak peeped for about two hours. Sunshine on my shoulders was a blessing after nearly three days with no sunshine. Corinne came up for a BLT out on our deck, surely she was another blessing! I was having symptoms of "cabin fever".

The town held "town meetings" each day; emails were sent out giving details of rescues at night to shelters, locations of stations for Red Cross aid. Helicopters from Ft. Carson with pilots experienced in war zones and night vision goggles made 500 rescues at night from Lyons, air-lifting children and pets with their folks to a large church nearby for shelter until other emergency housing could be located. Many were still in their homes in the area of Estes Park but unable to leave because roads were washed away. Fish creek, truly only a creek, rose out of its banks damaging sewers and electric cables. Neighborhoods became flood plains. The power of water is incredible. Books will be written about this storm, already the largest in Colorado history.

My days blended together. I was always able to get to town, sometimes a circuitous route depending on where I was headed. Many areas were without available toilet facilities, without electric power and without cell and phone connections. It seemed loss of any such connections depended just on where one lived. I was without phone—cell or land—for a day or so. My family were all in communication with each other, but where was Mother? Knowing he was the one in the family with truck and most accessible, Peter called from Colorado Springs: "Grandmother I can bring you water and food if you need some or are you O.K."? I was so appreciative of his call and assured him I was just fine. Wet carpet had been cut and hauled out by a fine young man Briggs had hired from a volunteer pool. Every church had volunteers coordinated at the History Museum, turned into a Volunteer Center. The Community, indeed, had come together, neighbors helping neighbors. Many putting themselves in harm's way to help a stranger in need.

Kathleen texted me their concern about my safety. When my phone service resumed she chided me not too gently that I should have let someone know I was O.K. I was thoughtless, not thinking that my family could not know at all about me just listening to the news.

FEMA, the National Guard, and other "Feds" arrived Sunday morning. The Larimer County Sheriff expressed his deep gratitude when the burden of managing all the problems attendant with the flood was passed to the various federal agencies. I could just feel his intense relief as he told us he had only three hours of sleep the last several nights. Our town, and the county and fourteen other counties declared disaster areas will be at least a year or more recovering from such upheaval as we have seen.

I contracted with Briggs to have "air movers" (large fans) and two very large dehumidifiers brought in by a national "Rescue" company and dry out the furniture, the Pine chest, the panelling of the "undercroft". This was to take five days. Pro-Tech (furnace company) worked parts of three days to get the newer furnace working in the "new" addition. It had shorted out by having too much water overflowing from the humidifier and onto the furnace. Until the house was pronounced "dry" by the moisture meters I could not leave for St. Louis.

On Thursday, September 26, Michael called early in the morning to say he and Katie would come over from their home in Tabernash to rescue me. He was checking daily on the Trail Ridge Road re: its opening and closing. This might be the last day it would be open before we were scheduled to fly to St. Louis and Ohio. The fans/humidifiers were to be moved out at 10:30 that day. I was to be packed for St. Louis and close the house by 3 p.m. Somehow I found that much energy. The kids moved all the deck furniture into the Garage and all the plants into the house. We made our escape from Estes Park over the divide, prepared to relax and enjoy our last four days in the mountains this year.

Spring Will Come in its Time

My second Great-Granddaughter was paging through on of her new books. It is one for her age. It is constructed like her other books, not with paper pages to turn but thick cardboards. No longer does a youngster need to be admonished to "be very careful, take the corner to turn the pages". That lesson will be learned later when books with pages will be in the playroom. However, Iris is reading the pictures. She sees illustrations that are Signs of Spring. It is near May 1 and signs of spring are observed. Spring should be awakening. We speak of "hard winters" or "late springs", recognizing that four seasons some years might be six or some other viable or modification of four.

This year 2018 seems to be struggling to awaken. The Greek goddess of Spring, Persephone, is still in the Underworld with her kidnapper, the God of the Underworld, Hades. In the last two weeks we have had radical changes. Sometimes 75 degrees in the afternoon dropping below freezing at night. Meteorologists one night on the weather channel predicted snowshowers. This was a new term for me. Living in Ohio in a winter I thought it was a kind of weather I had not experienced in Missouri. Sure enough, the next day right on the TV's schedule, the morning had several passing episodes that were "heavy snow showers". Similar to rain showers except white bead-like particles fell like a light blizzard. This snow-shower was at first light but quickly picked up wind to become blizzard-like and enduring furiously about four minutes. Not a trace of a bead of frozen raindrop was to be seen on the ground.

One morning about mid-April, I became aware that "my" forest, bordering the backyard meadow, seemed to have the very faintest tint of green. Could this be my first sign of Spring? In only one more day the honeysuckle shrub had been washed with green coloring. Tiny buds along each cascading stem were opening. The border plants are natives of Ohio and somehow know not to open too much. Like the heartiest daffodils, the honeysuckle buds will survive the erratic temperatures and elements of these pre-season days. Perhaps, we should have more season names. One could be Fore spring. Perhaps, swinter?

    I know that 2018 is not so unusual as I think it is. Only a glance at historical weather reports attests to this fact. Oh, how we look forward to Spring and the changes it will bring. And, at the end of summer and the weather changes again, we look forward to autumn. I am pleased to have a change of seasons. Each one has special joys for me. No one is a favorite. I have lived into my tenth decade always in a temperate climate. Having no basis of comparison, I cannot say this is best. But I can say that I really like light and sunshine. I would find Alaska difficult I think because of the long dark days in that region. I do not enjoy cold windy days. But I have had some of that living in Colorado some winter times. I have had several two to three months in tropics but to live there full-time would not be a good life for me. I relish every change of season.

April 29, 2018

P.S. This winter, I would have liked more sunshine.

Excerpts from notes made at Shaw Nature Reserve Workshop, April, 1995

CARPE DIEM...
- to be not afraid to be lonely
- to develop more creativity
- to pursue long time interests just for the self-satisfaction that might bring
- learn more about architecture, botany, writing
- heighten well-being and pleasure being alone in an activity

Can these be learned, adding new dimensions to life in hand, on my own?

REFLECTIONS/REFLECTING
- on the pond at the arboretum
- quietly sitting on the road to the Trail House
- listening to the call of a tufted titmouse
- times can bring sadness as the links of love have been broken
- on the storehouse of joyous treasured memories

IN A SPECIAL SPOT
- A shadbush, a balloon of white framed by a column of dark green juniper
- redbud shining brilliantly in the mid-afternoon; sun casting shadows on the ground
- tiny droplets of water like diamonds, cling to grasses at my feet
- I have captured the moments with gratification, and *joie de vivre*.

Days at the Knolls, January 11, 2020

The days at the Knolls at Oxford have amounted to about 5 weeks since disaster day December 17, 2019. That was the day of my most recent move. I must not say "last move". That sounds like I may not have another. But how could I possibly not move again? I've not counted my moves, though each one was reported in my recent writing titled "Moves".

I recall that each one was precipitated by a circumstance. Usually it was planned for except this last one to the Knolls @Oxford. Plan was for Two Men and a Truck, movers who "care" so their slogan says.

Dawn on Dec. 17 was rainy; only 3 men instead of 5 showed up and no truck. Packing moved smoothly, wrapping each piece of stuff to be moved in single HUGE piece of "movers paper". WASTEFUL!! But they were creatures of habit. SHAMEFUL.

Too many boxes to count but into one of the 3 rooms they were designated as packed. What designations for each room would become apparent as they progressed with the packing.

One took on the looks of bathroom since one room was empty except for a stool and a shower curtain. A second one had a bed, chest, dresser, apparently a bedroom. The remaining room had tables, lamps, sofa and TV—it looks a bit like a living room, dining room, reading room.

Often I have to open 2 doors out of the 3 to find the room I want. Three rooms have evolved this way:

1. bath—sink, shower, toilet, linen storage.

2. bedroom—bed, dresser, closet, small table/lamp

3. Eclectic—dressing room, wardrobe. It houses all seasons of clothes, nearly all my wardrobe except coats.

The third serves as a storage area, still has about 5 unopened boxes. No point in ever opening them except of curiosity regarding contents. Over the weeks I have sent many boxed belongings to WGI White Garden Inn when the "storage" seemed to be reaching its max. Most days I may move to open and sort one of 3 doors 2 or 3 times to locate what it is I want at the moment. I just allow time for there hunting expeditions. I am resigned to never again be completely organized and have no unopened boxes.

Pine Winds, August 2012

Pine Winds, Estes Park CO

Pine Winds, purchased in 1983

CHAPTER FOUR
Travels

Maurita and Linda in Patagonia, 1998

Those years aboard Ceilidh *were very good years, cherished by all of our family for three generations. Usually through 46 years of marriage with my captain, Neil, I was the reluctant dragon on new adventures. But I trudged along, came to relish every new experience. He taught me well, as I have ventured forth alone on new trails in the mountains and more waves on other seas.*

"Backroads" in Switzerland

Quotes around the title of this Memory Memoir indicate that we were with a tour operator called "Backroads". I pictured we would be walking through Alpine flowered meadows beneath awe-inspiring snow-capped peaks, like an environment in which "Heidi"* lived. Vistas were beyond my expectations: broad green valleys with fences defining pastures, the dreamed-of earthen track was ofttimes as wide as double sidewalks paved with millions of tiny pebbles. Cows with bells provided constant melody.

Though we travel with a group we are not a group meant to stay together. Our "guide" meets us after breakfast in our hotel, provides us the route "for the day" and then checks "out", not to be seen again until the appointed place for dinner. This group and this plan were certainly not like the Elderhostel from which my traveling companion, Ricki (nickname for Claire), and I had just attended. Here we were with about six "thirty-somethings" singles, one or two couples, one single male, most attractive and most disinterested in any of the other singles, one couple who did not intend to do any more with the group than fly. Two couples, physicians, 60+, and the two of us 70+. We set forth in a drizzling rain that became rather steady for the first several hours. The Swiss tend to walk rather than hike and on this rainy day we noticed natives carried umbrellas. Ladies living along our walk often had "house-dresses" as we used to say, and walking shoes with square 2" heels. The young career folks had elected to do this walking trip as something "different" in travel. It was not a camping jaunt but one that afforded some "night life" in the hotels in which we lodged each night. Our luggage was transported for us so the "30-and 40-somethings" could have appropriate evening ensembles.

The second day we climbed in the sunshine. The young ones set forth as if they were running a sprint, stopping to rest soon. I had learned to set a pace and keep it which I did arriving at the group at rest. "Don't you have to rest"? was their first question. "No, we will join you as you go ahead". We became a bit more acquainted and as always, the same queries: How do you stay in shape? Hope I can do this when I am your age? Ricki was ever annoyed; I explained: "I have never felt a need to 'work out'. I have walked to school all my life, chased after four children, washed all my windows and done my housework. There was grass to cut, gardening to do. I have done my share of walking my whole life. I even walked to the University. We were a 'green society'. About age 60 we began spending our summers in Colorado and I did some serious day hikes". They seemed satisfied that we could walk along through the Alpine meadows. It was not a time to race, but a time to take time to enjoy the landscape, time to wonder at the awesome splendor; to "ooh" and "ah".

And visit along the trail. I often wondered how old "they" thought I was! It was then not polite to ask a woman her age. Today I am asked many times even by strangers. This I still find it impolite. But it does not offend me. Changes come so rapidly in our society today I would be frustrated and grouchy all the time if I dwelt on our mores, morals, and folkways.

The single, attractive young male seemed attracted to Ricki and me in the evenings at table when he returned from his days "apart". I noticed he was really not included in his age group for whatever reason, but that he seemed quite comfortable with the two of us. I'm certain Andrew was comfortable with his Grandmother, too. We were substitutes for her in his lonesomeness.

"Backroads" does not need to plan lay-over or "rest" days as train trips, gondolas, ski-lifts, short bus rides break up our walking day. These plans also afford us the opportunities to see other villages, other hotels, each one more luxurious than the last, and some added experiences like riding up to the top of a mountain or a waterfall.

After several times in various conveyances, I could run and hop on like those native Alpine folks and gleefully ride to the TOP. We were up over residences, probably some of Heidi's ancestors. With fascination I watched haying operations, cutting, and raking with hand scythes. The raking was usually women's as we have in the Rockies to accommodate the rise and fall of the terrain. These trails, almost like back roads, went straight down or straight up.

To arrive at the town of Geissbach for our last two nights we had a total of five conveyances: train, cable car, bus, ferry, and a funicular! Hotel Geissbach was a dramatic closure to these days in Switzerland. How incongruous it seemed to arrive in such a palace in shorts, boots, and a backpack not be at all uncomfortable. And then to shower, dress for a dining experience, the menu I recorded in my journal: "Salmon with Brioche seasoned with fennel, Infusion of Mussels (excellent), Veal with Basil sauce, Broccoli buds, assorted cereals, sliced cinnamon apple sauce with puffs of pastry, Wine".

I was intoxicated to be awakened by the pounding waterfall and a day bursting with sunshine.

Heidi, a favorite book of my childhood. Too thick, pictures too quaint, but still a good story of life in the mountains of Switzerland not too changed in many ways.

*"Backroads" trip August 1994
Lifelong Learning Class February 2014

Cruising the British Virgin Islands

We did our first cruise in the Virgins in 1976 on a weeklong exploration with several of our children. It was a different kind of vacation, camping on a 39 foot boat rather than camping on land. Neil had been a Skipper with the Sea Scouts as had our son, Lawrence. That was cruising on the Mississippi. My experience was on "dates" in High School with a Sea Scout cruising on Creve Coeur Lake, most often with no wind.

Needless to say, we all needed lessons. Along with chartering the yacht we had Captain Allen for our teacher. He was from South Africa but was available in the Virgins while his boat was being repaired. It was our luckiest break of that year. We were all eager to learn; he was eager to teach. At the end of that cruise, Neil and I purchased our first sloop. Thus began 14 or 15 odysseys to these waters. In those years, each of our children crewed with us, several becoming excellent skippers, all enjoying the experiences of sunning, snorkeling, swimming, beach walking, and seeing the fascinating undersea world. In those years, several married and their spouses came aboard. One daughter honeymooned on *Ceilidh*. Her groom could not skipper so his best man took the wheel for one week, and his in-laws (Neil and I) skippered the second week. It was easy to be alone as honeymooners, even on a cruise. Days ashore they only had to be back when the boat pulled up anchor.

As I write now in 2016, I can read our logs from those cruises. What pulled us back year after year? It took us several days each year to acclimate to the life aboard; days there was no time to read or to just watch the pelicans dive. Concentration on charting our course, equipping the galley, getting our "sea legs". We needed time for our city-tired bodies to relax and to fall under the spell of sun-splashed waves and star-studded nights. Patience and faith the sea teaches, we looked forward what each new day would hold.

In the 70's there were still dirt roads in Roadtown, then

still a village. Cruise ships had not come yet. Treasures from the sea or coconuts from beach walks were all we could bring back from these vacations. The best shopping was on our beach walks. Shelling, driftwood, coconuts the natives could open for us to gorge on the meat and milk.

I like whelk shells—elongated with delicate shadings of color, smooth symmetrical face winding upward to one solitary point in the center. It is like an island surrounded by surf or an island with white beach circling it like my favorite, Sandy Cay. I think we need to have aloneness as this island on my shell. How nigh to impossible to attain any solitude in our bustling society, boisterous, noisy, people, and computer print outs, schedules to keep us as on a revolving wheel. In this web of relationships, I hear a small voice saying "Be still my soul". The whelk says to me "center-down". It is my island shell. John Donne was right when he wrote "no man is an island". The sea did "still our souls".

I label this shell found at random on a beach walk my "unknown shell". Still nearly perfect though encrusted, but beautifully designed with three concentric circles leading up to a little peak. How long it took to develop so beautifully, patience and faith like building relationships with people we encounter, developing teams to function smoothly, furthering our goals and designs of our life.

April 6, 2016

From Creek Paddling to British Virgin Islands

I do not remember paddling as a toddler in the Creek "at the Farm", but I do vividly recall my first swimming lessons. One of my mother's "Pillars of Parenting" was the firm belief that her daughters would experience activities in our young years that had not been afforded to her. Learning to swim was primary.

How she located lessons for me I have no idea. These were held at the Bishop Tuttle Memorial pool located via a long bus ride downtown. For eight weeks Mother and I made this trip; sessions that laid the foundation of a lifetime of swimming for me: recreational, competitive, and teaching.

My first Instructor did have a unique system of teaching for his time, one I never encountered as I taught in the years to come with the Girl Scouts, the Red Cross, or the YMCA curricula. I, an 8-year-old non swimmer, put on water wings in a harness suspended from the ceiling of the pool. Theory: children had no fear of water—that is often the great inhibitor of learning to swim. There was no need to breathe, no gulping of water as my head was out of the water. He then taught us to do the breaststroke, admittedly the most complicated stroke to learn. He chose to do this (I have subsequently reasoned) because it is a stroke that can be done without learning to breathe while swimming, a stroke that can be used if a rest is needed, therefore, a good one to learn initially. That first encounter with the breaststroke still stands me in good stead as I swim now just for exercise and recreation (relaxation at my age!). It has been used competitively and is the foundation of some lifesaving instruction.

On to many years of camping, always with a focus on swimming and boating in my teen years. I did manage to "make the team" for some competition in high school and college. I did not excel but enjoyed the experience. Traveling across St. Louis to participate in a swim meet with Principia High School was a high point. In today's world this would be a common occurrence but in the 30's my High School went off-site (back to the same Bishop Tuttle Memorial pool) to swim, rented a bus (as the school had no "bussing") and drove into mid-city to have this meet. I find this, in retrospect, the genius of Miss Helen Manley, the District's director of Physical Education, who moved on in her career to notable recognition in the nation. She had a passion for furthering Physical Education. Health and Sex Education were two other aspects she introduced into our curriculum before the schools found this whole area to be of great import. As our team "coach" she went to these great lengths that we might swim.

I took my first Junior Life Saving course at age twelve. I do not know how much my male instructor weighed, but I do remember a terrible struggle to "rescue" him from the depths of deep water. I failed the first time, but jumped back into the next course offered, passed when I was a little stronger.

Senior Life Saving and Water Safety Instructor I next took on. These certificates were part of my "resume" entering Lindenwood College. With a stipend from NYA, one of many programs of President Roosevelt that were developed during the Depression, I taught beginning swimming at the College. In the 40's a requirement for graduation was to pass an elementary swimming test. I found teaching swimming challenging and interesting. A clear image in my head is of one of my students, a college freshman, who was paralyzed with fear of water. With six weeks of patience and encouragement Vivian finally let go of the corner gutters in the pool and "bobbed" for the first time!

I taught adults and children from that time until I "retired" about age 60. The motivation adults must learn is as high or higher than kids; the joy expressed by mentally challenged children in first floating or "blowing" bubbles was contagious to me. Teaching Lifesaving to teens I felt most important as those skills afforded one jobs in the summer and many further water activities boating, float trips, sailing. Today's kids have many fast moving aquatic power "toys". Water safety is probably more important than thirty years ago.

I regret Mother was not an apt pupil. She tried and at least became comfortable just moving about in the pool. A good sport!

One of my last opportunities with the Red Cross at the Webster pool was one of my least enjoyable. I was to assist a male instructor, my pastor at the time, with his class of Senior Life Saving. I have seldom felt any discrimination because I was a woman. Here I did. I knew he was a man who reputedly was seen as one who did not hold women in high regard. Perhaps, this was the reason I felt he did not give me much responsibility as his assistant.

As an adult I have had some of my most fun times in all these activities. Float trips in Missouri with other families are fond remembrances of weekend camping trips. Each adult sibling and several grandchildren have sailed several years on our own sailing yacht in the British Virgin Islands. We have a host of friends, too, who over sixteen years have shared experiences with us on *Ceilidh*. Only once were old Life-saving techniques needed in an emergency. Crewing with us one year, Rosemary, a fair swimmer, had a small panic attack while swimming not too far from our boat. No time to call out encouragement. I struck out to the tired swimmer and all those words came back to me: "Put your hands on my shoulders and just lay back in the water. I will take you to the boat. Look at me". Breaststroke into action. My head up. I repeated: "Look at me". She obeyed. She relaxed. I pushed her to the ladder.

Neil & Maurita canoeing

I cherish those many float trips, just one of many experiences I no longer have. I do wish for a swim in the warm waters of the Virgins and that could be reality again. But for now the Webster Y and the Estes Park high school pool are my pools. The latter one is the largest pool, Olympic size, in northern Colorado. Windows on one side give me a view of the front range of the Rockies. What better place to enjoy a leisurely swim, using the sidestroke so I can see the view!

Going "Down Under"

My eldest daughter, Linda, recently flew from Ft. Collins, Colorado to visit with me for a week in her old "hometown". She comes about once a year or so and we visit some old haunts she wants to remember. She washes windows I can no longer reach and goes "through stuff". This year my priority was to look through "Grandmother's Attic" otherwise known as "under the bed". Storage in my cottage is limited. There I really did find some "treasures", journals of travels I had kept over some 20 years dating from 1980. What a delight it has been for me to reread the jottings of so many sojourns, trips. I want to write some excerpts from "Down Under" knowing that the entire journal will probably not be read by any of my family for whom I am really writing these Memoirs.

    I do not know from whence this expression "Down Under" comes but on this planet, we do indeed go down under from North America to Australia, my destination in 1995. This was a tour sponsored by the Missouri Botanical Garden to visit Western Australia, studying the flora of that region. I traveled with a small group of, perhaps, ten with Dr. DeBuhr who, at that time, was director of the Education Department at our Botanical Garden. Being a recent widow, I gave thought to those with whom I traveled always wanting to feel comfortable in the event I had any kind of mishap. I was an instructor/guide at the Garden, working closely with Dr. DeBuhr, and had no hesitancy about this trip. It was a most comfortable nearly 15-hour flight as I sat alone in a row of three seats being amply supplied with food, drink, reading time and material, knitting, "watching the full moon rise casting a silver streak over the quiet sea beneath us as we approached the landing". (Quotes in this memoir will be from the original journal.) On this trip I roomed with Ruth, a long-time acquaintance in Girl Scouting leadership. It was co-incidental that we were the two "singles" in the group. I knew she often wore purple but had not known that she had all purple socks, under-pinings, "purple cotton swab sticks, even a purple top on her deodorant" beside her purple toothbrush.

The Royal Botanic Garden, about the size of MBG, seemed so much larger as it is contiguous to public gardens surrounded by the city and the Harbor. Dr. DeBuhr's joy was as a taxonomist, having done his doctoral work in the state of Western Australia. My sheer joy was in the shapes, textures of the wide diversity of flora native to that continent. The succulent garden with wide sweeping brick walks, the Palm Grove first planted in the early 1800's was like nothing I'd seen. A boat tour around Sydney Harbor, the fourth largest natural harbor in the world, was stunning. To think three million people live in this city overlooking this beauty. Some in five-million-dollar mansions; others in Beach houses.

Next day, so I read in the Journal, we headed for the Blue Mountains, dense eucalyptus forests not too far north of Sydney. These were one of the factors helping to keep early members of the penal colony contained. I had not known (or remembered) that early settlement of Australia was as a place for prisoners from Britain. The stark-naked bark of the Eucalyptus trees rise above the highly diverse understory of the forest.

Off to Perth after this bit of sight-seeing. It was time to fly to Perth, our ultimate destination, three thousand miles from Sydney. Sitting alone, I relished the quiet. Neil and I could have quiet times traveling together, but acquaintances, new companions always seem to have a need to palaver. A new driver toured us around Perth, along the Swan River Valley, so named because of the black swans so numerous and tame. Watching them walk on the water as they gathered up speed to lift off brought giggles to all of us. As we stretched our legs on the shores of the Indian Ocean, an image from my third-grade geography book to mind. I pinched myself to be sure I was really standing on that ocean pictured in my book.

At last, the next morning we boarded *Priscilla* our "Bush-Baby" to begin our exploration, our real botanizing, in Western Australia, a state relatively unpopulated. A place where we would sometimes stay in the best accommodations available though they would not ever be recommended by any AAA. They would be clean "Mom and Pop" places with often the best food on all the trip. Our driver, Mike, guide, resident botanist, master of the Bush-baby was highly skilled in driving across tracks where there was no road. The sides of *Priscilla*, our Bush-Baby, drop down for tea and coffee stops and for lunch. *Voila*! There was our Aussie Chuck Wagon in operation. I was free to walk ahead just by asking our driver the route he would take. Following his instructions, I would just get picked up along the way having stretched my legs.

I want to quote my writing from 1995: "Our first stop was a wetland of incredible diversity just by the road. To name a few of the flora—the Green Kangaroo Paw, certainly the most unusual natural green I have ever seen. It looked sprayed like green plastic flowers or the artificially colored icing that has too much food coloring!...The purple orchid looking like it had been enameled in a kiln. And then I spied a large reptile of some sort. Mike, wading in barefoot, scooped up a Bob-tailed skink for us to pet. It yawned, flicked out its tongue, seemed to enjoy being cuddled".

We botanize from the van. Mike can drive, spy a flower, stop, back up...and we all pile out for a better look. I, without a camera, seemed always to be last to look. Others in the group saw the world through a lens. Even stopping for a "facilities" stop at Tony's place we can walk "in the weeds" and find many varieties of flora, fascinating and profuse. One day we stopped at the Combsdale Wildflower Farm that is owned by a South Dakota farmer (and owner of the motel in which we bedded one night). He showed us his drying shed, telling of the various processes of preservation. Lovely wreaths and arrangements. I do not recall if he exported his creations. We did some rock-hounding, too. I carried home a piece of quartz (common in Missouri), but fun to have an exotic in my home collection. Brought home some Rose Quartz that I had not known. Since that time, I have been to a large area of Rose Quartz near my home in Estes Park, Colorado.

September 21...two weeks of our trip have gone so quickly. Seeing the countryside, enjoying our morning "cuppas" served from *Priscilla*, picnics for lunch usually in an important area for plants, visits to National Parks and delightful arrangements for nights. One night was unusual in that we ordered our breakfast before retiring and were told it would be passed to us between 7 and 7:15 a.m. With faith we went to bed and, sure enough, at 7:00 a.m. our tray was passed through a little door carrying bread for us to toast, milk in our "frig", fruit compotes and cereal readied, and broiled tomato and sausage for my roommate. The two of us enjoyed "room service Aussie style". That day fields of rape created a landscape like a chartreuse and bright green quilt. Squads of Regent Parrots strolled across the road.

Driving along the Southern Ocean was yet another experience for me to relish as a place I only knew on a map, never envisioning I would ever be here. The Southern Ocean starts as Australia's coast turns to the south, the ocean between Australia and Antarctica. It was at Perth that our GIs in WWII were stationed. Then it was really an outpost I learned from a friend sometime after our trip. Today it is the largest city in the state of Western Australia, 6000 population. The Kerri forests are in that area, the third largest flowering trees in the world, our Sequoias and another Eucalypts forest are the two taller. This area was settled by Aussies in the 1920's for returning soldiers. Plats were given to farmers, furnishing them basic tools. Now its economy is dairy farming and apples. Granny Smith apples are from here.

Music is played most of the time "on the road" when Mike is not doing some discoursing on something botanical. One day he defined the types of forests we would see: Forest trees defined as single-stemmed trees with a crown forming a minor proportion of its height. Woodland trees are single-stemmed tree with branches a short distance above the ground level with the crown a major portion of height. A Mallee tree forest is full of short shrubby like, multi stemmed plants. How beautiful a eucalyptus forest can be, giants with pale smooth upper barks are strikingly handsome. The eucalyptus we know in our country are the "weeds" of Australian species.

The last morning of our Missouri Botanical Garden tour came all too soon. Three to go to St. Louis, one to Auckland, two to Cairns, and two to Alice Springs. I was bound for Cairns and another week of new adventures in Queensland. Australia is a vast country of great diversity, yet unsophisticated, except in the cosmopolitan city of Sydney.

February 12, 2014

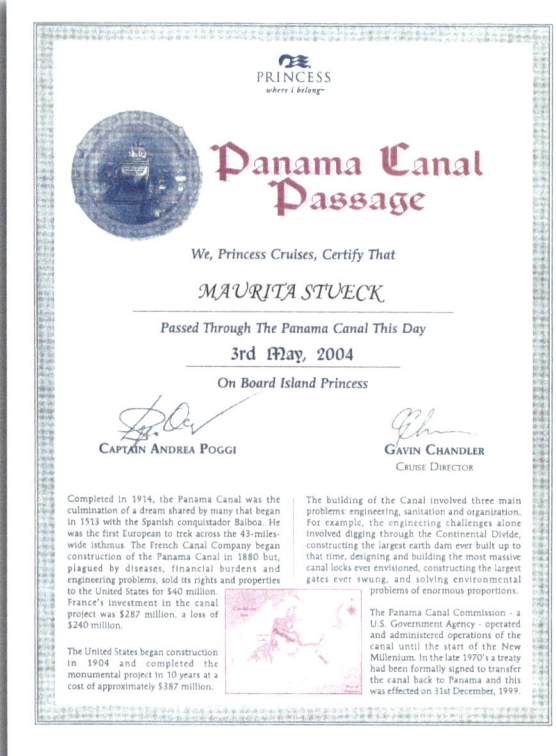

A cruise with Joe

Memorable Assissi

To the town of Assissi
There once came a group
From far o'er the ocean
We soon were a troop.

We stayed at the Sole
With Emma in charge
The staff was tremendous
Our hearts were so large.

We ate all the pastas,
The zuppe and breads,
The salads and cafes
Were really well-fed.

We studied and listened
And learned a lot
Like Anna we're certainly not.

With Laura in great voice
We climbed up and down
Saw vista of beauty
In each hilltop town.

Saint Francis and Chiara
Their churches we saw.
Rufino, Maria,
And two hundred more.

We studied the dovecotes,
Learned everyday more
The art and the music,
The history and lore.

Buongiorno e grazie
Buona sera, cioso
We spoke and we gestured
We're into it now.

One night while we slumbered
There came some shocks
We woke in the morning
To find the torn rocks.

Domani andeame,
Each one on his way
May peace and may goodness
With us always stay.

*May be sung to the tune
"On Top of Old Smokey"

Travel friends

No Good-byes

"I just dropped by to say 'hello'", Rosemary called as I watched her picking her way around stacks of bricks along the front walk. I go up from my task of laying our brick walk. "Come on in. I am glad to stop my job for a while".

It was late Fall of 1950. I had only recently met Rosemary, a newcomer and new member of our St. Louis AAUW Branch. She, a native Californian, and her husband, Larry Stewart from New Hampshire, had recently been married and moved to St. Louis where he was working at McDonnell Douglas.

Rosemary, vivacious and ebullient, was easy to welcome. She was carefully carrying a lovely white crinoline holiday ornament, layers of crinoline built into a tree-shape decorated with little stars. I treasured this hand-crafted holiday decoration for many years. Making craft items like this was done in numerous ways in those years. "Stay-at-home" moms were "the norm", but we did not have the title.

Rosemary and I co-chaired a new part of our AAUW Branch, Recent Grads. In the beginning there were only six or so who had been out of College less than 10 years. Within a year, we had grown to 30 or more and found our best friends developing within this group. Alas, Rosemary and Buzz (as Larry was called) only stayed in St.

Rosemary, Buzz Stewart & Maurita in Pacific Palisades

Louis a couple of years. Today, I think this would be called an "internship". California beckoned Rosemary. She missed home and Lockheed offered Buzz a position with his talent as an aeronautical engineer. We stayed in touch at least by Christmas letters. So often friends thousands of miles apart lose touch. This happened frequently in the 50's and 60's as corporations tended to do a lot of transferring of young employees. Monsanto, McDonnell, Southwestern Bell did so regularly. Somehow the Stewarts and the Stuecks found ways to follow our separate careers and family-building.

In the mid-70's, we connected closely again through our mutual travel interests and sailing. Rosemary entered the travel business not long after her two children entered school. Having a bad case of "travel-itis" she found that in the business, she would have opportunities and discounts to afford travel for the two of them. In 1976, we acquired a 37' sloop berthed in the British Virgin Islands. The Stewarts crewed first for us in the next year or two.

Rosemary, dressed a bit flamboyantly for travel from California, swished into our Marina on Tortola, Buzz coming along behind ready to come to attention as soon as his "Captain" (my husband) said "Welcome Aboard". The twenty-plus years since we had seen each other simply melted away. It was the second chapter of a friendship that was to last sixty-two years.

I do not recall how many years they crewed with us. Buzz was the most experienced crew we ever had; his naval training surfaced after years since WWI. Buzz was the son and brother of Admirals. He knew every sea chanty and sang lustily as we cruised. His repertoire of other songs, anecdotes, stories told with droll humor was vast and shared. We could laugh across the waves or when becalmed. I had the utmost confidence in his maritime skills. To get him to question anything the "Captain" said except in a dire emergency was next to impossible. Crew obey order in the Navy.

Neil and I did visit the Stewarts once or twice at their home in Pacific Palisades where they had built when they returned to California. The Palisades were "way out" then; Rosemary's parents could not imagine why "the children" would want to go there. What a lovely time we had with the host and hostess showing us LA and its environs! How inviting the hot tub on the deck as we looked out to sea!

They came to Estes Park one Fall to attend the Scottish-Irish Festival, one of the largest in the country. Buzz, devoted to his Stewart Clan, came with slacks, pajamas, maybe undershorts, a 4-in-hand tie with 4 different Stewart plaids. We had tickets for the Ceilidh Thursday night, the special dinner for Clan members Friday night where we were "piped" into the dining room, Parade in Clan dress, visit to the Clan "booth". I have attended the Scottish Festival in Estes Park for 25 years, but never had the opportunity to go with a member of a clan, the most enthusiastic Scots men. Great fun as always with Rosemary and Buzz. Looking back, I find it interesting that our interests developed along similar paths though we were far apart. Cultural Arts appealed to both of us, engineering, of course, home building, maintenance and the "home arts"—decorating, cooking, entertaining. And most of all, travel, and sailing. Their Christmas cards always pictured some exotic place seen in the year.

Our travels covered the U.S., camping most every year with the family until our eldest had even had one year of college. Family vacations after that seemed to gravitate to the Virgin Islands. Each of our children came aboard at least two or three times, all four at least one time or more with their respective spouses. The Stewarts did not do such family vacations for whatever reason.

Buzz passed away about five years ago. I continued to call Rosemary several times through the years. She became housebound several years ago. The phone was our only way to communicate. About a month ago, I called one time, found her lively, still a bit ebullient, still in their home overlooking the Pacific, but with a full-time caregiver.

Yesterday, her son called me because I had left a birthday message on her answering machine late in October. She had died a few days before her birthday, and he was trying to call folks in her address book. I so appreciated his calling. He said: "How did you know Rosemary"? I briefly told him, "In St. Louis when your Dad was working with McDonnell."

I have written this memoir for Rosemary's son and daughter.

November 6, 2012

Old and New Stand in Harmony

It was Midsummer's Eve June, 1996 in Svartsbaeken, Sweden. It is an ancient celebration related to the Summer Solstice. Now it is celebrated the Friday and Saturday nearest June 24 and the biggest holiday in all parts of Sweden, next to Christmas Eve. Every local community erects a May pole, not to be danced around, but to be entwined with boughs of leaves and bunches of field flowers. Food, dance and music gave us a lovely day, a generous slice of Swedish small-town folks. I was with a small group traveling Scandinavia with Hinshaw Tours. Our leader, Robert Hinshaw, is a new friend of ours. Ricki, my traveling companion, made his acquaintance in Estes Park. We are housed these first few days near the town (5000 population) of Svartsbaeken in what a Quaker Retreat Center is now. The town's name is found on old maps dating back several hundred years. This was the first of many experiences we were to have where the old stands next to new in perfect harmony. Like new friends and the old: "One is silver, the other gold".

Three days before the Midsummer's Eve celebration we had the "getting acquainted" day, also known as sight-seeing. Rimbo was nearby to show off its textiles, its Viking grave sites, its Viking fortifications, its Iron works with lunch at its still attractive Castle.

A visit to a Seventh Day Adventist school, another to a Day Care Center where children were learning to read using computers showed present day emphasis. Pupils do not start school until one is seven.

Each day there was time for strolling along the river, walking through meadows, and reading. We had music—usually folk music—with Julia and Tori the directors of the Retreat Center playing fiddles. Julia was Robert's daughter. Hence our visit to the Retreat Center. This is the National Retreat Center for all Quakers in Sweden. Only one time did we participate in a Quaker worship service. Not one word of encouragement for us to attend, only that we were welcome. Having known of the work of Friends through AFS groups coming to Webster Groves I wanted the experience. After all, to have new experiences as well as fleshing out my knowledge of history beyond books was my rationale for travel.

Stockholm, the "Venice of the North", was only 50 kilometers from Svartsbaeken so a day in that colorful city was another dimension where gleaming skyscrapers stood next to "Old Town". We appreciated the great church of St. George, a golden cathedral from the 14th century now a Lutheran, brick cathedral with an ebony and silver altar. Though the worship was in Swedish I knew when they repeated the Lord's prayer. The cadence is the same.

Young singles are living in condos. We visited a young lawyer in his urban apartment, c.1760. St. Louis singles are seeking quaint neighborhoods in St. Louis dating to 1890. But is St. Louis serving a beverage made with Elder Blossoms even though Elderberries are native to St. Louis? It would likely be beer. Sweden serves beer as the drink of choice at meals, though it is 1.5% alcohol. It is permissible to drink before driving. It is not possible to buy such low-alcohol content in St. Louis. I am a non-beer-drinker even though my forbears from Germany were brewers. But in Sweden I found it rather nice with a meal.

In one day, we visited a Viking ship built to fight Poland trying to gain Sweden for its king in 1628. Now it had been hauled from the deep to become the centerpiece of the Viking Museum. History must remain alive; we lunched at one of the many new McDonald's.

We had evening programs on present day education, health care, farming practices, care centers for the elderly or more music by fiddlers. One fiddler was a hundred-years-old.

This was a well-planned trip in every respect. Ricki and I shared many trips. Our best ones were small groups, often as this one, planned in concert with local residents, contacts of the leader and a mix of Old and New.

*word from song: "Make New Friends"
February 10, 2016

Recollections of the PDRC

We did not call our family vacations for three or four decades "road trips", but only vacations for two weeks every summer. Without exceptions I remember them as camping adventures. Times for family fun, times for opening windows on the world not possible during the school year. We managed to touch every state in the lower "48" except North Dakota and Oregon. Daddy was the principal navigator and I the PD, the program director. At the time I was not titled but assumed the tasks necessary to keeping harmony in the group. I am thankful every day that we could travel these thousands of miles with no serious accidents and have kids share happy memories with me. I did have hidden agendas often.

There were the years of just two of us and then there were three or four, finally there were six. Station wagons were a necessity and I still have one now called an Outback. How we fit is one of the mysteries of life. We had no tv in the car, no cup-holders, no videos, only a radio!

Singing was one of our mainstays for covering the miles happily. Rounds were the most fun especially "Grasshoppers Three". "Grasshoppers three a fiddlin' went, hi, ho never be still. They had no money to pay the rent...But all day long with their elbows bent they fiddled called...". (gestures here) This favorite of our son's had a reprise at his wedding reception many years later. Daddy really had difficulty carrying a tune, and while driving could not concentrate on singing too effectively. When we all tuned up for the "Orchestra" song he was assigned the part of the drummer. This was a "two note" part, "the drum playing two tones and always the same tone, five one, one five, five, five five one".

We devised many games dealing with geography. Taking turns, "It" called out a place name beginning with his designated letter and the next person had to name a place (or river, mountain, etc.) beginning with the last letter of the first named place. Maps were allowed for reference and, of course, the highway signs of places just passed. When that game became tiresome, we rested a while.

Lunch stops were invariably in a rest area (if we were on I-70) or better still we found a state park or a city park in a little town. It was in one of these out-of-the-way picnic spots that we encountered a sheriff also having a "break". A real-life sheriff in uniform was a highlight of the day for our 4-year-old Larry! Cross-country driving in the 50's was pre-interstate, though we had divided highways. As kids grew into older elementary grades, they could plan our routes to navigate us to the park where we would spend the night. We were always tent campers, graduating from one small tent to one large tent and on one of our last family trips to New England to two hammocks, one 2-man and a third one. By that time, we had a daughter-in-law.

I remember some nights of "worry" for me. In Maine, I was concerned about the bears. Being animals with poor eyesight and a reputation for being not too smart I just trusted that one would not bump into a hammock. Camping in the West we were always very careful to have our food cached high in the trees or safely in the car. One night in the Tetons I was alone with the girls; the boys were off "backpacking". Snuggling into my sleeping bag I remembered I had left our cooler out! At the same time, I heard heavy breathing outside the tent. I stopped breathing while Mr. Bear pried open our cooler...I thought to myself: "Be really quiet and let him pilfer our food"!

Our kids were not always angelic and quiet. The noise level sometimes became just too distracting. What to do? The PD spoke with authority, a time to roll down all the windows and shout as loud as each one could until I called time...Time was called when Daddy and I could no longer take this shouting, but kids were quiet afterwards for a time. Another devious "time-passer" was to be absolutely quiet for what each one thought to be a mile (or if that was not long enough for silence, I said two miles), though not too long my goal was accomplished. Larry figured out somehow that he could count telephone posts and know it was a mile.

As the kids grew each one brought new ideas for activities

in the car for the times, we had to cross many miles between rest stops. Katie would make up stories for the youngest, Sara. With Sara's head in her lap, she would tell a story while tracing a finger around on her face.

I recently found several sheets of legal-size yellow paper on which Daddy had listed every single year's vacation. I have a scrapbook on many of these trips, copies of the songs we made up with details of the adventure. But best of all I have many memories and could write a book on the advantages of family trips, visits to our National Parks, camping and city visits. I tried to incorporate times in the important cities each trip. This necessitated "city suitcases" along with our duffels.

Vanderbilt Graduation of Bridget McNeil, 1999

Granddaughter Bridget's wedding, with Joe and Kay McNeil, Outer Banks, NC, 2003

Reflections from The Sea

Here we were, two landlubbers yearning to sail the ocean blue with our family. It was the summer of 1975 and we were boarding our flight to the British Virgin Islands, the port of Roadtown, Tortola, to charter a sailboat.

I had done my only sailing on Creve Coeur Lake in a C-scow with Sea Scout Bill, in whom I had a special interest; he being a Senior in high school and I, a Junior. Neil's experience was as skipper of a Sea Explorer Post, sailing on Carlyle Lake and Alton Lake. We were to learn to sail while on our chartered 39' sailing yacht.

Aboard this first cruise we had son Larry, his wife, Karen, our eldest daughter, Linda, and youngest, Sara. Our captain and teacher was Alan, from South Africa. He was sailing around the world and lost his mast. Stranded in Tortola while his ship was being repaired, he obtained a job aboard charter yachts. It was a golden opportunity for us. He found our family quite compatible. His only *caveat* was that we NEVER mention politics of South Africa.

Neil was an eager, highly-motivated student. Larry, (as he was called until he was 50 years of age) and Linda were excellent sailors by the end of the 10 days. Sara learned that when she did not "listen" to us about the sun in the tropics she would have an EXTREME case of sunburn, never to be forgotten.

I managed the galley (not much different than camping). Alan and our family became good friends, good sailors, and Neil bought a boat the last night we were on shore with the owner of the "Moorings", the first charter service in the BVI. This cruise was the first of about fourteen. The stories of those years could be a Memoir of book length.

Here I only share some reflections from the sea voyages. I learned that when we first arrive there is no time to reflect, or even sit down and relax. Shopping for supplies, equipping the galley, stowing our gear, helping our crew, ofttimes inexperienced, to be comfortable. We had to concentrate on charting our courses, getting our "sea-legs". Hoisting the main, we could set sail.

We had time then, to fall under the spell of sun-splashed waves, the star-studded nights. Time to read, time for thoughts. We did not know what treasures the dawn of each new day might hold. We did not know what obstacles each day might bring. What weather? What winds or no winds? A secure mooring or one that I felt a need to watch half the night?

BVI Sail 1996

Snorkeling was my favorite activity other than just swimming in quiet waters of an anchorage. With a snorkel and mask the undersea world and here the complexities of the coral reef were revealed. I am saddened to read that coral reefs are dying in many areas world-wide. As the temperature of the sea rises because of heat generated from shipping, recreation and industry, animals creating the reefs succumb to ever so small changes in their environment. But forty years ago, I relished carrying my water-proof book of fish identification with me to help me know the fish NOT to encounter and the names of the friendly fish and other sea-life.

I collected many and varied shells from many and varied beaches. I called up images of the animals that created the shells. The whelk with delicate shadings of color spiraling upward to a point reminded me of Sandy Cay, a tiny island surrounded by sand. We need to attain times of alone-ness, of solitude in this too-busy world. It seems increasingly hard to find any time of stillness and quiet, especially in the urban life where I live. I give credit to Charles Morgan as he describes this need of solitude as "the stilling of the soul within the activities of the mind and body so that it might be still as the axis of a revolving wheel is still".

It was often the end of the first week of a 2–3-week cruise when Captain Stueck felt totally relaxed and had the time to just watch the pelicans dive. We had the confidence to relax under sail, to get on the "Cadillac Tack" as Linda called the long reach. In these many years we explored the British Virgin Island, the American Virgins, and even sailed down to Martinique and St. Lucia.

We explored the Islands ashore, picked mangos along the beaches, attended church, became acquainted with some of the natives as we had hired a captain the first year, we owned our own boat. He was the first black captain for the Moorings and taught us so much, as he had been sailing these waters since a boy. We enjoyed our "local" family friend many years.

Alas, we saw our small town on Tortola, with only one paved road, and one vendor on the beach selling limes he kept cool in the sand at his special spot, and electricity just a few hours a day flourish into a commercial town with even a cruise ship coming in the last couple of years we were there. With such progress came a time when we could not leave our dinghy and our motor unattended and needed an escort back to our boat after dinner ashore.

Those years aboard *Ceilidh* were very good years, cherished by all of our family for three generations. Usually through 46 years of marriage with my captain, Neil, I was the reluctant dragon on new adventures. But I trudged along, came to relish every new experience. He taught me well as I have ventured forth alone on new trails in the mountains and more waves on other seas.

The Importance of the Garden

One early morning my dear friend, Betty, called, "good morning", she greeted me, "I am going to sign up for training to be a Guide at the Garden. Want to come along, too"? I asked for the particulars, time, length, expectations of being a Guide and almost on the spot agreed. I had just shed much responsibility in Scouting and felt it would be fun to get involved in something else. Little did I know that morning conversation would lead to thirty years or more into a field that I had considered as an undergraduate.

Strolling around the Botanical Garden on several visits this year I recall some special tours and classes under my guidance. Variety in topics and students gave me many challenges. Being assigned a tour with students from the Missouri School for the Blind I called the teacher, introduced myself and asked: "What are you studying in the class? What would you like your boys and girls to gain from this field trip"? She replied quickly: "We do NOT want to visit the Garden for the Visually Handicapped. I want a regular tour just to help the kids to see the Garden! Some of the students can see light and dark and they will buddy up with those that have no sight". Obviously, I would have to do some special preparation to help these kids see the garden.

I planned my excursion around trees and shrubs that have an abundance of parts to feel or smell. What fun I had with these objectives in mind. Class arrived on time. In the next hour I learned as much as the kids. Well-behaved and intent on learning,

MBG pins and name tags

these students were highly motivated, participating in every activity. Some from time to time made observations that I, with my sight, would not note. One foot off the sidewalk onto grass, one child stopped immediately knowing she was on a different footing. Are we so sensitive with sight? Not one hesitated to feel the bark of a tree, a bud on a bush. Sighted students, I have learned, often are hesitant when he or she can see the part of a plant in question.

Another time I had a group of adults, scientists visiting from Russia. An interpreter began speaking along with me just as interpreters do at the United Nations, on TV, in interviews. Hearing my voice in one ear and his Russian in another I could not handle. Politely, I asked: "May I say a bit about a particular plant and, then pause, and you can translate"? He complied and the tour went on happily. The men were quite interested and asked questions as we strolled along. I wondered what he was saying. He could have been talking about me! At the end of the tour one asked: "Where can we purchase Cactus seeds"? That was a question I had never been asked. How many gardeners do I know who plant cactus seeds? Collectors of Desert plants usually just buy these exotic specimens. I promised I would get an answer promptly and send to him. I suspected why they were interested in buying seeds of the Cactus. None of this family grow in the New World.

Four-year-old classes came to the Garden in droves, or so it seemed, in the spring. A class could walk over from nearby schools all holding onto a rope to keep the group "in tow" literally. Some guides made it quite clear that a tour with preschools was just "baby sitting" and managed to not have preschoolers scheduled. Talking with a friend of mine who teaches that age, I quickly could design activities to heighten their observations and enjoyment of the Missouri Botanical Garden. There were clouds floating in a blue sky, there were many different colors of green in leaves. "Feel these 'lamb's ear' leaves", I suggested. "How do they feel? What do you know that feels like these"? There can be vocabulary in every activity. It was part of their school curricula.

A great deal more challenging were 8th grade students

from the Inner City of St. Louis. In one class (not a tour) we were discussing the cell structure of plants. A handsome young man threw down his pencil, leaned back in the chair saying: "Why do we have to spend time learning about cells"? That question from a boy probably going on 15 did set me to wondering "Why?" too.

Maurita and Linda in Antwerp, 1996

Yampa and Green River Rafting trip, 1996

In South Africa with Ricki O'Mara

Big Five Club

This certifies that

Maurita Stueck

has successfully tracked down
Africa's Big Five at MalaMala
Lion, Cape Buffalo, Rhinoceros,
Leopard and Elephant

Date _25 September '99_
Manager _Hilla Boshuizen_
Ranger _Rowan Smelton_   MalaMala:
Jonathan Wells

Totes for Identity in Queues

Women have always carried bags; women around the world carry bags to markets wherever they live. Bags tell a lot about the carrier. As we queue up, forming a line at the checkout counter or the Dairy Queen, we seem to have bags that identify us. One; might say "The Science center" or "Pacific Place" or "Webster Hills United Methodist Church". Some years ago, I was to meet a person I did not know in the railroad station in Lyons, France. I said: "I will meet you under the clock and I will carry a bag from "the St. Louis Art Museum".

My newest tote is printed "I Love History", an advertisement for the Missouri History Museum. And I do love history, especially St. Louis history. I trace this interest kindled to my father. He did not intentionally set out to spark my interest. As we casually drove around on errands, jaunts to forest Park, the Zoo, he just told me stories about his growing up in St. Louis. A very early one I remember was a drive down to the Mississippi riverfront during a season of high water. What impressed me most was "Hooverville", squatters in corrugated tin-roofed shelters where people were living. He did not say any more. No doubt they were the "homeless" of the Great Depression. The area was on the riverfront, cobblestoned as it is today and dubbed "Hooverville" after the then-President Hoover, who bore the blame of the citizens for the Depression.

I recall feeling right at home when I volunteered in a classroom at Clark Elementary school near Soldan. That was my father's old neighborhood and High School.

Further interest in St. Louis history stemmed curiously from one of my most interesting volunteer positions, co-chair of "St. Louis Scene", one of many projects of the Volunteers for the St. Louis Symphony about 30 years ago. As volunteers, we mounted Events to entertain most usually spouses of corporate men coming to St. Louis for various meetings and conventions. It was a most satisfying operation employing skills I had and could put to work. We had to research, write the scripts for the city tours, train the guides, contract for luncheons, all the parts of operating any small business. It was my first introduction in marketing, planning tours and handling groups of women. I found it quite satisfying to have our participants brag about St. Louis, telling me: "St. Louis is the best kept secret".

The challenge part was learning more about St. Louis history and sharing with not only the guides whom we recruited but with so many groups of out-of-towners. While facing my audience, I became quite adept at guiding the bus driver, although he had a tour itinerary. After perhaps six years, the number of women accompanying their husbands to conventions decreased as the economy slacked a bit. Sadly, our business slacked off too and the next chairs gave up the St. Louis Scene. Volunteering in a position became almost a part-time job, working as many hours as an employee. We had to act as professionals because whole groups were depending on us for a day at their conventions.

After my very good friend, with whom I had co-chaired, and I had retired, we were asked several times to plan a tour for a particular group. One of these tied in with history of the Salem-in-Ladue Methodist church. We traced and toured the history of this congregation now in its third or fourth location. It was a German Methodist church still standing near the river, a Methodist church in St. Louis before Methodism had a conference in Missouri. Another tour was designed for incoming clergy to become acquainted with the whole St. Louis area and its various neighborhoods and places just to be better acquainted with St. Louis outside of the neighborhoods they served. That is when I learned where the "Ladies of the Night" served.

For a while after that I was employed by a "professional" entrepreneur doing the same sort of "travel" tours. But that too ended because of a lack of business. I know of no business in operation now that plans events for incoming groups. If there is, volunteers would not be doing the job. The employees would be professional. Without exception my most interesting challenging and worthy volunteer jobs are now all paid professionals.

My interest is sustained and broadened with travel that I have done to a great extent in the last twenty years. History fascinates; only the teaching often does not. And now my memory needs to be sharpened.

Linda and Maurita in India

Travel Business

The travel business is big business. I ponder often as brochures some to be classified as magazine-size come into my mailbox. Cruising on rivers of the world, "Road Scholars" adventuring to many countries of the world, hiking trips, biking trips, trips for elders, trips for families. I ponder and muse, "Why do folks travel"?

My family teases their Daddy, my husband, believing that he has a gene in his DNA specifically to travel, inheriting it from his Maternal Grandmother. It was passed on to his Mother and his Aunt Lil. He had been raised by these women who were traveling in the days c. 1920 when one went abroad by ship, carrying a steamer trunk!

My husband retired at age 58 so that he could travel the worlds beyond the borders of our country. As our family was growing, we only stayed in the USA. Retirement and years with the kids all away from home gave us the opportunity to study history and cultures in other parts of the world. Some adventures were "winners", some were just O.K. but I do not recall any "losers".

Our first trip overseas was to be present at a Tattoo which is a part of the Highland Games in Scotland. Here we were to be immersed in one of the big events in Scotland. We learned quickly that Scots never push through a crowd like we Americans. They simply queue up and everyone moves right along. It was quite a joyous occasion with enthusiastic clans attired in traditional costumes kilts of every color and description, Bagpipe bands massed and playing the traditional music that was familiar to us from the Highland Games we had each year in Estes Park where we spend summers.

Motoring north from Edinburgh we stopped one evening at an Inn. We felt quite out in the country and found the dining delightful as we had conversation with the local folks living nearby. We assumed in the neighborhood. Dinner was most enjoyable as we conversed with them. Scottish hospitality was evi-

dent. After dinner we adjourned as was the custom in such an Inn to the parlors, the ladies in one, the gentleman another. One lady turned to me and asked: "Are you traveling alone with your husband"? Indeed, a curious question. "Did we need a chaperone"? I simply replied: "Yes". I paused, not quite knowing what else I might add. She explained: "I asked because we have never met an American who was not in a group". Tour busses had traveled this route. Obviously.

Continuing our meandering north, another day we were nearing our destination but stopped for a bite of lunch at the Ceilidh Inn. There we got to talking with two women sitting in a booth across from our table. Both were knitting furiously in what we call a "fair Isle" pattern, classic one like we buy at home. Here they were hand knitting these lovely sweaters in which we find a label "hand knitted". Then we asked about the name of this restaurant, "Ceilidh Inn". They explained that a Ceilidh is a gathering for fun and frolic, not any holiday just song and maybe dancing. "Just a gathering", they said. Several years later we named a sailing yacht we had moored in the British Virgin Islands. Indeed, it was a gathering for our family and friends for all the years we sailed there.

I would highlight another trip I had after Neil passed away. He had taught me so much about the joys of travel. I felt comfortable going now with friends providing she would like the same kind of travel—no shopping—not 5-star but with a dimension of learning and adventure in exotic places.

Traveling Shoppers

I stepped into the so-called Blue Mosque in Istanbul, Turkey, and audibly gasped at its beauty, its exquisite walls totally blue tiles, hence its name. Built in the 1600's it stands as a must-see attraction with its six minarets on any guided tour of the city. I was feeling so fortunate to behold this masterpiece when I heard a bit of grumbling behind me from a fellow traveler, "I certainly hope we don't spend too long here as I do want time to shop in this Bazaar"!

I recalled another time on a trip with the Missouri Botanical Garden highlighting the Gardens of China. My daughter, Katie, was my companion this time. Our bus took us to the Botanical Garden in Shanghai and let us be on our own to explore these Gardens. This would be a delight as we both were much interested in flora. Katie and I returned to the designated *rendezvous* to find no one. Checking our watches, we saw we were early. Looking around a bit we saw no one. Before I became panicky our leader (Intrav travel "rep" had been with us the whole trip from St. Louis.) found us and simply told us "the group" had decided we were too long at the Garden and had gone on to shop. Katie stamped her foot and said rather curtly: "I came on this trip to see the Gardens of China and Shanghai is important. It was not too long". The guide told us how to get back to our hotel, a short walking distance away. Katie and I found a delightful restaurant in a nearby skyscraper to eat by ourselves. "All's well that ends well"as we often would say in such times. I learned subsequently that several in our group had made connections for shopping at specific places before they left St. Louis. There are varying motivations to travel. They had little interest in gardens!

Returning from another trip it was necessary to go through customs, of course. At this juncture in traveling, one goes and does as a customs officer directs. In traveling with a group, the process varies a bit from being just an individual. On one trip (only one thankfully) a plan was devised whereby the huge tax levied on one huge shopper was to be shared by each of us! I was as confused then as I am now, except to say each of us was not taxed for the overage of one. She had shopped and shopped and shopped. She should have used a calculator as she shopped! Another time I recall, the shoppers were dismayed because on a Sunday all the shops were closed. Such grumbling on this tour in Italy! "You mean we just have to walk about this town"? became the cry of the "shoppers".

My husband enjoyed shopping, especially if we were in a country where bargaining was THE way in the marketplace. I did not like bargaining at all and would often just wander off by myself leaving him to his game. One time I really benefitted. Belonging to an investors syndicate, Neil, my husband, bargained his way to bring a personalized cartouche from Egypt for each wife. Neil established his connection and made all the purchases. He was pleased with his bargaining. I had no way of knowing how much success he had but I do know I treasure my gift to this day as do the other wives I still see.

Maurita hiking with a llama

I have many other purchases Neil made for me, as I often was with him or he found a fellow traveler with knowledge he needed. His shopping was not in any way browsing or spur-of-the-moment, but to be useful treasures from our trips, all of which I thoroughly enjoy. They range from bracelets to paintings, crystal to carpets. Each represents a product of a country. Only the carpets were bought because the tour guide took us to the factory. No doubt his cousin's business or he received a commission from the dealer.

January 21, 2016

Westward Ho!

Planning our next family vacation every year was a kind of hobby with my husband who had a very serious case of Travellaria. Growing up in a household in which a maiden aunt traveled the world, he really inherited his wanderlust. Fortunately, his plans always fit our budget. This dictated that we traveled by car, that we had only two weeks of vacation, and that children always went with us.

Friends suggested that our two families meet in Yosemite, California the summer of 1957 and camp in Tuwulome Meadows where they were well-acquainted, as the mother, Betty, was a native of California. In a matter of days, the plans were being shaped by two men.

At this point in time, I was about thirty-eight and four children were about ages 1, 4, 6, and 9. Having never been west of Denver I thought California was much too far to drive, camp in the mountains with youngsters. The other family had the same ages and quantity of kids and had made this trip several vacations.

I began to make my case for not going. "Honey," I said, "don't you think it is a very long way to drive in just two weeks"? No response. "Perhaps, we ought to think about just going to Colorado". His father had a cabin near Pike's Peak and surely that would help my case. "But I have never been to the High Sierras and they are stunning," he replied. I rested my case for that session.

Deep inside I had some fear of this whole trip...distance, highway driving anxiety, kids getting sick, weather, etc. No one else was on my team, least of all, Aunt Lil and Nana, grandmother and maiden aunt who had volunteered to keep the one-year-old we would leave behind. Nana had been to Yosemite Valley in 1915, Aunt Lil had walked the Oregon coast in 1921. Of course, we should take this trip. I resigned and vowed to be a happy traveler my first trip across our far West.

We made preparation; packed up our blue Station Wagon inside and on top, procured maps from AAA and headed out Highway 66. We moteled at night, picnicked for lunch in parks of small towns, made up games, sang. The three abreast in the back seat, were happy travelers for the most part. The advantage of "road trips" was that we could make stops and run awhile when the energy ran too high in the car.

The real adventure began when we arrived in the Meadows to camp near the Nellums family that had arrived some time before us. Bob, Betty, Mary, Bobby and Rich were all there to help us unload and set up. Our families had camped many weekends together for several years. All of us knew the routines.

Hiking in the Rocky Mountains, 2010

With tent up, gear stowed, kitchen set up we went over to their site to relax a bit. Turning around what should I see but a bear picking up our "Summer Kitchen", a.k.a. an Army footlocker, and waltzing down the trail with it! Noise, banging on any handy item were keys to scaring the bear who dropped our equipment. First adventure completed.

Hike the next day up to Lake Elizabeth, one of many serene jewels nestled in these mountains. Only a short walk, just enough for our 5-year-old. Lunch, dipping into the cold lake, warmed by the sun on our shoulders we lazed through time. Turning back down to our camp, Katie soon was tired. Before the days of packs to carry kids, she completed our walk sideways on my back. Not the "Fireman's Carry" on shoulders, but Saddleback, sideways on my lower back. No problem, my life-saving training came into good use.

It was on this trip that I did my first "mountaineering" on what was almost like the "bunny" slopes for skiers, but the highest I had ever gone. Perhaps, it was only 400' feet above the 9000' at which we camped. Nevertheless, Lempert Dome, a large dome of gray granite was imposing and the Nellums said: "You just have to climb up there while you are here in the Meadows". I was not sure just "why" but did as I was bid. Betty firmly insisted: "Maurita, you take one child so you can have a free hand and Neil, you take the other to keep one free hand. Katie will stay with us in camp". That decided, we took off as directed. I was in my tennis shoes as Boots had not become a part of my outdoor wardrobe. Where had I ever needed boots walking around city parks or even Missouri outstate?

Starting up with granite footing underneath, Linda's hand held tightly in mine, it was easy walking. Soon I suggested to Linda: "Let's sit down here a minute and rest a bit". What I really could have said was: "Let's stop here a minute while Mother figures out where to put my foot next..." And so Linda and I progressed, Daddy following, with Larry stopping more and more frequently to find the best footing. Someday I must ask Betty just how high this dome is and how far did we go. I'm certain it was not a big hike by any means. But it was my first. My appetite was whetted, as I have done miles in the mountains of Colorado.

Memories tumble into place as I write. Another day was a birthday celebration for Bobby, who was about seven. Being skilled in outdoor cooking, I constructed a reflector oven of a corrugated box, lined with aluminum foil to bake a cake in front of the open fire. It was baking well and looked about finished when the box began to smoke, as so often happens before flames erupt. This called for quick action: out with the cake, on with the water bucket kept nearby for just such a purpose. Cheers went up, no harm done to the cake and the celebration could continue. We had all comforts we needed in the backcountry, many more than our forbearers had. Our city friends did think we were a bit wacky to, first, take our kids on vacations, and, secondly, cook, even cook with wood, while on vacation. Today our family heartily approves of all the camping and road trips we did roaming into all the lower forty-eight except for North Dakota. How fortunate my family was to have a Daddy leading us to places I would never have ventured.

April 22, 2011

Travels on The Mother Road

Route 66 has been brought into the 21st century, restored by videos, turn-by-turn driving instructions, known to my grandchildren through songs of Woodie Guthrie and Nat King Cole recorded again. Known as the Mother Road by historians, it is now on the "Bucket List" for many tourists. Tour buses drive into former restaurants and inns along Route 66 delighting the old (or new) owners of the establishments. Business has picked up through Arizona, Nevada, and points west for purchase of souvenirs, T shirts, and mugs.

The highway, first opened in 1926 though not paved entirely for many years after that, heralded a new way of travel. For the first time, families could own and drive the family car all the way to the west coast. The gateway to Los Angeles started in Chicago, came through St. Louis, still the largest city it goes through between here and Los Angeles. Travels on the road weave in and out for most of my own life.

In 2000 I remarried and lived in southern California for several winters. My husband, Joe, had lived in Redlands, California, and we liked nothing better than to explore our environs. He had much knowledge to share with me.

Cajon (say Cahone) Pass was often on our trail as it was the gateway to Los Angeles, San Diego, Palm Springs, Palm Desert, all places we liked to visit. It was a natural pass used for centuries by Native Americans, Spanish explorers, and the emigrants from the East driving their private cars.

One sunny Sunday afternoon, I perched on a rock outcropping overlooking a highway coming around a bend far below me. It was a piece of historic Route 66 now skirting the new highway over Cajon Pass. I thought of my grandparents, emigrating from St. Louis, driving to Santa Ana, California in 1925. Of course, they had navigated right along the road still visible there below me. My, how small it seemed compared to our new highway. I could not even imagine what a trip that must have been!

"66" was our only route to travel southwest through Missouri until I-44 was built in the 1950's. My travel to Missouri School of Mines at Rolla, Mo. for party weekends with Neil (my future husband) was driving on this road, still quite nicely paved but only two narrow lanes. Our cars were obviously not as wide as in 2011.

Travels with Joe took me over several stretches of the Mother Road in 2000–2004. We drove from California to Colorado, Missouri, and Ohio in the several years of our marriage. Traveling with the family in our working years, I did not often have the time to explore off the beaten path, but with no children, no work, Joe and I had time to take by-ways as we crossed the country. Here we found old "66" and dusty, quaint stops. One time we did take Highway 66 to avoid a new interstate.

Approaching Highway 15 between Las Vegas and Los Angeles on a Sunday afternoon, Joe suggested we not go that way because of worse-than-usual traffic coming south from Las Vegas. Usually, traffic was too much for me in all parts of southern California, so any other way was fine with me.

East of Victorville we took "66" all the way into San Bernardino. It was quiet, no traffic, rest-stops, few settlements, and very good road. An easy drive so I could take the wheel!

The historic route is well-marked through St. Louis. I drive it frequently where it is called Chippewa, or Watson Road. When we first moved to Webster Groves in 1950 our best route to downtown was "66", then Chippewa to 12th Street. Later, we called "66" Watson Road.

Ted Drewes is a noted hang-out on Chippewa. It was a bit far for our kids in High School, but Sara did go there a lot when she was in College.

Just "Google" Route 66 and you can have hours scrolling through all the links.

February 2, 2012, Groundhog Day

Utah Winter Exploration

I find comfort in living in my Dogwood Cottage, a single scrawny dogwood on the patio giving the name. It is dubbed a cottage because it is too small to be called a house. It has small nooks of storage, not much light. Even though there are large windows, it is tucked in below a nearby large apartment building and overshadowed by several large Maple trees. Daughter Katie recently on a short visit to St. Louis observed: "Mother, everything in your home is so old"! To this I readily replied: "And so is the owner"! We giggled. I took no offense.

I do live with pictures, objects, a few knick-knacks that reflect where I have been, where I have traveled, interests I have. These items trigger most memories of pleasant times and places. One is a small painting that I bought on a ski trip to Park City, Utah a few years ago. My husband, Joe, was a passionate skier and readily accepted an invitation to go with his best "ski buddy" on an expedition with the Santa Monica ski club. Of course, I went along, happy for any trip with Joe and quite able to fend for myself while the skiers were out. I only did cross-country skiing; real skiers don't do this, saying: "It is too strenuous". I think it is because it is not exciting, exhilarating and has no mystique around the sport.

Nevertheless, I looked forward to being with the group and felt I could probably find other wives no longer skiing. On arrival Joe quickly became acquainted with all the group. They had a common language and need talk of nothing else but which slope? Condition of snow? And how high each might go.

I wanted to do some snow shoeing, a new experience that would be for me. The yellow pages led me to find a reservation for just such an excursion the next morning. This turned into being a private lesson with a young instructor faced with what prospect he knew not. He learned right away I was a novice. (I did not mention I had only been two times.) He took me to a place with a dirt road leading off the asphalt, a trail without much snow and flat. It looked simple and uninteresting. I realized he had to "test" me a bit. One does not take an 78-year-old lady into the wilderness without knowing something about her physical condition. I passed the first run with flying colors. Piled back into the car and went to level two. There was enough snow to make it prettier and more like an adventure. I made a date with him to go again tomorrow.

Just as I knew I could, I met another non-skier wife to come along the next morning. Again, we were the only two customers. Snow shoeing is not popular in Park City. This day was simply an incredibly quiet walk through a deep Aspen forest. A narrow trail he had broken for us just barely wide enough for us to glide through between the trees. We were in a rather extensive forest of Aspen. Surely there were multiple clones and several generations of trees. Our excursion was longer. Hot cocoa and cookies were brought for hand-warmers and nourishment. Knowing that our husbands were on the ski slopes, we were guided out of the forest into a clearing, the ski slope down which our skiers would come. In just a few minutes here they came swooshing by, too intent to even give a side-ways glance. My thought was: those guys do not get to wend their way slowly through the Aspens, enjoying the quiet that snowfall gives to the forest. I have never had the opportunity to downhill ski, have enjoyed walking on my cross-country skis. I have no "wish-I-had" feelings.

I do not travel to "shop" as I have noticed some do with whom I have traveled. I usually buy a "treasure" from a trip. This 5x7 photograph of Aspens in Snow is just such a memento: small enough to travel in my luggage, small enough to find a place on a wall. The companion picture is a wolf in the forest. When I walk by on my way down the hall I may have a glance, a pause, and I can feel the quiet of the forest. I may even feel the warmth of the Cocoa-stop in Utah.

Maurita and Katie in China

Maurita, Katie & Dr. Peter Raven in China

Maurita and Katie in China

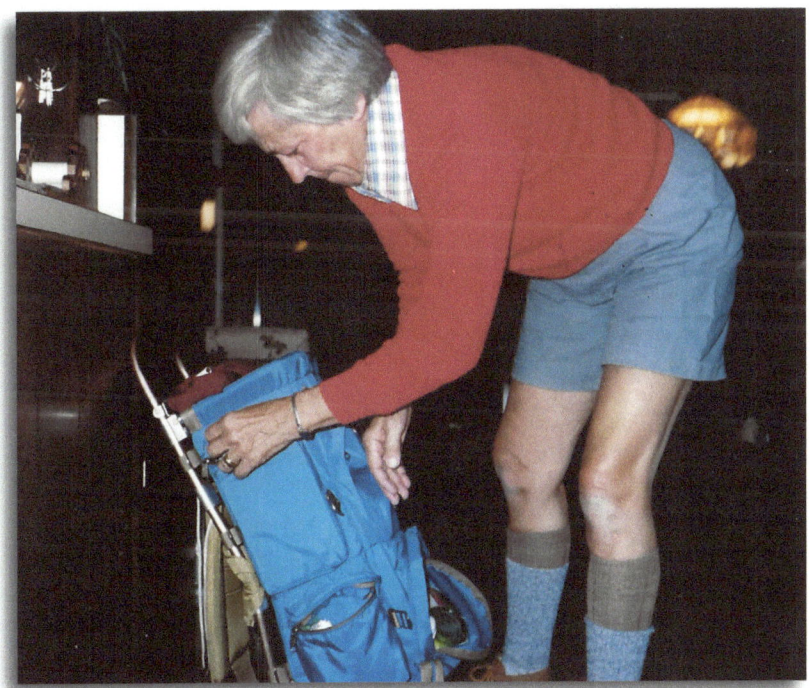
Preparing to Hike with John Mahan, 1986

Linda and Katie with Maurita at Levenworth, WA—Sleeping Lady Resort where Laura McNeil was working

Joe Birch and Maurita hiking Arches, 1997

CHAPTER FIVE
Philosophies

Methodist church pins

My purpose of writing is to share my life with others of two or three generations. I have outlived all my family members of the past two generations. The perspective I have of family ties is one that I want to share. Each dawn I receive is a gift that can bring feelings of much gratitude. Some days I have more energy than others. Not every day is very productive. My balance is only fair. I concentrate on pushing away unhappy thoughts. I do not let depression set in.

Only Change is Constant

His head down, his fingers moving swiftly across a palm-size electronic device, he was near walking into me. "Excuse me please", I cautioned. He moved aside, never looking up. I continued to navigate with some discomfort through the crowded concourse. With no further difficulty, I arrived at the Delta gate and settled down for an hour's wait until I could board my flight to Cincinnati, Ohio. The Southeastern branch of my family was gathering for Thanksgiving. As I looked around at the assembled travelers, memories swirled around in my head, an avalanche of memories over the last 40 years. I quickly realized change was the one constancy!

No longer were travelers dressed nicely, as he or she looked forward to meeting family or friend, fiancé, or employer. No longer concerned about being in public or even a modicum of modesty. Flip-flops, bare feet, shorts shorter than swimsuits, T-shirts, "sweats" were all in fashion. Women did not have skirts (unless ethnic) or suits. There were two young men in suits that I knew to be having a business meeting tomorrow in Cincinnati. I could not help overhearing all the arrangements.

Two toddlers entertained me as they crawled around and over the chairs. I was really watching them more closely than their parent, who was deftly fingering her device. A third child, about seven, was wired to her own pink e-device.

One elderly man was just sitting. I held a book, the pages of which I had to turn. There were several others reading books. This was not a generational activity, as some children and some 30-somethings were prepared to turn pages.

Once boarded, we were admonished to listen to the Attendant giving pertinent information about his aircraft. If not listening, most were quiet. When it was time that electrical devices could be turned on, all the laptops, cell phones, I-pads, etc. popped out.

I enjoyed the images of many other flights that kept popping up. There was a flight to Denver over the Christmas holidays one year. I was the only one on that flight not wearing ski clothes, nor did I have my family with me. When my family traveled, we had road trips as our budget could not provide for flying. When laptops first came on the market, that was the electronic toy EVERYONE had.

On my most recent overseas flight, we still had some nice amenities: a hot towel in the morning after an all-night flight, complimentary juice, and water every several hours, blankets, pillow, conversant attendants as they are not all busy all night and I like to walk around. Flights can be longer now. In November 2014, we had a non-stop flight from St. Louis to Cincinnati now…No longer does TWA take us from St. Louis non-stop to many places. Change is constant in air travel.

One thing that has not changed is the exiting procedure when the plane lands. Of course, we are told to "Keep your seat belt fastened until we arrive at the gate". But the message "We have arrived" comes without any voice. Everyone gets up, madly creating the crowded aisles for five, ten minutes, maybe 15 minutes, before we really can de-board. The system does not change.

I may even see the day I will join the wheelchair brigade to go through security, off to the gate. It might have great appeal being pushed through the concourse with my attendant saying "Excuse me please". And I will have an e-book, so I will not have to carry a 771-page tome as I did this Christmas.

There is nothing permanent except change.

January 22, 2015

Observations of Important Events

Memoirs have become a popular style of writing in our 21st century. It is not a new style, but it seems that in recent years it has become a kind of writing that many prominent persons are producing. I am not prominent except in this newly formed group of friends who are speaking as Writers. I am dubbing myself a Memoirist at this time. The dictionary has several definitions. One I choose to use: "A report or record of an important event based on the writer's personal observation or knowledge".

I am reporting on my observations of a recent eight-month preparation for a wedding in my family. In this case, the bride is the daughter of one of my nephews. Her mother is a wedding consultant and organizer of weddings. In my position as merely a great-aunt I could observe without any input. My experience has been planning my own wedding seventy-two years ago and three weddings for my daughters. Two of these, incidentally, were six weeks apart one summer.

In reporting these weddings, I could not help but compare the rituals, the guest lists, the arrangements for the wedding, the preparation and the expectations of family, the bride and groom and the mores and folkways of the times. What changes have been wrought over the years. Just a few of the many in both generations 1940's (and the 70's my daughters). The wedding event was the *raison d'être*, the culmination of the planning. Everyone received an invitation to the wedding. However, we had a reception in every case and the guests invited to the reception found a small card in the invitation. Fast forward, everyone was invited to a sit-down dinner. Therefore, no one, a mere friend or relative, did not receive an invitation to the wedding. The party and dancing the night away seemed to be the *raison d'être*, wedding almost a minor part of the event.

Gifts were a part of the 40's, and the seventies as now. Guest registry is a new way of the bride receiving gifts they want, even to put money into a Fund for the couple's wedding trip. This idea was new to me, but obviously not to the later generation. I have found it to be the custom in European countries not for a wedding trip but to help set up housekeeping. Past generations did not set up housekeeping and live together. Some did in the seventies, but not as it seems to me "everyone" does. In my experience a few years ago as a wedding coordinator at church all of our weddings gave only one address. Of course, in earlier times it was definitely the custom to write thank you notes for gifts. It seems not so important a courtesy nowadays. More and more it seems destination weddings, not in churches and not in one's "hometown". Cruise ships count on weddings "on board" for extra "revenue". Hence my observation that the ceremony, the marriage of two persons, is not the main part of the event.

But on to my observation of pregnancies today. Needless to say, the specialist of Ob-Gyn has grown and learned so much not even suspected 30, 40 or sixty years ago. But still we have so many infants born right here in our own county without prenatal care. Infant mortality is still a huge problem in many countries. In this report I am just an observer of changes over the generations. One, maternity clothes seem to be nonexistent. I do not know why. Is it being pregnant is a source of pride? Is pregnancy more important than early years? I recently was invited to a "Reveal" party. Doughnuts were ordered at the local bakery. Guests were invited to "come as you are" with little tykes and all the family to the Bowling Alley prepared to bowl. That morning I was delegated to go to the Bakery and pick up the doughnuts. This was the only preparation for the party of which I was aware.

When everyone had arrived at the Bowling Alley and were assembled and quiet the hostess called out to "hear this". The boxes of doughnuts tightly sealed were to be opened and reveal the color of icing that the baker had used. It's a Boy! Blue Icing! Whoops and cheers and three pregnant girls at the party quickly compared notes…All boys! I had much more fun observing the reveal party than any of the weddings!

And so decades lay ahead for these young parents and their offspring. More changes will come for them to observe. My imagination is not sufficient for me to even imagine what changes will be wrought. I know my grandchildren will adapt and adjust just as my generation has had to do. Today my generation is considered by some as "the Greatest Generation" but the issues today for our planet will be solved by another Great Generation.

2/11/18

Great Grandchildren 2019: Arlo Desmond, Ayla and Milo McCasi and Iris Desmond

Family Ties

In writing several times recently "my morning pages", I have touched on changes of family pathways. I have given more serious thought to families over several generations. Some stay in close touch. Some only at Christmas. From time to time, I have expressed to my children that I have prayed that they will stay in close touch after my passing. Of course, they say, "Of course we will", but I can see small cracks with the last granddaughter being married.

Beyond my immediate family with the loss of my sister two years ago, the extended family has already moved away, with one or two exceptions. However, at the same time, my niece is no longer so close to her two brothers. The fact that my sister and I stayed in St. Louis together after marriage made us closer. If either of us had moved, we may not have stayed in close touch. Other factors (family secrets) contributed to some of the fracturing of these family ties. I was blissfully unaware of some of these fractures in family ties. There were clues but things were never spoken.

Looking back, my maternal family had several reunions of the eight offspring of Mama O. My grandson, Wes, made a video of my father's 16mm home movies. That project helped keep us in touch for a while. Much of the family did stay around Little Rock, AR. From my perspective, it seemed they stayed in touch. However, living in St. Louis, I was never told when my uncle died but letters did arrive eventually. This created a "crack" in the family tie. A "Round Robin" letter was enjoyed for many years. The envelope circulated with relatives' letters of news. It stopped when time was not taken to pass it on to the next sibling on the list.

I consider the activities I can no longer do but at least I have my Rocky Mountain hiking sticks to help my walking now. I use two walking sticks when hiking in the mountains but around Mt. Pleasant, I would look too much of a hiker. Both sticks are safer and help avoid overuse of one shoulder. Now I find that my love of the natural world is right in my backyard. This morning I watched a butterfly visiting the crowns of my phlox. I thought now how much energy it takes a butterfly to find its food. Butterflies bring happiness to many people. I thought of how I could reignite my purpose in my almost century of living.

My purpose of writing is to share my life with others of two or three generations. I have outlived all my family members of the past two generations. The perspective I have of family ties is one that I want to share. Each dawn I receive is a gift that can bring feelings of much gratitude. Some days I have more energy than others. Not every day is very productive. My balance is only fair. I concentrate on pushing away unhappy thoughts. I do not let depression set in.

Ostner Reunion, 1948

Circumstances of careers, moves, marriages and deaths do pull children away. We drift away or we purposely decide not to keep in touch. Thinking about my father's family, circumstances prevented family in NY and CA from seeing each other often. I recall Aunt Aileen visiting a few times. My cousin, Elizabeth Chapin, from NY did visit me as an adult in W.V.

I have not put forth a great deal of effort in keeping in touch through correspondence and phone calls. It is partly my fault. Some families do break up. Classic case of Hatfields and McCoys.

Today the factors of where we live are not as relevant to staying in touch as a lack of commitment. The reasons to "hang in there" and stay in touch with family are known but not given a priority by many today. Families stay in touch only if the relatives want to maintain some connections. Now, I want to write to my cousin, John Lee, for news about my family.

Evolution in Education

It almost seems that study and changes in our primary and secondary education has been ongoing most of my memory. New methods, changes in curriculum, new groupings, new teaching techniques, books, and educational tools have evolved over the years. Articles and big issues facing our society today loom larger than ever. Reading this week, the lead article in *The Christian Science Monitor*, a well-respected weekly news magazine, highlights several schools across the country who are most innovative in "blending learning." Now there is some new language in the field of education. My mind's memory surfaced as I mused on changes, I have seen in my schooling c.1930's, my children c. 1950-60's in an urban community. It is important to note that urban and rural communities were quite variable in those years as they still are to a lesser extent, perhaps.

In my suburban St. Louis community, kindergarten was my starting point at five years of age. I walked to school two-thirds of a mile on city streets. The streets I had to cross are not near as big as I remember them! I stayed in the same complex of three buildings through ninth grade. Kindergarten was a lovely room, where all of one side of the large area was made of glass. I remember the sunlight streaming into that room, but not much else. Big change today for five-year-olds. All day kindergarten AND pre-K have come to be regarded as quite essential to child development. My children were in "Nursery Schools" but only if parents could afford this care. It had not yet been recognized by citizenry and legislatures as so essential in preparing children for schools. Today there are parents who are not in favor of early childhood education or money for states to fund public Pre-K. I was lucky to have had the kindergarten experience.

My elementary school education was quite progressive for the time. There were two "sections" in my first-through-sixth grade. We knew that two rows of us 20-25 kids were doing work that the other three rows were not doing, but I have no memory

Walking in flowers, Westcliff, CO

of why or did we talk about it. If my parents were aware of what "tracks", as this system would be called in today's parlance, nary a word was said at home. But in the middle of my second grade, we were put into third grade, thereby skipping a half year. This could be done easily as we have two classes in every grade, one starting in September, one in January. Same plan allowed me to spend only one semester in 5th grade. By then I was back on the same cycle as I started, just one year ahead of some of my classmates. I learned in a college class in Educational Psychology that this was known as a "double track", an innovation in its time. I expect some of the iPads, computers in kindergarten, a host of other innovative, creative uses of technology K-12 education will become commonplace in the future as "tracks" are today.

By sixth grade, we had three teachers and we passed from

room to room just as we would do in Junior High. Middle School in some areas is grouped with seventh and eighth; ninth goes to High School, a kick-back to 4-year high school. Changes today: students have many teachers in most High Schools, students in innovative schools do some on-line learning either at home or in the classroom frees the teacher from time teaching topics easily done online to having more time to help individual students or having group discussions.

We had some courses that have been in and out of favor as educators made more studies and had more or less money. We studied Civics (Social Science), we had only two years of math, now many states require four; we needed only two years of science and since STEM became very important those courses are now highly encouraged. Schools have computer labs, special science labs. There is far more emphasis on competition in Sports than we had. I have spoken with some Physical Education teachers who have expressed concern that there is too much emphasis on the Varsity sports and less on the mission and goals of Physical Education as "it was". One high-school Phys Ed teacher said: "Sports are taking over the Academics".

"We are putting Geography back in our curriculum", a teacher in a suburban school recently told me with a bit of pride and satisfaction. "Guess that is a good thing", I replied. "I have read that some High School graduates cannot name our states or find major countries on a map". Some say such facts can easily be "Googled", so why spend time in school?

If a great educational revolution is, in fact, on the horizon teachers will have more time to help students with personal skill building needed to cope with the ever-increasing complexity and technology in our world. Such a challenge it will be. Parents will have to give priority to teaching family values, cooperating with the schools, and making time for and with their children.

Mindfulness

I read many opinions on "How to be Mindful". How we need to slow down and stay present to lead us to a happier, less stressful life. Sounds a bit like "simplicity".

Notes I jotted down after surveying countless articles and the internet.

First, mindfulness is about putting down all the balls we juggle and enjoy monotasking.

Another is to keep a "gratitude journal" maybe not every day but perhaps 2-3 times a week. This might be an a.m. meditation or an evening devotion to have a concerted consistent intent to think and write down at least one thing for which you are grateful. This is more than a note or think about list. This would be a conscious thought of gratitude for a friendship or a book when needed. Write freely with no thought of grammar or spelling. Studies show that if you do this for a full three weeks it is said to boost your energy level and increase your vitality. This can help lessen symptoms of depression. Research is unclear but this can lead to a feeling of good health and improved kidney function. Those who kept a general diary did not get this good health. But only those who wrote specifically noting gratitude. From Robert Emmon's book *Gratitude Works*.

In reading through old mail and some new articles, essays on meditation, Buddhist theology and on through a wide range of topics; one of my findings resulted in a new name for "Pens". I find these point me to a new interest.

This is a new science of health and happiness. This is a mindfulness movement to help us manage our stress; breathing lessons to help us bring in a happier mood, deepen our sleep and have less anxiety.

My Country 'Tis of Thee

The "State of the World" in November 2011 is indeed woven with wars, poverty, and starvation in so many places. Values I have held dear for a lifetime are dissolving all around me in so many areas. There are currently groups from coast to coast testing our Constitutional amendments with "sit-ins", "sleep-ins", and a new movement of peaceable dissidents dubbed "Occupy Wall Street".

At the same time, I think of Egypt recovering from a Revolution, now preparing to create a new nation, a democracy with new constitution, legislatures crying for new attitudes in their society to mesh democratic practices with Islam, most of the population. Such tasks seem daunting.

But this morning, November 15, my Journal will reflect that patriotic spirit thrives in some, if not many, places. I attended a concert by a Brass Quintet founded by a retired military woman. Held at the Sheldon Concert Hall, an acoustically-perfect auditorium built in 1909, the audience attracted were the elders and elders plus of St. Louis. The generations that still revere our flag and all it has stood for these 250 years.

The babbling talk in the audience became perfectly quiet as the Color Guard marched forward, standing tall and straight as possible. Everyone stood and retired Veterans saluted. No talking as the flags were posted. These generations had been immersed in respect for the flag. I ponder: "Will my grandchildren live with such respect? Do they even now give much thought to our freedoms fought for"?

Civics is no longer taught in school. A 14-year-old said to me last summer, "I know we have picnics, hot dogs, and fireworks on the 4th of July, but why do we celebrate"? Who said, "Those who do not know history will repeat it"? An Elder.

I believe our country, with all the issues we face, still has freedoms that cannot be imagined by a host of people in the world. I have faith that we have the talents to save our planet from our own greedy selves.

The Way We Lived

The road traveled by women from 1960 to the present day (2011) has been researched in detail and compressed into a four-hundred-page book I have recently read. After hundreds of interviews and mini-biographies Gail Collins has woven a highly readable story of the dynamic changes for women in these years. I want to add a prologue from my own experiences. I was not quite 40 when her story begins; what was the status of my gender my first 40 years before 1960? And how did I feel at the time of the genesis of the "women's movement" that changed the world I had known?

As far back as I can recall, my mother programmed me to go to college so that I could support myself. I remember well that I had no goal to be married until after I had worked a while. As history evolved WWII brought changes to the way we lived long before Betty Friedan arrived on the scene in 1960. I finished college, supported myself, and after the war, got married.

Coming back home to be married I did not ever plan to go to work. I was of the generation and in the "middle class" who could afford not to work outside the home. I abruptly turned from "professional" to "volunteer" in the community, quickly leaning to domesticity. Workshops in cooking, learning to sew, reading up on interior design, entertaining, and becoming involved in church activities, League of Women Voters and AAUW. Soon we were parenting four children.

Never did I have the feeling of being a "desperate housewife". Sometimes through the ensuing years I felt I was not doing my part in this marriage, of feeling I was a "kept woman". My husband never felt I should work. He made it quite clear that I WAS certainly "doing my part" in our marriage. We had a clear division of the multitude of tasks around the home, parenting together, management of the finances, vacation plans. Today with only about 10% of married women not working outside the home, Fathers are expected to help a great deal more at home. The book referenced in the beginning of this essay suggests her findings do not find this to be true. Women working outside still do most of the housekeeping. Neil always was on hand to take over the kids so I could go to night meetings of AAUW, church circle and continuing education courses. And on "party" nights he helped clean up after the guests left, though I had the task of all the preparations except male tasks of "carving" and outdoor grill cooking. He did all the traditional "husband" tasks: home improvements, garage, cars, yard and garden heavy tasks.

From time to time through the years I felt some discrimination as a woman. I wanted a credit card in my name from American Express, the card of choice then for overseas travel. That was just before my first trip overseas with a daughter. Hmm, no way would that be issued in my name alone. That was in 1977. I just went without a credit card and used traveler's checks. Very soon thereafter it was suggested that women get credit cards in our name to establish our own "credit".

In the society in which we lived from 1940—1960 there were mores and folkways and laws we did not question. Abortion laws, segregated housing and schools in St. Louis, some religious discriminations. These barriers began to break down little by little.

When I was in West Virginia, below the Mason Dixon line, in 1945 the two Girl Scout leader's clubs (one African-American we called simply "black") and one white merged. A big step. A highly respected African-American member of the Board stepped up and said: "We do not need to discuss this issue, just do it". We did just that. There is not a social aspect of volunteers working in Girl Scouting; hence, our success, I think.

Perhaps, it was a myth, but I did believe in my "before 40" years that a man would always be able to negotiate more effectively buying a car or dealing with a garage mechanic. Neil did make major decisions though I always felt I did have input.

I was not an activist with those who "marched" nor was a I one of the flaming feminists. At times I felt their actions would backfire on their causes. I did not hesitate to have an interracial meeting at my home, to work with any one of color in community activity, to volunteer in St. Louis public schools with predominantly black kids and faculty though I often felt an outsider as indeed I was.

The road for women has widened far in my adult life. Two "bread-winners" now is almost a necessity. Curiously, the percentage of young women highly educated at prestigious schools in law, medicine, business, and engineering and, yes, even the clergy, though 50% in some cases recent studies show that after having children 25% may not continue to work. The issue of disparity of pay to the sexes has been an issue for most of the 20th century. Today Gail Collins** found that married women in the same job as single women may be paid less salary.

In my thinking, I regret women are still largely in traditional careers of nursing, teaching and fields of social work. Here they still are paid less than other professions, men are discouraged from those fields because of pay scale, and these positions often do not even garner as much respect as they used to.

Women have broken many barriers in the latter half of the 20th century for which I am grateful. An old Chinese proverb, now attributed to Mao, wisely states: "Women hold up half the sky". I do trust that my daughters, Granddaughters, and now a Great-Granddaughter will believe this and continue to help "break barriers" for women in our country and around the world.

**author of *When the World Changed*

April 26, 2011

Play, Then and Now

When I was about seven, I learned to walk in high heeled shoes, my mother's. At the same time, I was giggling over how funny the room looked when I put on her glasses. It was part of "dressing up". Except for the glasses I had many costumes with which to play at this creative, imaginative past time. The absolute all-time favorite creation was a dress, heavy with black beads of various sizes and shapes laid over a turquoise satin dress that I would describe as a "shift style", an authentic 1920's dress. Our "dress up" trunk had a complete wardrobe of "grown-up" cast-offs: pocketbooks, hats, gloves, shoes, coats, and sweaters. A fur neck piece was the *piece de resistance*. With these costumes we could imagine and play whole afternoons with one or two other girls. There could be tea parties, dances, and shows. It was often an intergenerational group as I had my little sister (six years younger), and her neighborhood playmates came with their big sisters. We could be indoors or outdoors, on the porch, in the basement or upstairs, imaginative play for our young girlhood years. We could play by ourselves, never bored on rainy or winter Saturdays.

Dressing up we made decisions, shared our goods, helped the younger ones to be a part of our play, were not bored, and were giving some thought to growing up. As a young teen in camp, this kind of play continued to another level dramatizing ballads for "campfires". We sang, we scoured our tents and the Craft center to find costumes as highwaymen (one ballad I recall), worked out the script, performed. We were developing inner resources, working together.

Board games or paper-and-pencil games were activities for "after-school" if it was raining and for family fun-nights. These remained popular all through my childhood through teens and young adult. My children played some of the same ones as Monopoly and many more than I had-Chutes and Ladders, Sorry, Checkers, card games too numerous to count. Parcheesi was played by my Mother and she with Grandchildren. It is still a favorite over four generations. Games at home parties were important entertainment when we were young married couples. No expense for this fun!

My husband made blocks that became a staple item in the playroom. I so regret giving them to the Nursery at church. I did not realize how fast years pass and we would have grandchildren to enjoy them.

The blocks were made from sycamore (never had splinters) in a myriad of shapes—triangles, squares, rectangles, arches, rounds—thus could be built up in many ways. There were so many that several boys and girls could be building at one time. I watched Crestwood Mall built and "the builder" (my son) took me around to all the stores he imagined. Bridges and streets could accommodate those little "Match box" cars. Imaginations were not limited by any commercialized blocks found today at "Toys R Us".

A new refrigerator arrived one day, a joy to me and necessary for our growing family. The box in which it came was put to the best use of most any toy that year. Residing in the basement playroom for as long as it could be taped together, the Box is still remembered by all the children. It served for many games, dramas, secrets, shelters, caves, Indian hide-outs—no end of uses four or five kids could find for the Box.

While Grandmother took care of the kids on "Mother's Day Out" she often supervised the building of a train made from shoeboxes. The train could be elaborate with buttons for wheels, but that was not necessary as cargo could be pulled about without wheels. Play, "just childish fun", or stimulating creativity, requiring that ideas be generated together, disputes to be settled by players.

Play, family activities, outdoor/natural world times growing up and parenting seem to have been an important part of my life and I trust an important part of the lives of my children who had the time to play and not be so very structured, organized, and supervised as the trend seems to be in the 21st century. Children and teens are victims of commercialization: electronic, "tech toys", and marketing.

PLAY was the focus of the lead story of the *Christian Sci-*

ence Monitor today addressing: "Why educators now see make believe, free time, and imagination as more than just childish fun". I found I was on the same page as the author!

January 26, 2012

Foodology

2013 and it seems everyone is obsessed with food. The Missouri Botanical Garden is having a summer-long plan for food exhibits, the obesity of citizens of the country is becoming a national issue, articles on food abound, "talking heads" on tv ramble on with recipes for a family dinner in 30 minutes, the government has prepared a list of foods to consume every day, school lunch rooms tout nutritious lunches. And my son asks that I write about foods I ate when I was growing up. There is a topic about which I can muse!

As I recall there were some unspoken family principles that did revolve around food, but we were not reading and discussing every day; the country was not obsessing on diet, weight, calories, organic and gluten-free foods.

1. We ate breakfast. Hot cereals alternated in the winter: oatmeal, cream of wheat, Ralston, oatmeal, cream of wheat and Ralston. Corn Flakes was the only prepared cereal until my late girlhood when All-Bran and Wheaties were introduced.

2. We sat down to dinner as a family approximately 6:02 every night Tuesday—Friday when Daddy arrived from his working day. Saturday was flexible. Sunday was Dinner after church.

3. We ate what was "put before us" and all ate the same foods.

4. Daddy said "Grace" and the same grace every night.

We lived in an urban environment and raised no food. Therefore, we ate that which Mother could purchase at the Market. Occasionally, on summer afternoon excursions we could buy local produce from a roadside vendor. Our fresh food was limited in the winter: carrots, beets, potatoes, heads of lettuce, turnips, the so-called root vegetables that could be stored over winter. I think apples could be kept from the autumn harvest.

Winter staple items on our table were from cans: gray spinach, gray string beans, dull green peas, yellow corn and my favorite, beets. Pasta only came to the table as spaghetti. Mother's desserts diversified our meals: custard, bread pudding, always with chocolate sauce, cakes, and cookies. Chocolate chips had not yet been designed so we just had sugar cookies or oatmeal. Pies were infrequent as they were made with lard on Mother's "not good for us" list.

Mother's knowledge of nutrition must have come just from reading *Good Housekeeping* or the *Ladies Home Journal*. She gave us Cod Liver Oil by the awful spoonful. She knew an "Apple a Day kept the doctor away". We had meat, potatoes, green, gray or yellow vegetables. Okra and Eggplant were NOT to my liking, but I ate those vegetables she seldom cooked. Perhaps, she did not like them either. It was unfortunate that Rombauer's *Joy of Cooking* with so many delicious ways of preparation was not on her shelf. Alas, only the *Boston Cooking-School Cook Book* was used. This brown "bible" of cookbooks c. 1925 was not comparable.

Several meals every week seemed to be the same menu. Monday night we had liver (only calves' liver) baked potato and canned spinach. These were foods on Mother's "good for us" list. I learned long after I was married that Daddy did not like liver or spinach and he was not home for dinner on Monday nights. Sunday dinner after church had a roast for a special dinner. I do not have to mention that in the 1930's we watched the cost of food very closely. Our meals the rest of the week were not meatless. We had ground round beef appearing in countless ways. Friday was always fish; it was available fresh at the market in our predominantly Catholic community. In that time, Catholics could not eat meat on Friday. There was canned salmon and tuna for us at other times.

I mused in the first paragraph that we were not obsessed with food. We ate with no grumbling. No doubt these memories are rose-colored now. We did have some talk and visiting while we ate. Daddy's quizzes for us were fun. He had a lot of arithmetic games to play while we were at table. He would say: "Take 4, add five, subtract 3, what is the answer"?

Patterning the games as we grew we could add up many numbers, multiply, and divide and come up with an answer. The games, challenging and fun, probably helped us with our arithmetic. We did not need a calculator to find the answer. My Grandparents came back to St. Louis in the Fall. Such good items they brought from that sunny land: oranges, lizard-skin avocados, grapefruits. A burlap bag of English walnuts was sent from them for cracking over Christmas. Such treats!

    When I was in High School I was responsible for dinner on Friday night. Mother went to the symphony Friday afternoons and Daddy picked her up to bring her home. No doubt she went on the streetcar though I did not give much thought to her transportation. I just knew that they expected dinner to be ready when they got home at 6 p.m. I became an expert at preparing Round Steak with canned tomatoes over it. A baked potato and green vegetable accompanied this delectable meat dish. There must have been some dessert as we always had dessert. That was the beginning of my cooking experience. Mother did have one night off from cooking and as a bride I did feel comfortable in my kitchen.

    Eating out was an event for special occasions. I only recall meeting Daddy for lunch at the Missouri Athletic Club one time when I was 15 and feeling extremely grown-up. As a teenager I did go to church suppers on Wednesday nights, not to dine with my parents, but to sit with other kids at our own table.

    My children sat at our family dinner table. No doubt they remember Tuesday was Girl Scout meeting and dinner was a little later as the girls and I, their leader, did not get home until 6 p.m. Monday night was Boy Scout night and dinner had to be rushed to get Daddy and brother off to 7 p.m meeting. Sunday night for many years was a Pancake Supper in front of the fire. I wonder what their Memoirs will include about their family dinners. Their schedules of work and activities in the community, especially sports, have made eating together a special event. Eating out has become a norm.

February 28, 2013

Our Rapidly Changing Society

Feeding the multitudes will continue to be studied and researched. I do think bio-scientists will find ways to feed the billions of people in the world and even help us in America to eat more wisely than we do now. We will have food that will never perish, laced with chemicals to keep it "like fresh". Again, those with wealth will have organically-grown fresh veggies and fruit produced in greenhouses with good growing medium, if not soil.

I think STRESS is a factor that will be an increasing problem. I have seen it come into every part of our society, rapidly advancing in the last three decades. Higher status occupations will have higher stress levels. There are many at work on this problem that was never mentioned when I was 20. Now 6-year-olds are stressed!

Though many people endeavor to be out-of-doors and active in sports, I see that most are just observers of the natural world, not understanding our place in it as humans. They do not realize that conservation should be a most important study in our lives and imperative to our continued survival on planet earth. Let us walk with a friend, listening to sounds around and not with a Walkman plugged in our ears.

In the United States, our population is approaching the time that we will no longer have a clear majority of any one race/religious group in our land. We almost have one-third of the people we call "African-American", one third "Hispanic". And one third "White". (These are labels used by the Census Bureau.) We still are the legendary "melting pot", but pieces of the "soup" become less distinguishable. I cannot fathom how these demographics will ultimately change our governance, our world societal attitudes, the family, the status of women and our religious institutions. Will we still live by the Ten Commandments? The "Golden Rule"? Beliefs I have held about marriage and the family?

Glimpses into my Treasured Memories

Approaching the 100th anniversary of the Girl Scouts of America, I want to share some treasured memories. How is it possible to do this? I shall try "On my honor; I will try to do my duty to God and my country; to help other people at all time; and to obey the Girl Scout laws". That was the way it was when I first became a Girl Scout as I neared my eleventh birthday and made this Promise, about 78 years ago if my arithmetic is correct. I have been a registered Girl Scout since that time, sometimes a girl in Troop #1 University City, some years a

Troop 152, University Methodist Church; Fay Estes, leader 1939

Field Director in Professional Girl Scouting and many more years as troop leader (always a Cadette troop), committee member, parent, member of the Board of Directors, District Chair, Trainer, Established Camp staff, unit leader, Program Director, Day Camp Director, Day Camps Coordinator, tasks too numerable to name. Each one bearing memories…99% happy, satisfied. Continuously over the decades jobs and tasks gave me diversity, new skills to learn and new interests.

I met some notable people. As a girl, I was fortunate to

Lady Margaret Thatcher dinner at Rolla, August 1994

know "Robin", the Executive Director of the St. Louis Council. She was a legend in her time who gave me one of many special opportunities I had being a Girl Scout. This was a scholarship given by the Kiwanis Club in St. Louis to attend a two-week session at Camp Miniwanca, an American Youth Foundation camp in Shelby, MI. It was my first time in a non-Girl Scout camp. I was a rising Junior in high school. "Robin" was Ruth Adele Sampson.

Another notable memory is of meeting Mrs. Franklin Delano Roosevelt when she was our First Lady and Honorary President of the Girl Scouts of USA. Being one of 12 delegates to the first Western Hemisphere Encampment held in 1940 at Camp Andre Clark in Pleasantville, NY. I, with my tentmate, Olga, from Newfoundland, were to welcome Mrs. Roosevelt to camp and escort her to our primitive unit. Walking up behind her on a one-track trail, I noted darns in her lisle hose and her "walking shoes", just like my mother wore. Perhaps, they were known as Oxfords and were the shoe of choice in 1940 for the not so rugged out-of-doors. Mrs. Roosevelt made each of us feel very special. Though she was called "homely" by the Press, on that day I found her simply radiant, exuding pleasure and interest at being in our camp setting.

While my memory is still backing up, I remember being enraptured at meeting Lady Baden Powell (she said "Pole"). She was the wife of Lord Baden Powell, the founder of the Boy

Environmental Law Center

Scouts just two years before Juliette Low founded the Girl Scouts. Lady Baden Powell brought the Girl Guide movement to the world, fashioned I suspect after the Boy Scouts. She was a visitor to Charleston, WV, in 1945 and I was delegated to squire her around our Council, a "show and tell" tour. At the time I was field Director of the Kanawha County Council of the GS, responsible for the Public Relations Committee activities. Such a committee has another name I am sure today, but the tasks are the same, expanded with contemporary names. Lady Baden Powell was a most gracious British lady, just as I expected.

    There were other notable adults having greater influence on me as our trails crossed. Though not of national or international fame as the aforementioned, their stamp on my life was far greater. Miss Stevens (her given name, Eleanor, I learned as an adult, of course) volunteered to take my troop on bird walks, tree walks, and star parties over the course of my first 6-7 years of Scouting. I do not know how often. I do know that those activities plus our Troop camp trips left an indelible mark on my life. My undying interest in Botany had the seeds planted with Miss Stevens. Because I could not afford my own binoculars, I took to the tree and the starry skies and not the birds.

    Mrs. Dunbar, the mother of one of my best camp buddies, first suggested I might be interested in Professional Scouting. She arranged an interview with a National Staff member in our region regarding such a career. In that age (c. 1942) one had such an interview when applying for a position with the Girl Scouts plus a month-long training at Camp Edith Macy, national training camp for adults.

Being a Girl Scout in Junior High was not particularly a "cool" thing to do in 1935-6. I suffered a bit of teasing as Jackie, the next door neighbor, sent a shower from his water pistol onto my newly starched Junior High uniform as I went past his house on my way to some special scout activity. Meetings were on Tuesday night now and it seemed pretty "grown up" to go out on a school night. My leaders from then on through Senior year of High School were teachers at the high school—my typing teacher and a gym teacher. They were quite acceptable. Miss Steven still seemed to be around sometimes. And now I was in the older group of girls, still a wide-age range with ages 11-18. Senior Scouting was brought into the program when I was just about to be a Junior in High School. There was one Senior Scout troop in University City, but I decided to stay in Troop #1 as I had only one or two more years. My underlying reason was, really, that I was not "in the crowd" that belonged to the Senior Troop. I stayed in Scouting primarily so I could go to camp in the summer. That was Mother's Law: "You cannot go to camp if not active in the troop the rest of the year".

In this short essay, I have lifted highlights of two decades, 1933-1940+. Perhaps, I will add other chapters: Girl Scouting in WWI, Girl Scouting as a volunteer back in St. Louis 1950-1980. Girl Scouting as a retiree. Girl Scouting for my Grandchildren.

The Promise I made, I try still to live by. Girl Scouting has changed…No longer does a Scout "Obey", she helps where she is needed. I will have to ask Laura to tell me what it is she promised when she became a scout.

I believe the strength and lasting quality of the Girl Scout movement has been the ability of its leaders to change with changes in girls and in our society.

August 18, 2011

Maxims and Proverbs

Because I did not have employment in the years I was partnered with my husband raising our family, I never retired. Therefore, I cannot write about my retirement. Through those years I was a Volunteer. Sometimes on the lists of Board members or in describing "what I did" I would say or write "Community Volunteer". One friend said in response to such a question, "Professional Volunteer". That is surely an oxymoron, an "acutely silly figure of speech".

In the last eight years, plus or minus, I have found Life Long Learning the most stimulating dimension of my "retirement". I have delighted in signing up for classes about which I knew not. I had never heard of François de la Rochefoucauld. Dear reader, perhaps, you do not know of him either. That was a class in which I enrolled.

A noted French author, he lived in the 17th century and gained fame writing his Maxims. This was the time of Salons' popularity for the nobility. In our class we discussed the Maxims selected by our facilitator. I was interested in each one as it could be related to my life or my society life today.

Recently I ran across a log from one of our cruises in the British Virgin Islands when we moored our sloop at The Moorings. It was a page of 20th century maxims just as if we were in a salon of La Rochefoucauld. Not so famous, not so intellectual but handwritten by my Captain Neil. Maxims, quotes he liked, some original. In the twenty-four years since he passed away, I have "run across" bits of paper, scribbles just such as these pages in a black and white paperback Composition Book from school days. I incorporate some of these findings into my memoirs. These give some hints of the values he held, just glimpses of the Grandfather or even the Father the children never knew.

"Good friends and good books are my most valued possessions. May God help me learn the value of cultivating both till the end of my time". 11-16-89

"Every disappointment is for the better". We had a shipwreck and were at Leverick Bay, Gouda Sound, BVI awaiting repairs. 11-18-89

Some of the following remnants from this "found treasure" seem to be from his readings. From the Talmud: "The old who are not wise should not be called venerable".

A note on my mirror: "This is the person who must be responsible for your happiness".

Origin unknown: "Wisdom is a moral quality revealed more by actions than by words".

Chinese proverb: "I hear and I forget. I see and I remember. I do and I understand".

Values of Old Age and government cannot tax patience and acceptance, humility and courage. "Be concerned with the diet of the mind. Find pieces of writing that somehow strengthen you".

Neil read and recorded; made jottings for me to find and pass on as his legacy. Somewhere he must have read this from a Buddhist Monk: "We are the heirs of our actions"!

February 24, 2016

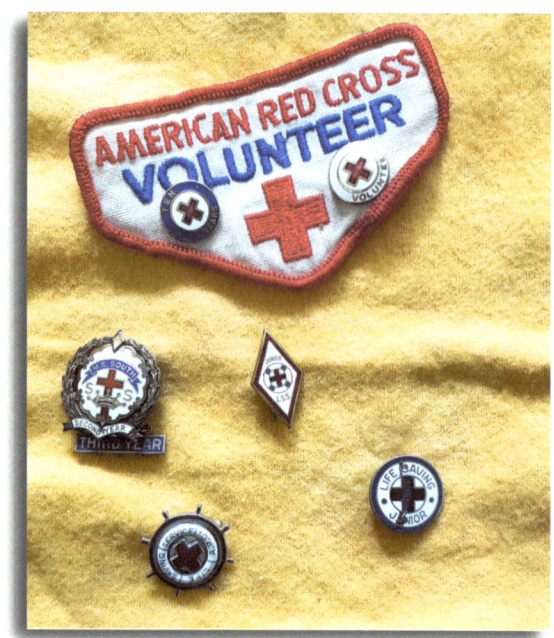

Red Cross Awards

Hillandale – We Are Products of Our Time and Place

In thinking about the design of my life, it seems I often think of the people who greatly influenced me. However, just as often there are places and experiences that have left an enduring stamp on the sculpting of my life. Although I have lived my entire life in an urban setting, I was quite fortunate to have spent untold weekends, several summers and most vacation time in camps and overnights with Girl Scouts. We also had "road trips" every year when we had a two-week vacation.

In my younger years, many weekends (and sometimes a week or two a year) were spent at Hillandale, a family-owned property near Potosi, Missouri. The 8000 acres belonged to my Estes grandparents, Mudde and Fafa, although they never lived there. Mudde had named it Hillandale—but our family just called it "The Farm". Hillandale was 12 miles down a gravel road from town. Daddy, while still single, had built a two-story white stucco house with three bedrooms and two baths. The kitchen and the "great room" were for dining and living. The fireplace was faced with native rocks Mother had gathered from the land. Most were attractive quartz. One I recall had just the right hollow of quartz where we could keep matches to light the fire. The attic was a house feature new to me as an apartment-bred child. It was here that mother and daddy lived when they were first married. When it came time for my birth, my mother moved to St. Louis where I was born in 1922. I returned to live at Hillandale for my first two years.

In 1924, my father moved us to St. Louis to work with his father who was the general life insurance agent of Aetna Life Insurance. My father began a lifelong career in St. Louis, but we retained Hillandale. My grandparents left for California in 1925.

We had tenants, Ben (Mr. Rickner) and Mrs. Rickner, living on the place for security and doing subsistence farming of corn. What else could be done with the little soil in a pin/oak forested land in the foothills of the Ozarks? Ben patiently helped us ride on his donkey, milk a cow, and best of all, let me take home a little piglet to be returned the next weekend to the Farm. Such a chummy pet he was with dark gray hair, a wide ivory girdle around his tummy and a pink nose. Mother provided for his needs just as all other pets we brought home.

How very fortunate my sister and I were that two "city kids" had the freedom to run and holler and develop a "queen's bathtub" in a creek at Hillandale. For five decades we continued to enjoy the house, wild cave, fields, and woods. It was a retreat for family and friends. In later years, the generator for electricity and the water pump were never operable but we learned to live without those utilities. Our refrigerator was a "Spring House" down by the creek. It had a distinctive smell I can experience as I write. We had our kerosene lamps, one with a special Aladdin mantle that gave us entirely adequate light for our family "Flinch" games. A windup Victrola afforded us music of the 1920's—even a record of Caruso, the tenor of the time. We treasured a collection of 78's from our Big Band era (1930's-1940's).

The Farm was donated to the Missouri Chapter of the Nature Conservancy and later became part of the Daniel Boone National Forest. My father served as treasurer of the newly-formed Missouri Chapter of the Nature Conservancy in the 1960's.

June 2019

Generation Gaps

I need to prepare some writing for the "Friendly Readers" PENS group that is coming for our bimonthly meeting. No inspiration was coming, a Writers' "block". I turned to my old text from my first class in lifelong learning. The class was titled "Writing for others"; my "others" are my children, grands and greats. I realized that some of the words I used they do not know, or the meanings have changed and even the context is not even known.

Words have new meanings: grass can now mean pot. There are many ways people rendered services that no longer are needed—the "iceman", the scissors grinder, the "egg man". I will have to take a minute to describe these opportunities that some people took on to help others in day to day living. These people went door-to-door for sales.

Before there were refrigerators, we had an ice box iceman in the alley to get a chunk of ice on a summer day. And we had a milkman deliver bottles of milk to us. We could leave a note for him to put the bottles in the house if we were not home to get them out of the metal box outside the back door. These bottles, also, furnished us the cream that we had to skim off the top of the milk. Daddy used this for his coffee and cereal. When the dairies learned to homogenize the milk, cream no longer rose to the top and other cream had to be bottled separately. There was even a Bookseller: one for encyclopedias, another for "The Book House", a long shelf of books for every age. And we had a meat man who brought Mother veal steaks for special dinners. It was not too many years before we had neighborhood markets that put the traveling men out-of-business.

Conversations sometimes referred to parts of our world in the 1930's and the 1940's such as the CCC, the Civilian Conservation Corps, where many were employed by the government.

Our family had some special traditions celebrating birthdays and holidays. My tenth birthday was a special one for me. I got my first 28" inch bicycle. I was free to ride all around our rather large neighborhood with little traffic until I was older. Then I could go into the Loop and to Church. I felt free that I could ride out of University Heights.

Every year we saw the Veiled Prophet parade with us going a long time prior to the start. The "Veiled Prophet" came every year to start the social season when the year's debutantes started their social whirl. And the Shrine Circus was another annual event our family attended. It was there that I first saw huge fireworks displayed. Today such displays can be seen in every suburb, Macy's, and Washington DC.

Hollywood movies were just coming in the late 1920's. I remember my first time going to a movie at the Tivoli, a neighborhood theater. I went with Aunt Helene and Uncle Bailey, though my mother disapproved, thinking I was too young at 5-years-old. It was titled "If I had a talking picture of You" with Jane Gaynor and Charles Farrell, new stars in Hollywood.

We dyed Easter eggs and parents took them right away so that the Easter Bunny could hide them. Our nests were in our apartment and I, being the big sister, let little ones look for the nests. I knew after a year or two just where the bunny would hide the best nests in our apartments. There were just so many places, most of which I can remember as I write this memoir.

School picnics at the end of the school year were a highlight of my Junior High years, seventh through ninth grade. The 9th year we went to the Highlands, the large Amusement Park in St. Louis. It was there that I lost fifty cents as it flew out of my pocket on the "Flying Turns", the only spending money I had. It was there that I pleaded and begged one of the guys named Neil not to rock when the Ferris Wheel stopped at the top…to no avail! I was still pleading with Neil years later when he was "husband" not to rock at the Shrine Circus.

We did not have vacations trips as I was growing up, as Daddy was self-employed and every day went out to make sales of insurances. We had many weekends at Hillandale. I went to camp every summer starting at age ten. Employers did not give vacation as they do now. Just keep in mind, as you read this, the

Depression was beginning 1930 and then we moved right into World War II. There was no Peace ON Earth until 1947, as we had to "clean up" after the War.

I was a privileged child with always two loving parents and never went hungry. I always had two pairs of shoes—one "saved" for Sunday School. I was able to attend College when only 25% from my Progressive High School even started and maybe 10% finished 4-years.

What Changes Have Been Wrought?

Three of us huddled to view a small television on John's desk. I waited in breathless anticipation for my first visit on Skype. Linda, the eldest of my children, John, her husband, talk on Skype often. John explained: "We are calling our good friends in Kathmandu, Nepal. They are getting ready to go to work but want you to meet their mother". Sure enough, in just a minute or two, there on our screen were the three Napoli folks and we Mothers were formally, verbally, introduced.

This is incredulous to me growing up when just a long-distance call just across the state was a kind of communication not used frequently. When Neil (my future husband) called me one time from the Philippines during WWII, it was a one-time, very short conversation. What changes have been wrought in my nine decades!

Development in the fields of communication continue to develop fast even for the Millennium Generation—those between the ages of 18-30. I see this as a most positive change in many ways. As with most technological changes I see negatives in the ways these changes are used in many cases. Texting has come about with the cell phone leading to "smart" phones, Blackberries, iPhone, with additional capabilities beyond those I know. The rather constant use of these devices had led young and old away from any face-to-face conversation to the point where writing is an obsolete skill for our Middle School and High School ages. This is born out by standardized test scores. Discussion of the uses of this new communication closes for me saying: "Moderation in all things is my mantra".

I see other changes on the horizon. Living alone has become a new norm. In 1950 only 9% of our households were living alone, and even those were often "short term" on a stage until one could "settle down". Today there are 18% of households living alone. Without statistics I see some reasons this has happened. Housing is more economical to raise young people, urging them to move out and away from parents, "spinsters" no longer want to live with the married family members, single men and single women no longer want to live together and appear as gay/lesbian couples. They express their joys in living singly. Studies being made can never be too reliable. But I can make predictions just as I feel that independence should be relished and give one a sense of maturity. Living alone may help us discover who we are and what our calling may be. Dinner table talk will be past, multi-generational activity will diminish over the years and more and more elders will be stacked into community living. Those with means in retirement will have lovely, upholstered lounges in their quarters while others will live in poor conditions with little or no support as they age.

    We moved one last time in my "growing-up" years soon after my 10th birthday. This time into a Dutch Colonial home at 775 Harvard. It had a large yard, the last on the block. A living room was across the front of the house entered into from a porch (screened in the summer) the same length. A dining room and kitchen were across the back of the house. Stairs went up to a landing with a large Bay window and window seat. Turning, we went to the second floor with three bedrooms and a bath. A basement housed a fine new furnace, an "Iron Fireman" that burned coke, rather than coal. That was known to be better for the environment. A washing machine with a hand-turned wringer made Mother feel really up to date for 1936. The apartments we had experienced were just like steppingstones to this home where I lived until I went to college. Those years were a big chapter in growing up.

March 3, 2011

Where Have All the Stars Gone?

I remember a hit song in the 1960's decade "Where Have All the Flowers Gone"? Now a song could be "Where Have All the Stars Gone"? 99% of the people living in Europe and the U.S. experience some form of light pollution, that is some form of light in the night sky. 80% cannot see the Milky Way from where they live. In Estes Park, Colorado, where I live about half-time, I noticed that there were many more lights in town and many staying on longer in the night. Even before I had read statistics, I knew I did not see nearly as many stars in my sky as I had thirty years ago when we first went to Colorado.

In the 1980's, two astronomers concerned about the darkening skies founded the International Dark Sky Association. To be a certified dark sky park, a community had to meet certain tests and qualifications. Now where are the certified dark parks? Joshua Tree National Park has dark sky status, though it is only on the eastern edge it still is one of the darkest skies in southern California. The Grand Canyon National Park qualifies. This would involve passing city codes such as having only parking lots and apartment housing lights only shine light down, keeping lights out of the skies. Estes Park does not need to keep the town lighted all night. Residents there have earlier closing hours in town. I have driven through downtown at 10 p.m. not meeting a single car.

If 20 to 50% of the U.S. more broadly implemented nighttime use of electricity, this light pollution would be reduced as well as tons of carbon dioxide emissions. One study estimates that number at 44 million metric tons. Another unintended consequence of light pollution is the interruption of the flight patterns of migrating birds. The light of the moon and stars serve as guides. Effects on wildlife has been documented. Baby turtles and salmon spawning use light in their navigation systems. I have used the Big Dipper in my own navigation system. *

One year, I flew on New Years Eve from St. Louis to Los Angeles and was struck by how I could see every city and town across the plains all lighted up when I was miles above the land.

    Now, where have all the fireflies gone? As a child catching fireflies to put in a jar for counting was a summer night ritual. Did fireflies succumb like the songbirds or can we just not see their tiny lights in our lighted darkness?

    Stargazing with my Girl Scout troop (and knowledgeable leader) on our "overnights" or even just a weekly meeting at night in the city, we could use our constellation book and identify Orion and the Winter Triangle, Cassiopeia and so many others. Impossible today even at Camp Cedarledge only 40 miles from St. Louis. Electricity has come to camp, too. Light pollution has come to the country.

    As a child my family weekended or in summer spent a week at Hillandale, a large property owned by the family in rural Missouri. We had no electricity and used kerosene lamps carrying one around to all the rooms where light was needed.

    I have one treasured memory of a dark sky when I was hiking one year in Morocco. We walked by day and camped out most every night. One night we were camped in the Sahara Desert about 20 kilometers from the nearest village. My travel "buddy", Ricky, and I waited outside our tent until everyone in our row of tents turned off flashlights. NO LIGHT. But not a dark sky. No moon—only an uncounted number of stars. A billion? 2 billion? I could only stand, shiver, and try to think of something to express my awe. What God has wrought! *

"Dark Matters" *Sierra* Magazine, March-April 2018, p.31

Each Day a Gift

As I marked another year recently in this 21st century according to the little genealogy I have learned, I now have outlived all my paternal and maternal ancestors. This includes only two generations, plus parts of the third. My paternal Grandmother, Muddee, lived to be 97—her birthday was in July. Here I am still enjoying most of the days; each dawn is a gift I receive with much gratitude. Like all days of our lives each one can bring uncertainty. Not every day is productive. I may not feel upbeat. My energy level is not predictable. Balance may be only fair. I can concentrate, shushing away unhappy thoughts I don't want to set in.

Lulu Martha Carroll Estes, "Muddee," St Louis, 1884

Now It Must Be Told

In writing my Memoirs for the last four or five years I have believed I was a storyteller, not a writer. I have believed my memories were correct, at least, my memories cannot be disputed, unless proven otherwise. Each one is correct in my memory. Right? Well, maybe not.

Tonight, I spent about an hour deciphering my journal written in 1940. In detail and tiny writing mixed in with commercials, postcards, illustrations for the text I read of a trip to New York, Washington, Rochester, Chicago. It began with the description of an overnight train in a Pullman to Washington. I cannot dispute any of this Scrapbook. My traveling companion was Patty, a friend I had for life with whom I shared many adventures. Now it must be told that my memory is not necessarily organized at the time recalled. I remember events but not the correct chronology.

By asking my sister about some happening, such as when or where we lived, she shows me I am sometimes sketchy in my memories. Or is her memory sometimes confused, too?

As I was reliving this 1940 excursion this evening, I had no memory of the four-day sightseeing excursion nor the train trip with Patty. However, I do remember attending the First Western Encampment with the Girl Scouts on this eastern trip when I was 18. This encampment was part of the same trip. My memory is selective. In writing my Memoirs my memory has been selective in the stories I have told. I am not an historian who must be accurate in all statements and details. This must be why some authors write "Historical Fiction" and not Fiction.

But what tricks did my memory play on me re: the 1940 trip? Fact one: I did have my 18th Birthday at Camp Andre Clark, Pleasantville, NY at the Western Hemisphere Encampment. I did, at that camp, escort Eleanor Roosevelt to my unit. She was the First Lady at the time and the Honorary President of the Girl Scouts as every First Lady has been since 1912. Fact Two: Patty and I did go to Rochester, NY to visit my Aunt Alline cepting the kindness of my seat partner to loan me money to purchase the correct ticket. Since that time, I have always made certain to have money for a one-way ticket home. To this day I tuck cash for my shuttle from the airport to Old Orchard to have money for the driver.

CHAPTER SIX
Additional Writings

Maurita Stueck, 1999

Books on writing memoirs suggest it could be important to make floor plans and descriptions of places we lived. I attempt to focus on the aspects of where I lived that helped to shape my life through the years rather than focus on the particularities of the many places I have called home.

Christmas Letters

Christmas 2000 finds us embarked upon new frontiers.

Married in October, Joe and Maurita have moved about visiting friends and relations from Florida to California.

We can say that we are having a very good time getting there but are not quite sure where we are going!

Eighteen of our immediate family gathered in Estes Park, Colorado for our wedding. Three of our eight children were unable to attend and how they were missed. College man, Peter, Maurita's grandson, was at St. Olaf's, but did share Thanksgiving with ten of our family in St. Louis.

Having spent each Sunday of Advent in a different church, we are now to be in southern California for the winter months. There with the sun on our shoulders we can view distant snow-covered peaks from Joe's deck, one of our special places. We just want to LIVE FORWARD in the years we will share. Our life already has many blessings, real "chicken soup" for our souls, and we have learned that were it not for the rocks in our stream, the stream would not have a song.

Until further notice we can be reached in California, St. Louis, or Estes Park…three special places for us on this planet.

Christmas 2000

"How lovely 'tis to take the time
To greet our dearest friends
To wish them health and happiness
Before the old year ends.

Darkness comes late afternoon
And winter lies ahead.
But friendship is a glowing fire
When all seems cold and dead."…Nicolas Gordon

And I shall add that good friends are like stars. Though I cannot always see them I know they are always there.

    2007 draws nigh to a close. It has been a good year of joys and blessings untold for me...new friends, friends of long standing, (never old or elderly). Some most pleasant travels...tip toeing through the tulips of Holland in the spring, cruising the China Sea visiting the land of Vietnam in September. Visits with all 16 of my family from time to time from Colorado to Georgia, north to Wisconsin added the spice and frosting to my days.

    I sing "Glory! Glory, to the new-born King" this Advent season. Peace and blessings to you and your families.

Christmas 2007

Tidings of great joy ring out from every corner of Kirkwood, or so it seems, I have anticipated taking this time to compose a note to fill the space between my friends and me and to wish you joy in your life as we come to the end of this old year.

    2009 brought new experiences for me. Having never had any surgery (except one broken wrist) I now have a new part to my old body. A most successful knee replacement. I still wanted to make visits to family, see more parts of this world and hike comfortably in "my" Rockies. I traveled to Turkey this Fall, but the highlight of my peripatetic life was Thanksgiving with the Eastern Branch of the family in Ohio. The main attraction was 4-month-old Ayla, my first great Grandchild. Ayla relished being held ALL her waking hours by parents, 2 Great-Grandmothers, Grandparents (how could Katie be a Grandmother!), an uncle, 3 aunts, and a 2nd cousin "once removed"...Watching Katie and Michael as Grandparents was rewarding, however surprising, for me.

    With my family now spread from Washington State to West Virginia and south to Georgia I am so fortunate to have had several gatherings to keep us all "in touch". Mini reunions were held in Florida, Ohio, Georgia, and Colorado, of course.

"As I go along life's way
Reaping better than I sowed
I am drinking from my saucer
Because my cup has overflowed." (author unknown)

God's blessings be yours this Holy season.

Christmas 2009

Friends, near and far, as I sit down and compose this note it is pleasurable for me. I reflect on the many paths we have taken; trails we have crossed and the multitude of experiences we have shared. I try to keep in touch, but this year seems to have whizzed by and my good intentions are not always implemented. As I have so often quoted in years past, friendships are like stars in that they are always there even if they cannot be seen.

This decade draws quickly to a close. I look forward to being home in St. Louis this Christmas season, this year with two of my children coming "home", Sara, and Hannah (15) and Lawrence and Kathleen. I had Thanksgiving at Katie's and the Colorado cyclists, Linda and John, visited in October after riding their bikes from Kansas City. Again, I am blessed with health and wealth to be able to travel for visits and have parts of the family together at special times here in St. Louis.

One of the high points of 2010 was a week-long trip to the hill towns of Tuscany with Lawrence and Kathleen, a long-time dream of mine. Having been to Italy several times I always wished for Lawrence, the sculptor in the family. I do hope he had sufficient time to absorb enough art on this trip. Art, sculpture, architecture enveloped us. Even the design of the landscape of Tuscany is an art form!

I am filled with gratitude for many blessings, but my heart is heavy when I learn of the millions on planet earth living with war, sexual abuse, hunger, and fear.

May joy, peace and hope fill your days in this blessed Christmas season.

Christmas 2010

Reflections from Another Year

It was not hard for me to cross another threshold early this year. I had already downsized several times, changing my place of residence, my activities, and even my thinking to adapt the philosophy expressed some years ago the "small if beautiful".

January 2011, I moved into a small cottage, one of two, in Pacific Place. Unusual name in the middle of the continent. The design/builder of this urban Senior living-space is a native Californian; hence our name is appropriate. We have a "big house" with about 30 apartments across the drive from my house. The closely-knit group has become my "family". My son, Larry, commented: "Gee. Mom, it is nice to be back home again". My church is close by, the Symphony and Repertory theatre I attend regularly, visit my favorite Botanical Garden, go to Washington U. every week to Life-long Learning Institute. Here I found a class in "Memoirs" much enjoyed. Having dabbled in "journaling" a long time I look forward to writing my assignment each week. My peers span about 30 years. The recently retired up to 90. Other classes I attend offer more mental stimulation.

My family spreads farther and wider, ranging from Colorado to West Virginia, south to Georgia. One professor, Linda's husband, John, is now retired and we have two to replace him...Brenden (Katie's "middle" child) and his wife, Karen, each have appointments to West Virginia University. In addition, they have added another Great-Grandchild to the family. Milo, now four months, was the star player in "Pass the Baby" at Thanksgiving. The five other "Grands" are each sprouting various wings, giving me joys by keeping "in touch" via e-mail and phone calls. Writing letters is somewhat passe. All are in place as last year except our Laura (Katie's #3) has moved from her beloved resort community in Washington State back to Ohio to be employed by the Miami Machine Corp. a.k.a. the parent company. It is nice for all of us to have her back closer, although the Northwest is a wonderful place to visit!

One of the highlights of my year was a trip with Michael and Katie to visit Glacier National Park. Michael does a thorough study of where he is going, mapped out our itinerary, studied the history, geography and out-of-the-way sites, finding the only Buffalo herd in Montana. I packed my suitcase, my only responsibility, met them in Denver as they changed planes for Kalispell, Montana. It was a spectacular time in this part of our country missed in all our family travels. To be with adult children is one my greatest pleasures. I grieve so often that Neil did not know our children and their offspring in these years. I spent the summer in Estes Park as I have since 1982. Hiking but not so far or so high!

With a heart full of gratitude, I am blessed to cherish every day, especially the sunny ones, and my health to enjoy leisurely endless "small" acts of kindness and beauty amidst a world so troubled in near and far-away corners. It is, indeed, a bittersweet world.

May you receive and share God's amazing love now and throughout the New year of 2012.

Christmas 2011

Friendships are like stars in that they are always there. Your friendship through many years is my special gift. Years go by as if on a comet's tail. My family spreads across the country from Colorado to West Virginia, through Ohio and Georgia.

All were together for several days around Thanksgiving except for those I refer to as "the Colorado Branch". I see those four when I spend summers in Colorado. That I continue to do as long as I can board an airplane. I don't even have to take off my shoes now!

Thanksgiving was a time that I, the only one in my generation, was challenged to find time to visit with everyone. I played "catch" with a small beach ball with Ayla, now four-and-a-half. Her interest in this game was sustained almost longer than I could run and catch the ball not aimed too well.

My days in St. Louis have been blessed with a long Indian-summer, followed by single-digit cold temps rather unusual for St. Louis. My daytime driving affords me many opportunities: Life-long Learning at Washington U., church activities, Book-group with the PiPhis and AAUW. A very special activity is the digital simulcast of the Metropolitan Opera shown at our Art Museum coinciding with the Opera production in New York. We have seen "Falstaff" and "Tosca" and look forward to 3 others this season. We tell ourselves we are seeing better than if we were at the "Met". Not quite the same, but a glorious experience anyway.

This summer, living through rain, floods, in Colorado was, indeed, a new experience for me. Power of water was incredible. I have recently read about the Greater Good Science Center at California-Berkeley. A professor there says: "Now we are thinking...why people sacrifice on behalf of other people and non-kin". Believe me, I saw this time and again in the crisis in Estes Park! It was the message of HOPE we have at this time of Christmas.

Christmas 2013

*"People look east,
the time is near of the crowning of the year.
make your house fair as you are able,
trim the hearth and set the table"***

Every year about this time as we gather for holiday parties, we, the oldest generation, remark: "Cannot believe Christmas is almost here. It used to seem that 'Santa' was a long-time coming".

My family now numbers sixteen including our two Great-Grandchildren. (Next year we expect another on St. Pat's day.) We find ourselves coming together several times, though never 100%. How we have spread across this country: West Virginia to Colorado and several points in-between. I treasure each visit: Estes Park, Winter Park, Colorado, Ohio with the McNeil's home as command center.

Linda and I spent three weeks on a Road Scholar program in Eastern Europe. Neither of us had been to the Imperial Cities: Budapest, Vienna, Prague and Krakow, Poland. We spent about four days in each city in four different countries. I found it easy just not to shop rather than keep up with the different currencies. I was enthralled to see magnificent architecture, castles and cathedrals wrapped in history I had studied so long ago. These cities are walkable, paved with colorful cobblestones, many sizes, and shapes. My goal was to stay upright at all times; Linda's goal was to keep an eye on me while not hovering. One of our group wore a pedometer to record our steps each day. She reported 19,000 one day = 6 miles: seven the next. More reports were not forthcoming lest we became demoralized!

I extended my stay in Colorado thrilled with a glorious long "Indian Summer". I had come home for three visits with my sister who was recovering from a serious stroke in May. That was the one "damper" to a year where every day was a good day. There were disappointments, some not-so-kind actions, some lonesome days that I try to brush aside. I think on the peach blush on the mountains as the day awakes, the blazing red of autumn Maples, activities in my communities, the kindness of many friends. These are my treasures.

May you have bouquets of blessings in the days to come.

**These words are the first verse of a favorite hymn

Christmas 2014

Here 'tis another year has flown into the Clouds. Surely that must be where the years gone by are gathering. I come to realize that family and friends are the reins on which I want to take hold. The world is moving almost too fast for me to hang on. The truth probably is that I cannot keep up because I for one do not move so lithely as I did. But believe me, I vow to stay upright!

I have navigated through "Ohio Living Mount Pleasant" for fifteen months, fifteen months of meeting new folks and trying out new activities planned for us. Being under new Corporate ownership we are now longer called a "retirement village", as that term seems to have a negative sense somehow that it does not have in later years. However, I observe that no one here receives any paycheck from an employer. 99% have spent their former lives in Ohio most from southwestern areas. The introductory question is often "What brought you here"? Whether it was "good or not" I will never know. But at this time, I do enjoy watching my third great-grandchild grow up. My new name is Gigi, a short version of Great-Grandmother. It was about her first word.

Katie and Michael traveled with me to Alaska in August. We embarked on my 95th birthday and indeed that was the biggest birthday party of my life. The first evening was a "formal" dinner. I had six young waiters sing Happy Birthday to me. Each more good-looking than the last. To be hired on these ships I am sure "looks" ranks high on the requirements. "My" personal Butler surely looked after me the whole week with flowers and balloons every day!

Grand as the cruise was (even one day out to sea on the ocean) the week following was a great deal more of interest to us. Alaska with its 6 million acres is unlike any other state. From its purchase a new culture was added to our country, one we treated very poorly as we did the Spanish culture and the Native Americans in the southeast. On a six-hour train excursion we traveled through vast wilderness area with mountains most always in view. Mt. Denali rises half again as lofty as Long's Peak at 14,000. Denali at over 20,000 would dwarf our southern Rockies in Colorado. Giggled though at the "forests" of Black Spruce trees the dominant species in the Arctic. Could not help but marvel though at the adaptations it has made to survive at all! The very harsh climate prevents any leafy bowers and little growth. They are spindly and skinny. Put Alaska on your list if you have not been there.

I treasure your friendship and all the times we have shared. It is nice to keep in touch and it is difficult as we race around the places, we are but I find it rewarding. My wishes for your happy days ahead in the new year. Can you imagine what life will be for little two-year-old Iris?

Christmas 2017

The traditional Christmas letter for me is now a New Year's letter. If you saved my letter from last year, you could read it again.

However, we do have a new family member, Mitchell Brannon. He and granddaughter Hannah had a beautiful wedding in May, detailed to include rhinestones in her hair. Only Sara could have helped plan such a perfectly beautiful wedding. They are in Atlanta where Mitchell is continuing studies at Georgia Tech and Hannah with her new Masters degree is an Activity Director in a senior living community.

The only other big change are the ages of the Great-Grandchildren. In Morgantown, W.V, Brenden and Karen now have a 10-year-old gymnast, Ayla, and an "ice hockey" kid, Milo, who is 8-years-old. In Oxford, OH, Laura and Quinn have Iris, a pre-debutante turning 5-years-old in March. Arlo at 18 months is a climber.

Speaking of Ohio, I have moved again "to be near some family". One last move to the Knolls of Oxford. Home is now a 3 room apartment and going to three meals a day is a recipe for interruptions. All 24 assisted living apartments are on one level looking into a courtyard. Not many birds have discovered my feeders yet but it has not been very cold!

It has been fun to watch two Great-Grandchildren grow so quickly into pre-school age, from the "one knee" crawl of Arlo before he walked. The B&B White Garden Inn is nearby. Katie and Michael are living there until their new house is completed this spring.

The academics, Brenden and Karen, are teaching and counting weeks of each semester. Karen is finishing her department chair job and can get back to writing her book on immigration. Bridget and Darren are in Denver and visit when they can.

Lawrence in retirement has had more time for Ohio visits and is creating urban landscape sculptures in the form of public bus shelters and creating a catalog of sculptures on the University of Georgia campus. Kathleen is not taking on any new landscape customers.

Linda and Sara visited over Christmas and New Year's week and helped with settling into new apartment. I would not recommend moving into new communities. It takes so long to establish and understand rules and relationships. New doctors as well.

January 2020

My Thesis at the Outset

A speech given at the Maria Center, November 9, 1984

Thank you…I am pleased to be with you this evening, to greet those of you I have known, and I look forward to meeting others of you personally. We have a common interest in being together this evening—our interest in the program and operation of the Maria Center. Certainly, you and I have been most interested in the presentations by Sr. Joyelle and Sr. Michelle.

How to respond to the nice introduction that…has given me pause. To acknowledge this introduction with proper humility is harder than climbing a fence leaning toward me! I must admit though that I'm quite willing to hear those nice things even if she has to stretch matters considerably.

I've had to do a bit of soul searching in the last several weeks to find a rationale for my being here speaking with you. The invitation from Mr. Cognato as I saw it was certainly not sufficient; I have no reputation as an after-dinner speaker or even as a "drawing-card" for the people invited; I have no expertise in fund-raising. So, I have determined that I can only share with you some of my reflections on the gifts of giving.

Let me tell you my thesis at the outset. I believe that giving-giving of time, talents, money—fits God's plan. And further, I believe that the greatest gift of giving is the sheer privilege we have to give voluntarily to programs in our community.

This volunteer action and volunteerism is the strongest cultural force in our free society. The voluntary way of caring and support has always been the American way. Its absence is strikingly apparent in societies that are not free. Newly independent countries are trying to emulate our ways. It is people—individually or formed into groups—who have voluntarily developed and sustained interest in all aspects of our culture-education, art, social services, and special avenues of endeavor such as the Maria Center.

We have witnessed in the last thirty years greater and greater erosion of this volunteerism—greater dependence on government programs and more and more government control of our systems and institutions. Because of your expressed commitment to the Maria Center, I tend to believe that you are among those eager and willing to accelerate efforts to maintain institutions in the private sector that render care and support of multiple needs in society. And that you want to minimize compulsory giving and taxation for programs in education, human services, art, and music.

The first gift of giving, then, is this spirit of volunteerism that is woven into the fabric of our American culture.

Commitment—commitment to a cause (or causes), a movement, or more particularly to the people the cause represents or to the workers in whom you place your trust would be another gift of giving. We can achieve meaning in our lives by giving beyond our self. Giving is a way we can extend our lives.

Last evening, I asked a friend of mine what she sees as a gift of giving. Without hesitation, she said: "A new learning experience, an enrichment in my life". She paused, reflected, and then added: "When we give, we gain new understanding of many aspects of life; we have our horizons broadened and come to know persons who share these interests. Giving is a way to be involved in the community even though we cannot physically do anything".

A fifth gift of giving I sense is joy that comes from knowing we may have helped another. I am reminded of a young professional friend of mine who leads a busier-than-usual kind of life expending much effort in developing her career and her social life. However, she still makes time to drive a young adolescent to drug therapy sessions feeling that she might build a relationship that would add quality to the young life.

More often, it is our gift of money that will enable ardent skilled professional workers to make the way a bit easier for those who are stumbling.

I like to think of these persons as "road markers". God

has gone before mankind to prepare the way for His work. The "road markers" are those who will further clear the way, straighten some curves, and smooth the bumps.

This weekend, my husband and I returned from travel adventures in Greece. There we found evidence that long before Christ, man's concern for his fellow man was important. Perhaps, our very humanness dictates the need to give care and support, one to another. We were aware of many roadside markers, especially in Macedonia. Historians, archaeologists, and theologians have conjectured a heap as to their origin. In ancient times, it is believed they were, in fact, travelers' aids. Sometimes, simply a pile of stones to mark the way, ofttimes little structures that held oil for lamps, containers for water, food. They were called "Hermes" after the God protector of travelers in pre-Christian times. Today they are simple glass boxes or elaborate miniature chapels of sometimes miniature houses—but all have a source of light, some food or beverage, often religious symbols-but still used as traveler's aids sustained by individuals.

As early as 400 B.C. a sage wrote this bit of wisdom: "Whatever you give to other, give with love and reverence. Gifts must be in abundance with joy, humility, and compassion". That teacher in ancient days touched upon yet another gift of giving- an attitude of unselfishness and humility with no thought of self-aggrandizement or honor.

While in Greece, we trod through the excavations of Philippi, of Thessaloniki, the sites of early churches of Macedonia—walking in the footsteps of Paul, reflecting on his letters to the young churches. Paul wrote to the Christians at Corinth his view on giving. (New English version of the Bible, Corinthians 9:6)

Indeed, it is clear that the cornerstone of our Judeo-Christian teaching is that our duty to God demands that we help our neighbor. In doing this, we serve our God. The thesis with which I began—that giving fits God's plan—is the underlying controlling principle of our belief in voluntary giving!

In our contemporary days, one idea looms large to me… God wishes us to be giving people. God gave us the breath of life and added to it the opportunity to experience a depth of life through Jesus Christ. So, take heart. Grasping God's plan is not like a treasure hunt or diving for pearls—it can be plainly seen and acted upon. May we continue to freely share our time, talents, and money. For giving fits God's plan and holds many gifts for the giver.

CHAPTER SEVEN
Addenda

Bridget and Maurita in favorite blue suit

*Reflections on the
gift of memoirs*

Writings as a Girl

Dear Grandmother,

You and I have always been good pen pals, and neither of us really like speaking on the phone, so I wanted to put some things down in writing to send along to you. I just want to ensure you know how much I love you and how fortunate I feel to have you in my life. You have been such an amazing role model for me and, while I'm not always successful, I often remind myself to emulate your openness with everyone, your curiosity and desire to learn, and your can-do/make-do spirit. I also credit my love of travel to watching you and Granddaddy set off into the world and sharing that with us—to receive a postcard from you on one of your trips was always such an excitement, and it also meant that I could look forward to you sharing your photo albums with us on our next visit. And I really cherish all of the times we got to share after I grew-up—not many people are fortunate enough to be able to commiserate with their grandmother about the ups and downs of dating! :) Mostly, I just want to say thank you for loving me, accepting me, and always being there—the relationship I have had with you has always been very important to me and I hope you realize this.

Much, much love,
Bridget

In Remembrance

My mother used to ask me what she should write about. How do you choose from the millions of events/sightings that occur in 97+ years? Some of these memoirs I knew of course but some I did not. There are some repeated episodes but written in a different version. Chalk it up to normal aging memory or just continuing to remember the especially happy times.

I would always suggest she write about her feelings about events, as I wanted to know maybe how it is to get older! As I have retyped but not edited these writings, her humor struck me after members of her AAUW writing group had mentioned to me how much they enjoyed her writings. Her feelings were always there. I just was not always listening.

In 1977, I was between moves with Michael from Albany, NY, to Appleton, WI, having just finished my Masters. She applied for her first passport when I called her up and said let's go to England and Ireland to see gardens for three weeks. We spent a few nights at the Girl Scout house in London and then just went from one garden to another with no reservations. In Ireland, the local Roscommon Catholic priest took us around to some Gately families for tea in thatch roof homes. (Michael's grandfather had come to Boston from Ireland.) Michael and I then went to the BVI with Mother and Daddy for another wonderful sailing trip.

In 2008, Mother called to see if I wanted to see gardens in China with Missouri Botanical Garden director and friend, Dr. Peter Raven. I did some necessary office work from my laptop for the business that Michael and I owned. I hope I can be as interested in new cultures when I am her age. It was a fabulous, fascinating three weeks.

In 2013, Michael and I met Mother in Denver and flew to Montana to see Glacier National Park. She had not been there. While hiking we sang Girl Scout songs at the top of our lungs to keep the bears away. She had an amazing repertoire of songs for any occasion, including scaring bears!

In 2018 on August 18th we were on a cruise ship in the Inland Passage heading for Alaska out of Vancouver, BC. She had dinner with the Captain for her 95th birthday and celebrated all week. She especially liked the chocolate martinis during the entertaining shows. She hiked for several miles on the boardwalk through Sitka forests and then around Denali National Park as well. She had been on many train trips but the one to Denali was amazing.

I was so fortunate to have had such an interesting, loving woman be my mother. Her wide interests and study of issues continued her entire life. I am so thankful that my children and their children knew her as well. How lucky I was to have had these special times with her and for so many years.

Katie Stueck McNeil

The memoirs are precious to me for the throughline they provide to my maternal ancestors. They capture the family values as well as stories and traditions.

And, I hear her voice as I read them now. They're a challenge to live my life fully and an inspiration to imagine the legacy I will leave for future generations of my family.

Linda Stueck Mahan

I am so blessed and grateful for my Mother; who she was as a Mother and a person; her encouragement, sacrifice, her love of other people, righteousness and lifelong learning.

Love you Mother.

Sara Stueck Elrod

My mother had a very strong moral compass. She taught us by example to always do what was right, kind and helpfully to others. This compass interestingly did not point in a negative direction. She believed that, "If you didn't have something nice to say you should not say it". I do not remember her ever criticizing anyone. This, of course, was a blessing for me as I made some poor choices during the 67 years we were together. She was very supportive of my decision to become an artist, supporting all the wild and crazy ideas and things I made. As I bumped along financially only rarely did I hear her say I might consider getting a job. She was pleased when I became a teacher and had a steady pay check.

She would have made a great entrepreneur, being intellectually curious, hard working, patient and people friendly. As it was 1949, and my dad being of his time, she became a dedicated homemaker. This was always part of her story, accepting yet knowing it could have been different. She funneled that drive into her many volunteer activities in the school, Scouts, church and community.

My mother never wanted to interfere in our private lives. I think, she was entangled in her mother-in-law's world more than she would have liked and promised herself she would not be like that. Thus, we called her, we set up visits and we only shared what we wanted her to know. Seems she was fine with that because then she could move ahead with her life and create her world.

In that, I found her four very different daughters-in-laws there was ample opportunity to express negative judgments and give advice, she never did. She found the best in each of them, and in my pixilated choices. Her love for Kathleen, my wife, grew over the 25 years and they shared many interests.

Lawrence Stueck

Grandmother:

Hello, my name is Hannah and I stand before you honored to have been one of Maurita's grandchildren. I am the youngest by a decade and was still given almost 25 years worth of memories that I will now cherish. I prayed that she would be at my high school graduation, my college graduation and my wedding and she made it to all 3. She always made every effort to be there and I felt as if she was one of my biggest fans. I couldn't be more thankful for the time I had with her in this life. People tend to throw around the phrase "I don't know where I'd be without (blank) my grandmother", but for me that couldn't be more true.

She provided a way for a life that I otherwise might not have had. She provided the means to send me to a Christian camp in Colorado for 10 years, where I was able to learn about God and get over my fear of heights. She also provided the means for me to get through six years of school. I didn't realize what a gift it was then, but now having a family of my own, I know now just how blessed I am. I even majored in what I majored in because of her impact. I wanted to work with seniors and better their quality of life through diet and exercise. She was such a role model for living a healthy lifestyle and keeping in pristine shape.

My Grandmother is my biggest inspiration. She loved people. She cared about others and helped me see the importance of people and their experiences. She never met a stranger. She treated strangers like they were her friends, which truly impacted me more than I can even put into words. She once picked up a hitchhiker, with just her and I in the car. I panicked at how trusting she was. She taught me that you can still trust and be kind even in the world we live in today. Now this was probably 10+ years ago but it still influenced the way I view people today, who simply need God's grace and kindness shown unconditionally and for that I am thankful. She modeled hospitality so well. Even when she lived her last months in the assisted living facility in Ohio, she asked me if she could get me a drink or cookie. She taught me the importance of writing and growing in knowledge, no matter if you're in school or 60+ years post-grad.

I'll always cherish my summers out in Colorado with her, the simple joys and memories made at the cabin in Estes, whether we were learning about the birds at her feeders, taking a walk or hike, playing games like Old Sol, Scrabble or Mexican Train, eating a bowl of ice cream (always with a cookie) or just simply sitting around the table sharing past experiences and sweet sentiments. She made me appreciate nature. She took her time and appreciated the little things of life. Every time we took a walk she'd point out a bird, flower or plant and she almost always knew exactly what it was called. We have a fond memory of a hummingbird entering inside the cabin who we then named Ralph. We shared a lot of laughter as we came up with a plan as to how we would get him out.

So many memories.

Maurita was truly a special person that had a meaningful influence on the way I live today and I am so blessed to have had her as my Grandmother.

Here's a verse that I feel depicts who she was.

Proverbs 31:25-29 says:

"Strength and dignity are her clothing. She opens her mouth with wisdom, and the teaching of kindness is on her tongue. She looks well to the ways of her household and does not eat the bread of idleness. Her children rise up and call her blessed; her husband also, and he praises her. Many women have done excellently, but you surpass them all".

Hannah Brannon
August 2020

Obituary

Maurita Fay Estes Stueck
Oxford, Ohio

Maurita Fay Estes Stueck lived a long, rich life of hospitality and service to her community and family. Her devotion to others was an inspiration to all who knew her. She will be fondly remembered especially by her four children Linda Mahan (John) of Fort Collins, CO, Lawrence Estes Stueck (Kathleen McQuiston) of Watkinsville, GA, Katie McNeil (Michael) of Oxford, OH and Sara Elrod of Fort Oglethorpe, GA. Through her long life she also left many memories with six grandchildren Bridget Kennedy McNeil (Darren Kennedy), Brenden Estes McNeil (Karen Culcasi), Laura McNeil Desmond (Quinn), Peter Mahan, Wesley Mahan and Hannah Rebecca Brannan (Mitchell). Known as GiGi, she was blessed with four great-grandchildren, Ayla and Milo McCasi and Iris and Arlo Desmond. Betty Estes Gnaegy, her only sibling, predeceased her. She will be deeply missed by her niece Dr. Suzanne Gnaegy and nephews Michael and David Gnaegy.

She was born in St. Louis, Missouri on August 18, 1922, to Wellborn and Fay (Ostner) Estes. At an early age her family moved from the rural woodlands of southern Missouri to the St. Louis suburb of University City. There she flourished, enriched by activity in Girl Scouting and a strong education. She attended Lindenwood College (where she later served as a board of trustee member) and graduated from Washington University. Her appreciation of the importance of higher education for women led her to gift endowed scholarships to both institutions. She also established the Stueck Distinguished Lecture Series for civil, architectural and environmental engineering and an endowed scholarship in the name of Neil Stueck at the Missouri University of Science and Technology.

Following graduation in 1943, she bravely left her home and family to relocate in Charleston, West Virginia where she worked as a professional for the Girl Scouts of United States.

Maurita married childhood classmate Cornelius Frederick Peter (Neil) Stueck on October 18, 1946, in University City, MO when he returned from the Army following World War II. In 1950 they built a home in Webster Groves, MO. Maurita and the family were active members at Webster Hills United Methodist Church, in Scouting and community leadership while the family was growing up.

She channeled her lifelong passion for plants as a volunteer docent at the Missouri Botanical Garden. She also served on the Board of the St. Paul Theological Seminary in Kansas City, as well as many others including Girl Scouts of Greater St. Louis, American Association of University Women branches in St. Louis and active in the Wednesday Club of St. Louis and the St. Louis chapter of Phi Beta Phi.

In 1982, shortly after Neil retired from Stupp Brothers Bridge and Iron Company, they purchased a chalet—Pine Winds—overlooking the valley of Estes Park, Colorado. Her days spent surrounded by the natural and rugged beauty brought her deep joy and peace. Hiking the Rocky Mountains with family and friends well into her eighties she also enjoyed fellowship at the Estes Park United Methodist Church and volunteering with the Estes Valley Land Trust and Rocky Mountain Conservatory. Part of her legacy is the gift of written memoirs.

Her love of international travel led her to many countries where she appreciated the diverse cultures, people and history. After Neil's death in 1992, she continued her travel with friends, often taking one of her children with her—to Italy, China, Costa Rica (granddaughter), Chile, Guatemala, India, Bhutan, Australia, Poland, Austria, Hungary, and Ireland. These journeys are lovingly remembered by her children.

At the fifty-fifth reunion of University City High School Class of 1939, she reconnected with Joe Burch, a classmate whom she had not seen since graduation day. They married in 2000 in Estes Park, Colorado. For five years they lived in Redlands, California and Estes Park. Following his death she returned to the St. Louis area. She moved to Ohio in 2016 and lived at Mt.

Pleasant in Monroe and the Knolls of Oxford.

Maurita passed quietly of natural causes at the home of her daughter Katie, amidst the loving care of her children, on Tuesday, March 24, 2020. Per her wishes, she has been cremated and will be interred at Bellefontaine Cemetery in St. Louis with her husband. Due to Covid restrictions a delayed Celebration of Life was held at Stupp Pavilion at Tower Grove Park on August 8, 2021.

Bellefontaine Cemetery, Stueck family plot

Maurita with Karen Culcasi & Brenden McNeil, Syacuse doctorates

**Youngest granddaughter Hannah Elrod, graduating from college
Maurita attended all graduations of all six grandchildren.**

320

Commitment to Higher Education

Maurita was very proud to have obtained a University education at Washington U. She continued to attend reunions of her class and enjoyed hearing from the students who received her scholarships at Lindenwood and Washington University.

She also contributed to a Distinguished Lecture program at Missouri University of Science and Technology in honor of Neil Stueck's graduation from the school at Rolla, MO.

With generous financial and loving support, her four children all obtained University educations with Lawrence earning a PhD , Linda and Katie earning MS degrees, and Sara earning numerous degrees from Interior Design to Early Childhood Education.

Her six grandchildren all obtained University degrees with Bridget earning a JD, Brenden a PhD, Hannah and Wesley master's degrees, Laura and Peter both are currently continuing their advanced degrees and certifications.

Michael McNeil 70th birthday, October 1997: Karen Culcasi, Brenden McNeil, Maurita, Michael McNeil, Quinn Desmond, Katie McNeil, Laura Desmond, Bridget McNeil, Sara Stueck, Milo McCasi. Iris Desmond, Ayla McCasi, Hannah Elrod

Nannie Crook (b. 1/23/1842–d. 1/4/1865) married at Jack's Creek, TN on 5/1/1860 to Col. John Wesley Estes (b. 6/23/1832–d. 1/4/1865). These are Great-Great-Great-Great-Grandparents. Their son John Wesley Estes II was raised by Uncle William Jeremiah Crook.

Continuing the legacy of world travel, four great-grandchildren visiting islands of the Caribbean in 2019

www.ingramcontent.com/pod-product-compliance
Lightning Source LLC
Chambersburg PA
CBHW041624220426
43663CB00001B/1